BOB VILA'S TOOLBOX

Also by Bob Vila

THIS OLD HOUSE

THIS OLD HOUSE
GUIDE TO BUILDING
AND REMODELING
MATERIALS

BOB VILA'S GUIDE TO
BUYING YOUR DREAM
HOUSE

Designed by
Marjorie Anderson

Photography by
Michael Fredericks

Line drawings by
Jeffrey Bellantuono

BOB VILA'S TOOLBOX

The Ultimate Illustrated Guide to Portable Hand and Power Tools

by

Bob Vila

William Morrow and Company, Inc.
New York

It is the policy of William Morrow and Company, Inc., and its imprints and affiliates, recognizing the importance of preserving what has been written, to print the books we publish on acid-free paper, and we exert our best efforts to that end.

This book was prepared and produced by Gallagher/Howard Associates, Inc. The photographs are copyright © 1993 by Michael Fredericks (aside from those reproduced on pages x and xiii, which are reproduced by permission of Christine Kitch). The contemporary line drawings are copyright © 1993 by Jeffrey Bellantuono. The period line cuts are drawn from public domain catalogues of the nineteenth and early twentieth centuries.

Library of Congress Cataloging-in-Publication Data

Vila, Bob.
  Bob Vila's toolbox : the ultimate illustrated guide to portable hand and
  power tools / by Bob Vila : designed by Marjorie Anderson ;
  photography by Michael Fredericks ; line drawings by Jeffrey
Bellantuono.
     p. cm.
   Includes index.
   ISBN 0-688-11735-X
   1. Tools. 2. Dwellings—Maintenance and repair. I. Title.
TJ1195.V53 1993
621.9'08—dc20   93-9544
                                                         CIP

Printed in the United States of America

First Edition

1 2 3 4 5 6 7 8 9 10

I dedicate this book to my father, whom we all called Opa, and to my son, Chris.

Opa taught me many lessons in the course of Saturday building projects around the house in Miami. Sawing wood, mixing concrete, whatever he was doing, he welcomed me as his helper.

My hope is that Chris has similar memories of growing up around tools.

ACKNOWLEDGMENTS

To begin, I have to thank Hugh Howard, whose skills as a writer and packager helped make this book possible. My appreciation, as well, to Michael Fredericks for his photographs, Jeffrey Bellantuono for his drawings, and Marjorie Anderson for her design. Jean Atcheson did her bit, too, in making sure our sentences were literate and correct; as did Richard Bennett, in transforming thousands of bytes into a few hundred pages of handsome type. My thanks to our friends at William Morrow and Company, in particular Allen A. Marchioni and Adrian Zackheim, for the enthusiasm and good publishing sense they brought to the project. And to Morrow's Susan Halligan, Ann Cahn, Scott Manning, Larry Norton, Tom Nau, Lisa Queen, and Suzanne Oaks for their help in packaging and marketing the book.

I must acknowledge the people who got the project under way. My agents, Barry Weiner and Jonathan Russo, and my lawyer, Ronald E. Feiner, put me in touch with Robert J. Sann and Joe Mangione of Syndicated Multimedia Corporation, who in turn linked us with John Gallagher and Hugh Howard of Gallagher/Howard Associates, Inc.

My thanks, too, to my friends at Sears, Roebuck. At the Tower, there's Tracie Wiesman and Fred Ciba in particular. My thanks to the good people at the Albany, New York, store, especially Shayne Kennedy and Jeff Champagne, for arranging for the loan of tools.

As always, my appreciation to my colleagues at BVTV, Michael Ferrone, Jeanne Flynn, and Sheila Morris.

Finally, a few words of appreciation for the tradespeople and craftsmen who have taught me and my collaborators about tools new and old. At best this must be only a partial list, but special thanks to Bob Ryley, our Yankee carpenter on "Home Again," Michael Beecher, Jerry Grant, Robert Haldane, John Howard, Don Carpentier, Bill McMillen, Richard "Junior" Holgerson, and the many others from whom I and members of our team learned tool sense.

CONTENTS

Introduction *xi*

INTRODUCTION

I learned about tools from my father. He built the house I grew up in, and he made furniture, too, after he retired.

I remember as a boy how big my father's hands seemed, and how natural was the fit of his fingers and palms to the tools he used. One of my earliest memories is of lifting a masonry hammer. It was the heaviest thing I'd ever picked up. In my father's hands, it didn't seem big at all.

I've learned about tools in other places, too. I studied architecture in college, and in the Peace Corps I helped build precast concrete housing in Panama. Then I did graduate work at the Boston Architectural Center. But it was the housing stock of the Boston area that really got me going in the renovation field and there that I learned about putting tools to use.

In New England you're surrounded by all those wonderful early and Victorian houses. My wife, Diana, and I bought one in 1975. It was both an eighteenth-century house (some of it had been built in the 1790s) and a spectacular Italianate house, as a great big addition had been added to the original structure in the nineteenth century. A lot of people liked what we did to that house, and one thing led to another. Namely, "This Old House" and my new show, "Home Again With Bob Vila," both of which are indirect results of that renovation.

I still admire the New England classics – the Cape Cods, the

My wife, Diana, on demolition day

Georgians, and the rest – but more recently I've been able to take on a variety of projects in Florida and California and Chicago and other places. We've worked on barns, cottages, and ranch houses. Occasionally we take the dream-house approach, introducing top-of-the-market elements that only a small percentage of people can afford. But what I like best is working on a house that has come upon tough times. In the fabric of such houses you can see happier past eras, and the challenge is to make them once again into dwellings people will care about.

Preservationists often talk about the stories old houses have to tell, and I'm always fascinated to learn about the history of a place. But for me, the most interesting story line involves what's going to happen now. We make sure that we respect what came before, but my job is to think about who's moving in tomorrow. And, of course, what I can show the people who watch me on television about the techniques, the tradesmen, and the possibilities involved in each renovation.

A lot of the pleasure in the process lies in watching the transformation. You take one house, a pile of materials, some talented tradespeople, and a sort of chemical reaction results.

Let's add one more ingredient to that recipe. In the hands of the workers, amateur and professional, are the tools that are the subject of this book. Like the houses where they have been or are about to be – put to use, the tools you'll see in the following chapters are a mix of the old and new. Some are old designs updated for today's construction techniques; there are clever new tools, too, that are a step or two advanced on what came before. And there are antique tools that, when properly cared for, just seem to last forever.

I still own and use some of the tools that I remember seeing in my father's toolbox when I was a boy. He taught me to regard them with a mixture of respect and wonder, as well as how to take care of them and how to put them to use. For me, working with tools has something of the same appeal of those old houses and their individual histories. They both give me a strong and satisfying sense of continuity.

THE TOOLBOX AND THE WORKSHOP

This is the first of two books: *Bob Vila's Toolbox* will shortly be joined by a companion volume, *Bob Vila's Workshop*.

When we began planning this project, we quickly realized that it just wasn't possible to cover all the tools we wanted and needed to discuss in a single book. In fact, even in two substantial volumes like these we cannot pretend to have covered every tool and technique you'll ever need. But we've done our best to get you safely under way, even if my advice alone won't be enough to launch you on a professional career.

The line of division between *Workshop* and *Toolbox* is a simple and logical one. This book is about the tools you would take with you to a work-site, whether your project is installing a new vanity in your upstairs bathroom or the construction of a weekend house a hundred miles away. As its name suggests, *Workshop* is about the tools in a fixed, permanent workshop.

Thus, tools like the cordless electric drill will be covered in *Toolbox*, while the drill press will be in *Workshop*. *Toolbox* includes a portable table saw, but not a band or a radial-arm saw. They'll be found in *Workshop*. And so on.

LEARNING FROM THE PROFESSIONALS

The best way to learn how to use a tool properly is to work with a pro. In my television shows and in my life, I've always relied on professionals either to do the work or to show me how. A great deal of what I know has been learned from people who have been working at their trades for most of their lives.

But not everybody has had the good fortune to be exposed as I have been to so many experts. While I can pick their brains on my show, for my edification and yours, that isn't an option for the average person who, on a given Saturday, decides to embark upon this or that project. I've gotten a couple of good pieces of advice over the years about taking on new challenges that I think are worth recounting here.

Back in my "This Old House" days, I was talking to a very experienced contractor. I had interviewed him on tape, and after the cameras stopped rolling I apologized for asking so many questions. I was sure a lot of them were pretty elementary for him, and I thought he might think some of my questions were stupid. But he stopped what he was doing, looked me in the eye, and said, "Bob, there's no such thing as a stupid question."

You know, he was right. Especially when it comes to tools – many of them with sharp blades, powerful motors, or enough weight and mass to really hurt you – you should never hesitate to ask questions. An intelligent question may save you time and money, too, helping you avoid mistakes and wasted materials.

Read the instructions that come with the tool. Always obey proper safety procedures. And don't ever be in a great big hurry, either. Haste makes more than waste; it can result in injuries as well.

The other lesson came from a very accomplished contractor who happened to be much younger than I. He was a carpenter, but he was also a skilled plumber and electrician. He did his own design work, too, and as someone with drafting training myself, I admired his drawings. Not to mention the finished product, which was usually even better. The guy was good.

I asked him who got him started in the business. "I did," he replied. I asked him if he had apprenticed with anyone, and he said

Shooting for television demands a good deal of flexibility, especially in instances where the camera has to see exactly what a tool is doing. In this shot, the camera lens is peeking up underneath my arm.

The drawer and its contents, featuring the solutions to a thousand and one household headaches.

TOOLS FOR A KITCHEN DRAWER

I once heard a friend of mine describing his mother's tool sense. (He had no choice but to talk about his mother because his father didn't know a square from a squeegee.) The recollection concerned a drawer in her kitchen, the one over by the stove, my friend remembers fondly, right behind the kitchen stool. It appeared to be full of junk – yet therein were the tools to fix just about anything.

It was a regular drawer, one big enough to hold a silverware basket and a few hand towels. But in my friend's childhood home, that drawer was the source of a million solutions. A hammer, pliers, screwdrivers, and a few other tools were to be found there. They were joined by a broken salad bowl brimful of odd screws and nails and broken bits and pieces of this and that.

There's a lesson in that tool drawer that we can all apply. You see, even in houses with workshops in the cellar, it's a must to have a few basic tools in a kitchen drawer or some other small storage spot (a shelf in a coat closet, a small toolbox underneath the sink, wherever). The spot should be

no. I asked a few more questions before, with a certain impatience, he said to me, "You can't be afraid of something just because you don't know how to do it." Then he added, with a shrug, "You just take the learn-by-do approach."

To him, learning a trade or a skill wasn't a matter of formal training. In fact, almost everyone at a certain point has to learn by doing:

easy to reach and access. And it just might contain some or all of the selection of tools outlined below.

Tape Measure. A small one will do, perhaps a six-footer, a half-inch wide. It takes up half the space of a deck of playing cards. (See page 5 to learn more about tape measures.)

Square. A combination square does the most things of any of the hand squares, with the level and scribe built into its head-piece, along with the removable rule that can act as a straightedge. (See page 20.)

Torpedo Level. This is only about nine inches long, but very convenient for leveling your new dryer or refrigerator, not to mention helping with carpentry tasks that come up. (See page 24.)

Saw. A handsaw is very handy to have around, but a traditional carpenter's handsaw does take up space. An option is a small backsaw, though I also favor a compact folding Japanese saw. (See page 55.)

Utility Knife. If you're like my friend's mother, you already have a jackknife in your pocketbook (or pocket). Even so, a utility knife requires minimal space and performs a multitude of tasks. (See page 84.)

Drill. A push drill isn't much larger than a screwdriver, and can help drill holes for all kinds of purposes, among them pilot holes for all sorts of wood screws. (See page 101.)

Scraper. A two- or three-inch scraper will find its way into your hand for a good many uses; a razor-blade scraper helps, too, for such jobs as cleaning paint from newly painted windowpanes. (See page 114.)

Hammer. Every household needs a hammer, and probably the best investment is a small claw hammer. For a million little jobs around the house, the hammer is a great persuader. Buy one with a curved claw, which makes pulling nails easier. Given minimal space, a twelve- or thirteen-ounce hammer is probably best. (See page 130.)

Screwdrivers. A minimum of two each (small and medium-sized) Phillips-head and slotted-head varieties. (See page 141.)

Clamps. A couple of small (three-inch) C-clamps take up little space, and make lots of minor repairs possible. (See page 145.)

Pliers and Wrenches. An inexpensive pair of slip-joint pliers (page 159) and an adjustable wrench (page 165) are essential. A pair of another breed of pliers (perhaps water-pump pliers or linesman's pliers, pages 160 and 161, respectively) is a good investment of space and money, too.

Miscellaneous Supplies. A couple of sheets of sandpaper (one medium, one fine); a plastic bag containing some steel wool; a catchall container for odd nuts and bolts and screws. You'll see, that drawer will fill up with useful items.

Oh, there was one other thing about my friend's mother's tool drawer. A household rule in her house demanded that the tools be put back immediately after they were used. Harsh penalties (like no dessert, for example) were meted out to those who failed to comply. I won't tell you it should cost you a piece of pie, but returning tools to their proper place is a necessary discipline. Make it a habit.

Eventually, it comes down to you, the tool, and the unique problem at hand. This takes confidence, of course, which my multitalented friend has a lot of. But perhaps a good motto for any homeowner-hobbyist-renovator would be: Take it easy, take it slow, but just because you haven't done it before doesn't mean you shouldn't take it on.

THE BASIC TOOL KIT

If you have more than a mere drawer to devote to tool storage, here is a basic list of tools for which you are likely to find frequent use.

Tape Measure. A twelve- or sixteen-foot retracting carpenter's rule is a good investment. (For a more detailed discussion of tape measures, see page 5.)

Squares. You'll need at least a carpenter's square and speed square, and a combination square and try square are also good investments. The carpenter's square will prove handy when you need a straightedge, too. (See page 13.)

Bevel Gauge. A real favorite of mine, essential if you ever plan to cut a line that isn't a forty-five or ninety-degree angle. An inexpensive and, when needed, invaluable tool. (See page 21.)

Two-Foot Level. A two-footer is the minimum; you may find a torpedo level and four-foot level have many other applications, as well. (See page 22.)

Chalk Box. The chalk line within will not only enable you to snap lines but can act as a line level, while the box itself can function as a plumb bob. (See page 36.)

Handsaws. You'll probably need a carpenter's saw, with a cross-cut blade, perhaps twenty-two inches long with ten or twelve teeth per inch. A hacksaw and backsaw are also handy to have at hand. A compact wooden miter box will prove its worth the first time you try to miter a quarter round dowel for a shoe molding. A coping saw is a cost-efficient investment. (See page 42.)

Power Saws. If you opt to buy a power saw, the portable circular saw should be your first investment. A standard model with a seven-and-a-quarter-inch blade is likely to be the most affordable and all-around useful tool. If your budget allows, and your projects dictate, then a saber saw is a good second power saw, with its ability to cut curved as well as straight lines. (See pages 59 and 68.)

Utility Knife. Own one. You won't regret it, whether you're in the business of marking cutoff work, trimming plastic sheeting, or any of the many other jobs this tool will do. (See page 84.)

Electric Drill. If you buy any power tools, this should probably be your first. It will drill holes and drive screws with a small added investment for a drill index and driver bits. (See page 93.)

Chisels. A small set of four wood chisels and a single cold chisel will prove valuable time and time again. Make sure you store the wood chisels, in particular, with care, protecting their fragile edges from clanging against other metal tools. (See pages 106 and 111.)

Block Plane. For fitting trim, the block plane is easy to use and will elevate your level of finish. As with chisels, its blade must be protected carefully. (See page 119.)

Scrapers. A paint scraper, putty knife, razor-blade, and hook scraper are all worthwhile investments, particularly if you do any refinishing or stripping of furniture or woodwork. (See page 114.)

Palm-Grip Sander. If there is a good amount of finishing or refinishing work on your list of projects, buy a palm sander. (See page 122.)

Hammer. If one hammer is enough, buy a sixteen- or twenty-ounce claw hammer with a smooth bell (convex) face. It'll nail small finishing nails and tacks, and bang in large common nails, too. If having two hammers is an option, buy a small claw hammer (say twelve or thirteen ounces) with a curved claw; and a larger (perhaps twenty-ounce) hammer with a straight (ripping) claw. When buying a new one, make your buying decision on the basis of how the hammer feels in your hand. Balance, comfort, and confidence are all important. (See page 130.)

Depending upon your requirements, a soft-faced mallet, wooden mallet, ball peen, and club hammer might be useful (see pages 137, 133, and 133, respectively). Nail sets are an inexpensive and invaluable addition to the tool tray of the finish carpenter. (See page 138.)

The basic tool kit – with which one can do a lot of good work.

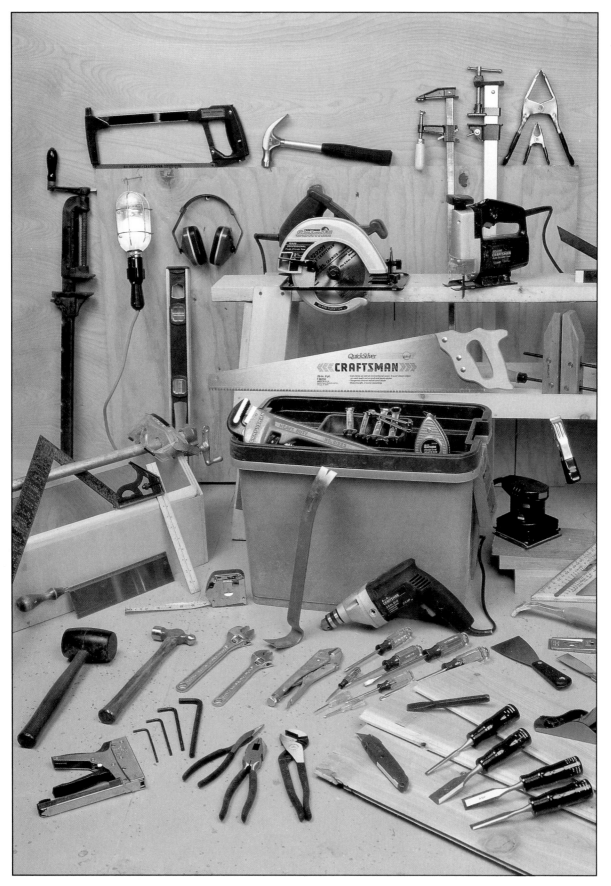

Flat Bar. A medium-sized wrecking tool (twelve or fifteen inches long) with a hook and claw on one end will extend the life expectancy of your hammer and enable you to take on the sorts of small demolition tasks that any renovation inevitably involves. (See page 155.)

Screwdrivers. Perhaps three each of Phillips- and slotted-head screwdrivers, including a pair of stubby drivers (they are roughly three inches long, handle and all). A minute driver, often called an instrument or jeweler's screwdriver, is also handy to have around. More screwdrivers probably represent a good investment of space (and money, as drivers that are perfectly adequate for around-the-house use are sold in sets quite inexpensively). (See page 141.)

Clamps. There are many varieties of clamps, each of which performs certain functions very well. At a minimum, I'd recommend your toolbox contain two each of four-inch C-clamps, twenty-four-inch pipe clamps, two wooden hand-screw clamps, and spring clamps. More is better here, too. (See page 145.)

Staple Gun. You'll find new uses for this tool every time you take on a renovation or construction job of any size. (See page 152.)

Pliers. A good set of basic pliers includes pairs of slip-joint (eight inches long), water-pump (ten-inch), linesman's (eight-inch), needle-nose (six-inch) pliers. (See pages 159, 160, 161, and 163.)

Wrenches and Sockets. An inexpensive set of at least six combination wrenches or a ten-piece socket set (see pages 163 and 167, respectively) are recommended. Two adjustable wrenches (one six or eight inches long, and another, larger wrench that's twelve or fifteen inches long) make a useful team for many jobs. (See page 165.)

Locking Pliers. I mention locking pliers separately because they can be used as a makeshift vice when clamped to a work surface. (See page 162.)

Allen Wrenches. For their small price, a basic set of allen wrenches will pay for themselves. They will allow you to tighten (or loosen) set screws on appliances, toys, and many household items. And when you need one, nothing else will do. (See page 166.)

Plumbing Tools. One of the things you'll soon learn if you're willing to take on plumbing chores is that pipe wrenches generally travel in pairs. You'll need two for loosening and tightening pipe joints; I'd recommend ten-inch and fourteen-inch models. (If your house is plumbed with copper water lines and plastic waste lines, save your money. A good pair of water-pump pliers will allow you to do all the trap work you'll need.) (See pages 176 and 160.)

As for other plumbing tools, your tool kit should be the partner of your ambition; if you have the wherewithal to take on certain jobs, you'll need certain tools. Like a basin wrench to change a

kitchen faucet, or a propane torch and a tubing cutter to sweat a fitting or two. (See page 71.)

Almost every home, however, has occasional need for a plunger and a drain auger (see pages 177 and 178).

Electrical, Tiling, and Plastering Tools. Again, buy what you need as you need it. (See pages 181, 187, and 195.)

Extension Cord and Droplight. If space is at a premium, buy a combination extension cord and droplight. Better yet, have one of each. (See page 181.)

Flashlight. Last but not least, keep a flashlight (or two or three) around the house.

BUYING TOOLS

This book doesn't pretend to be a buyer's guide. The engineers at Consumers Union do that better than I ever could. On the other hand, I do know something about buying tools, both from my own experience and from talking with hundreds of people in the building trades.

The first rule is, no single saw, drill, or piece of equipment is right for every user. The right tool for you depends upon your size, strength, and pocketbook. And on the kinds and quantity of work you want that tool to do for you.

A contractor-quality worm-drive circular saw is wasted on a weekend handyperson who'll use it twice a year. On the other hand, a budget-priced electric drill just won't service the needs of the electrician's assistant who drills hundreds of cable holes through two-by stock every working day.

You must make up your own mind about what you need and can afford. But there are guidelines I suggest that you consider.

This antique is called a twist or spiral auger. You may think it looks like something of a joke but, believe me, it's a serious tool.

One is that having more tools isn't necessarily better. In fact, you're probably better off having fewer, good-quality tools than many more tools, half of which you'll never use, or which will (like cheap sockets, for example) break the first time you put them to the test. It's like the bargain knives on late-night television. Sure, you get about a dozen of them, but none is worth much a few weeks later.

Particularly when it comes to power tools, the choices are daunting. A basic Sears or Black and Decker electric drill can be bought for well under $50. Yet some models are available – both from U.S. makers and the European and Asian makers such as Bosch and Makita – for more like $150. Which of them is right for you?

Keep in mind also that the most expensive tool isn't always the best tool for a given user. The most expensive models are generally intended for professional or industrial applications, and may even be labeled as such. If you are a pro whose livelihood depends upon reliable tools, go up-market. But you should buy what you need, no more, no less.

If you use your tools once a month for a minor repair or two, buying bargain-priced tools probably makes sense. But if you plan to put your tools to serious use, testing yourself – and your tools – with a series of new challenges, buy a tool that will last. Buying a tool, any tool, is rather like buying a car: Go ahead, invest in a Rolls-Royce if you wish, but if you have six kids, maybe you'd be better off with a minivan.

There are so many fine tools on the market that choices are often difficult. But do yourself the courtesy of shopping around a little. Consider your skill level, too, along with how often you use your tools, the area you have available for storage, and your budget. Then make your decision.

GETTING STARTED

There are experienced craftsmen who maintain that a beginner shouldn't use power tools but that toolcraft should be learned using the muscles of the human body. And it is certainly true, for example, that the ability to use a handsaw to cut a straight, accurate line is a great introduction to using a portable circular saw. You'll be able to appreciate what you know, as well as recognizing both the advantages and disadvantages of the electric tool.

My job, however, isn't to tell you which approach best suits a particular person. You have to figure out for yourself, on the basis of your confidence level, experience, storage space, and good sense what your needs and desires are. I *can* tell you, though, that doing a job well, whether it's building a structure from scratch or fixing a leaky faucet, is one of life's genuine satisfactions.

So go on, get out there, and put your hands to use. And, please, do it safely and carefully.

BOB VILA'S
TOOLBOX

CONTENTS

MEASURING AND MARKING TOOLS

Making something, making almost anything, shouldn't begin with the sounds of sawing. Regardless of the material to be used – wood, metal, or just about anything else – the quality of the end product will be distinguished, I've found, by how well the various pieces fit together.

Whether it is to be mitered, butted, joined with a mortise and tenon, or to stand alone, each piece must be accurately cut and shaped. The laying out process, which involves measuring and marking, makes that possible.

Different tasks require different degrees of precision. Machinists think in hundredths and even thousandths of an inch. Finish carpenters worry about thirty seconds, while drywallers need be concerned only with eighth-of-an-inch tolerances.

Whatever your task, before you cut you must know exactly *where* to cut. In short, then, to get almost any job under way, you'll probably require one or more of the wide array of measuring and marking tools described in the following pages. For assembly, too, accurate measurements are required for leveling, squaring, and aligning the miscellaneous parts.

You won't need all the tools discussed in these chapters; some are old standbys that homeowners and professional craftsmen alike require, while others are more specialized, tools peculiar to certain individual trades. Depending upon your skill level and the kind of tasks you plan to take on, though, you'll find at least some – probably a good many – that you'll need, as well as some ideas on how to use them effectively.

A clear, square cutoff line, complements of a tape measure and combination square.

C h a p t e r 1.
Tapes and Rules

If the clock helped make the industrial revolution possible – and many historians argue that it did – then the tape measure and other precise measuring tools made their contributions, too. In centuries past, even the best equipped craftsman didn't have the option of reaching into his pocket for either a watch or a tape measure.

Two hundred years ago, carpenters and masons had to content themselves with a homemade yardstick and a "traveler." The traveler was a simple wheel, with a handle attached by a rivet to its center, that was rolled along a surface to be measured. The user noted each time a marked point of the wheel came full circle. By knowing the circumference of the wheel, distances could be measured by multiplying the circumference times the number of revolutions.

Take my word for it, the trusty tape is a lot easier to use.

FLEXIBLE TAPE MEASURES

Today, the tape measure may be the carpenter's best friend, but in dozens of other trades, too, the tape measure can perform countless tasks. From dressmaking to dressing stone, all kinds of jobs are made possible by this compact and convenient tool.

Tape measures come in a variety of lengths, ranging from a few feet to one hundred feet or more. Depending upon the nature of your work, you may wish to carry a pocket-size model with you everywhere you go, keep a long tape in your glove compartment to measure off building sites, or have several different models available for various purposes. For most home applications, one of each of two kinds of tape measures will help you accomplish what needs to be done.

Push-Pull Tape. This familiar device is spring-loaded so that the tape retracts into its metal or plastic case when not in use. It is also known as a flexible rule.

The push-pull tape comes in lengths from five or six feet up to twenty-five feet. It can also be purchased in metric lengths. The blades (as the tapes themselves are formally known) come in half-inch, three-quarter-inch, and one-inch widths. Wider tapes are bulkier, but the wider they are, the farther you can extend them, ver-

How long is it, anyway? Opposite are a number of ways to find out. Flanking the folding rule at center are two push-pull tapes on the right (one twenty-five feet long, the other a six-footer) and a fifty-foot windup long tape (left). There's some drawing paraphernalia in the foreground. At the rear, there's a metal machine rule, and a folding carpenter's rule leaning against a grain-painted tool-box dating from the mid-nineteenth century.

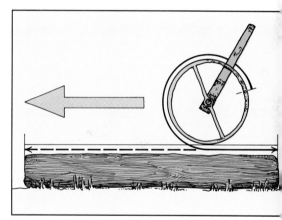

Also known as a traverse wheel, this antique tool doesn't offer quite the same convenience – or accuracy – that today's tape measure does. Usually made of iron with a rivet that connected the wheel to the shaft, the traveler was an eminently practical tool back in the eighteenth century in the hands of a skilled craftsman.

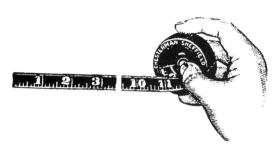

A turn-of-of-the-century tape measure.

tically or horizontally, without the supporting hand of an assistant at the other end. A practical size for most home applications is three-quarters of an inch wide and twelve or sixteen feet long.

The hooked tip of the tape has a pair of rivets that fasten it to the blade. The tip slides back and forth a fraction of an inch, compensating for the thickness of the tip when measuring inside or outside dimensions.

Many models come with a built-in locking mechanism that can be used to hold the blade in place, preventing it from retracting until the brake is released. The tapes on some models come bearing not only measurements (to sixteenths or thirty-seconds of an inch) but with stud markings at sixteen-inch intervals. Some also have other information like nail sizes printed on the reverse side. Many models also come complete with belt clip.

Windup Long Tape. This design is available in fifty- and one hundred-foot lengths. The tape must be retracted by cranking the built-in handle clockwise.

Used less frequently than the shorter tapes that retract automatically, this tool features a metal or fabric tape inside a steel or plastic case. Its primary uses are in situations where large dimensions are involved, such as in measuring structures or entire rooms.

The end of the tape features a ring that can be slipped over a nail to hold it in position and a hinged hook that can be opened to catch on a stud or edge. Both make one-person use of the tape practicable.

THE FOLDING RULE

Though less popular among carpenters today than it was a generation ago, the zigzag rule certainly has its admirers. I bet this handy device will be around at least as long as carpenter pants continue to

When measuring an inside dimension (for example, as illustrated here, the distance between two studs), the case of the tape measure should be positioned flush to one jamb, the tip butted to the other. The width of the case itself (here it's two inches) can then be added to the reading of the extended tape.

If your preference is the folding rule, its brass extension leg allows for accurate measurements of inside dimensions, too. It can reach up to six inches beyond the end of the rule, and its reading is to be added to the measurement at the opposite end of the device.

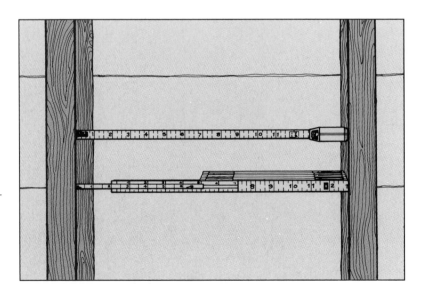

feature the elongated thigh pocket designed for it.

Most models are six feet in length. Folding rules today are available in either wood or fiberglass.

With a few flicks of the wrist, the folding rule quickly snaps open, its pivoting joints locking into place. It's particularly handy for inside measurements because it has a brass extension built in.

Folding rules are a bit more fragile than the durable tape measure (they break easily if mistreated), so use and store your folding rule with care.

RULES AND STRAIGHTEDGES

We all learned how to use a ruler in elementary school, if not before. Little did we know at that age how many varieties existed and how many important purposes were to be served by the rulers of the world. For home use, several different sizes and configurations are available and useful, depending upon the work you do.

The Bench Rule. As its name suggests, you keep this one on your bench. Typically, it's twelve inches long, with one edge marked off in sixteenths, the other in millimeters. The bench rule is handy for simple measurements, for adjusting your compass or dividers, and a miscellany of measuring tasks.

The Yardstick. Though not essential, the yardstick can be a handy tool to have hanging on the wall near at hand.

The Machine Rule. This six-inch-long rule is especially useful on the job site for reading drawings.

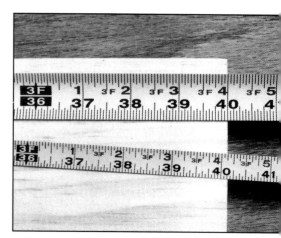

Note the difference in measurements, despite the fact that the tips of both tapes are aligned (outside the photo) on the same edge. The lesson? Don't run your rule out of parallel with the edge you are measuring. If you do, you will introduce error into your measurement.

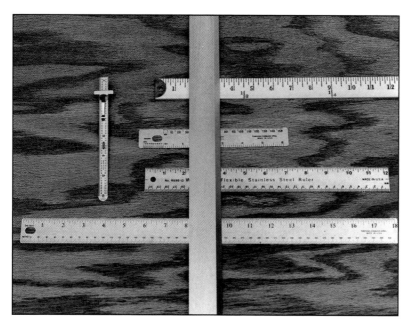

Running vertically are a six-inch pocket rule (left) and a two-foot straightedge. From top to bottom beneath the straightedge are a yardstick, a six-inch machine rule, and twelve-inch and eighteen-inch bench rules. You probably won't require so complete a set of rules in your traveling toolbox, but they all have their uses.

Straightedge. This heavy steel rule comes in a number of sizes (typically from one to six feet in length). One side is beveled.

Despite the absence of dimensions on its edge, a straightedge is invaluable for a number of tasks. You can use the beveled edge as a cutting guide. And when you hold the rule on its edge, it will instantly reveal whether a board or other surface is flat, convex, or concave.

GETTING TO SQUARE WHEN YOU DON'T HAVE A SQUARE

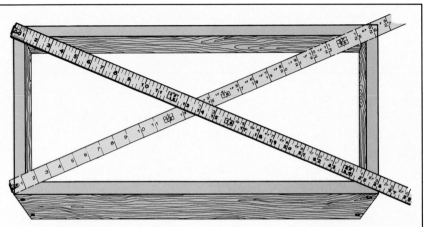

Even if you don't recall learning it, your high school plane geometry teacher probably taught you this trick years ago. In fact, it's been in use since classical antiquity. Talk about passing the test of time . . . .

When you are trying to determine whether a rectangular object has square corners (whether the object is as small as a jewelry box or as big as a building's foundation), extend your tape diagonally from one to the opposite corner. Then measure the distance separating the other two corners. Compare the two dimensions: if they match, the rectangle is indeed square. If not, you'll need to shift the sides of the piece until the diagonal measurements are the same (a gentle tap or two at one of the corners of the longer dimension should do it).

This pair of dividers is positioned to transfer a measured increment from the rule to the workpiece. Dating from about 1825, this antique pair is of a configuration known to tool collectors as a "dog pattern."

COMPASS AND DIVIDERS

Whether you're drawing a circle or getting ready to cut an arc onto a sheet of plywood, you'll need a compass. This age-old tool can perform a range of other duties as well.

The Compass. The compass enables you to draw circles or arcs. One of the legs ends in a point that is fixed at the center of a circle, while the other has a pencil or pencil point at its tip. Depending upon the nature of your work, you may require a simple drafting compass (for circles up to about ten inches) or a larger model.

The Dividers. Dividers are used to step off measurements, or to transfer dimensions from a drawing to a workpiece or from a model to a piece in work. These tools closely resemble the compass, differing only in that both legs end in sharp points.

A variety of purpose-made dividers can be purchased. There is also a whole family of related tools, among them calipers, inside and out, micrometers and slide calipers, and others, some of which are accurate to .001 inch. For most people, though, a single combination compass-divider will fulfill likely needs.

MAKING DRAWINGS

Making professional working drawings takes training and practice. For many simple, around-the-home kinds of jobs, however, even the inexperienced hand can devise working plans. With the investment of a few dollars and given a minimum of practice, useful drawings can be made – and later mistakes avoided.

The Drafting Board. While elaborate drafting tables can cost many hundreds of dollars, you may opt to purchase a portable drawing board, some of which these days come with a handy, built-in T square. Another option for the occasional draftsman is to use a desk or tabletop.

The Equipment. A basic drawing kit need only consist of a T square, a triangle, some graph paper, a roll of masking tape, and pencils.

Getting Started. For the beginner, graph paper makes the process a great deal easier. Tape a sheet to your working surface, aligning it with the T square. Identify the longest dimension of the object you're drawing, then determine the largest scale you can use to fit the object onto the sheet. Depending upon the size of the object to be drawn, the scale could be one square to a square foot, one square to a square inch, or whatever proportion makes sense.

Turning Pro. Once you've mastered some of the basic skills, you may decide to leave the graph paper behind and confront the somewhat intimidating emptiness of a plain sheet. If you do, you'll need a scale (it's a triangular ruler with different scales along each edge). There are plenty of other fancy implements to help, too (among them pencils with leads of varying softness for darker or lighter lines), but such subtleties aren't required to master the basics.

Quicker than you can say "Engineering Drawing 101," you can be a draftsman, too. All it takes is one T square, two triangles (one with a pair of forty-five-degree angles, the other with thirty- and sixty-degree angles), plus a compass, a ruler or a scale, a roll of masking tape . . . and a little practice.

THE STORY POLE

To those who have used one, a story pole does indeed have a tale to tell. To the un-initiated, however, the story pole may seem like just a piece of scrap wood with a bunch of marks on it. Then again, that piece of black basalt we now know as the Rosetta stone hardly looked at first glance like the great window on the past it has proven to be.

For the mason or the carpenter, the story pole is a time-proven trick of the trade. Functioning as a building-specific rule, the story pole

helps assure uniformity from one part of a structure to another. In fact, though, it is simply a board with markings, which vary depending upon the materials used and the design of the building.

For a mason laying up a cement block wall, the marks are eight inches apart; when laying brick, the marks are more like two and a half in-ches apart, depending upon the brick and the thickness of the mortar joints. For the car-penter applying siding, the spacing between courses depends upon the show of the siding and any adjustments made for door and window openings.

The carpenter's story pole is probably the trickiest, so let's look at how it is laid out and put to use.

Let's say it's time to re-side an old house. The new building paper is on and the old corner boards are still in place, as are the water table (at foundation level) and frieze board trim (at the top of the wall).

Cut a piece of straight stock to precisely the distance from the top of the water table to

A simple story pole saves the car-penter or mason a great deal of measuring time – and can keep cours-ing consistent from one section of wall to another.

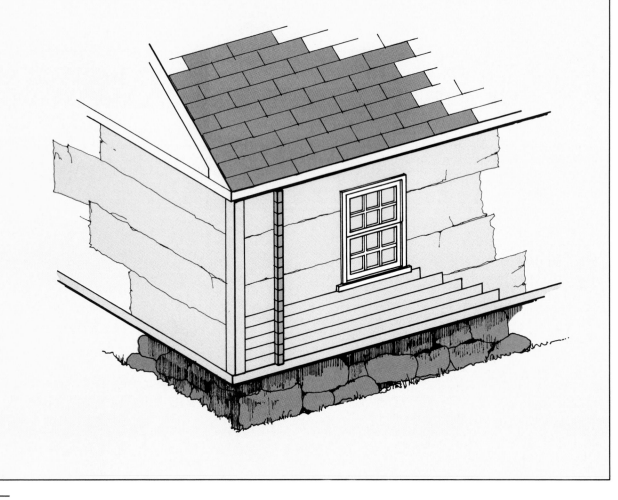

the lower edge of the frieze board. Tack it in place adjacent to the corner board with a couple of finishing nails (make sure it's plumb first, of course).

Next, determine exactly where you want each course of your siding to lie, making allowances so that the openings are met by full pieces at the bottom and top. Now, mark the position of each piece of siding on the story pole.

Quicker than you can say "Once upon a time," your story pole is ready. All you do now is transfer the markings from the story pole to the corner boards, window architraves, or other trim to which the siding will butt.

Story poles are easiest to use on new houses where everything is square and uniform. But even on an older home they can be a genuine time-saver. Before you go ahead and nail the siding, however, take your story pole around to any other sections you plan to side: You may want to compromise a bit from one spot to another in order to get as symmetrical a job as possible.

The story pole is used by the mason in the same way, to plan out the wall being constructed – *and* to make sure that all the corners match. A key step for both mason and carpenter is to make sure that ground zero – the point at which the bottom of the story pole is positioned on each and every wall – is the same at each location. A water level, chalk line, or some combination of other tools can help establish the proper point.

The story pole is sometimes used horizontally, as well, to lay out joist or other framing details that are repeated in a structure. And a variation of the story pole, the layout stick, can be a useful tool when doing cutoff work (see page 34).

If you're like me, there are days when 7/8 inch plus 3/16 inch plus 2 1/2 inch equals a mistake . . . or a headache . . . or both. On such days, you just might be glad to have one of the several models of calculators available that add in feet, inches, and fractions. Don't be surprised at the price tag, though, as they're a good deal more expensive than other pocket calculators.

Called timber or tree calipers, this giant measuring tool (it's more than four feet long) is designed to measure the diameter of a tree and to determine the amount of timber that could be sawn from it. Once the jaws of the tool are positioned around the trunk, the scale incised on the shaft then provides an estimate of the number of board feet that could be milled from the tree. It's a clever, though not very compact, calculating device.

Chapter 2.
Squares, Levels, and Plumbs

According to the old nursery rhyme, there once was a crooked man who, along with his crooked cat and a crooked mouse, lived in a little crooked house. Obviously, the crew that built their place worked without a square, a level, or a plumb line.

The truth is that the importance of straight lines and regular angles was recognized a very long time ago by the ancient Greeks, and even earlier by Egyptian builders. In this country, all the early builders' books, from the eighteenth century onward, devoted more pages to geometry and trigonometry than to tool techniques. That's because any object or building is made or built by connecting points (to form lines); by combining lines (to establish two-dimensional shapes); and then by adding the third dimension to create volume. Thus, accurately drawn lines and angles are the essence of the building process.

In this chapter, I'll talk about the tools that tell us what is "true" (that is, level or square) and what is not. These include squares, which are used to check the trueness of angles (usually ninety-degree angles); spirit or "bubble" levels that advise us when we're on the level; and plumb lines, which help us keep our work standing straight.

Each of these tools also has other uses. Many squares, for example, have inches and fractions of an inch marked on their blades so that they can be used as rules. Levels are handy as straightedges, too. But, at bottom, these are the tools that will keep you from being known as the person who lives in the little crooked house that's full of little crooked objects.

THE CARPENTER'S SQUARE

Every time I pick up a carpenter's square, it feels familiar. This is one of the practical, substantial tools that always seem eager to go to work.

Made of flat steel or aluminum, the carpenter's square is actually shaped like an **L**. Today's standard model measures twenty-four inches by sixteen inches. However, the flat square, rafter square, builder's square, and roofing square, other names by which this tool is known, are occasionally to be found in other sizes, including twelve by eight inches or twenty-four by eighteen inches.

Here's a mixture of the old and new, but all these plumbs, levels, and squares are still very much used. Flanking the window are a bird's-eye maple mason's level with plumb (left) and a two-foot mahogany level. In between, from top to bottom, are a torpedo level, try square, chalk line, line level, combination square, plumb bob, two speed squares, a rosewood try square, two bevel gauges, a solid brass carpenter's square, a water level, and a two-foot spirit level.

true (tru) n. *Level, square, or concentric; precisely shaped, positioned, formed, or adjusted. E.g. "We must use a Square Rule . . . of a very large Size, that our strait Lines may be the truer." From* Alberti's Architecture, *Leoni translation, 1726.*

In early nineteenth-century references to squares, the eighteen-inch by twelve-inch size is usual, but the tool has been around for centuries. It was used in Europe long before it was first patented in this country in 1819 by one Silas Hawes, a blacksmith in South Shaftsbury, Vermont.

The most common use for the framing square, as its name suggests, is for laying out and marking patterns in framing, roofing, and stairway work. The carpenter's square can also be used as a straightedge for determining the flatness of a surface. In the workshop, it's handy for marking cutoff work on wide stock. There are so many uses for the square, in fact, that a new model will usually come complete with a booklet enumerating its applications.

The longer, two-inch-wide portion of the square is the blade. The shorter leg is called the tongue, and it is one and a half inches in width. The outside corner where the blade and tongue join is the heel. The flat surface that has dimensions stamped on it is the face; its reverse side is known as the back.

The calibrations on a square vary with its age and the purpose for which the tool was intended. Early handmade models tend to have fewer markings scribed or inked onto their surfaces; more recent factory-made squares may have differing calibrations and tables stamped onto their faces. Virtually all squares are marked in inches and fractions of an inch, usually to eighths of an inch. The markings on the face of a rafter square will probably include a rafter table, which will enable you to calculate the proportional length of a rafter once you know its rise and run. There may also be a table of Essex board measures on the back that will enable you to calculate board feet, given the length and width of the stock.

Be aware, too, that dimensions on the back of a rafter square may be in *twelfths* (for reducing a scale in feet to fractions of an inch) and *tenths* of an inch (for decimal calculations).

The carpenter's square is a deceptive tool. It looks simple – it's a ruler with an elbow, a straightedge that turns a corner. Yet it is a great deal more, because it can function as a sophisticated arithmetical guide to many of the complexities of laying out a wood-frame house. (See *Raising the Rafters* and *Squaring the Stairs,* pages 16-17.)

To determine square, the carpenter's square is simply positioned inside the angle being examined, with the leg flush to one arm of the angle. If light shows through between any portion of the tongue of the square and the other leg of the angle, the angle is out of square.

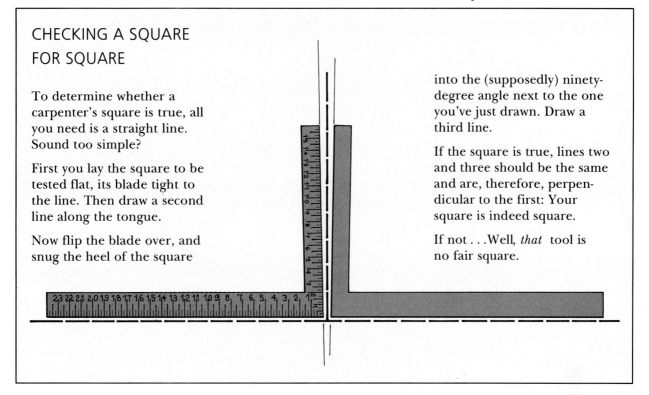

CHECKING A SQUARE FOR SQUARE

To determine whether a carpenter's square is true, all you need is a straight line. Sound too simple?

First you lay the square to be tested flat, its blade tight to the line. Then draw a second line along the tongue.

Now flip the blade over, and snug the heel of the square into the (supposedly) ninety-degree angle next to the one you've just drawn. Draw a third line.

If the square is true, lines two and three should be the same and are, therefore, perpendicular to the first: Your square is indeed square.

If not . . . Well, *that* tool is no fair square.

HAND SQUARES

Traditionally, the larger metal squares like the rafter square described above were thought of as carpenter's tools. In contrast, smaller wooden or metal ones were more likely to be found in the joiner's or cabinetmaker's tool kit. However, that line was blurred many years ago and today the well-equipped woodworker of almost any stripe finds many uses for both large and small squares.

Hand squares have been used for most of recorded history. Many handmade squares survive from earlier eras and, in a sense, the handwork ethic is still honored; even today, hand squares are more likely to be crafted of expensive woods and admired as much for their ornamental appeal as their practicality.

I've included several distinct varieties under the heading of hand squares, including the try square, the speed square, and the combination square.

Try Square. A fixed ninety-degree angle is formed by the thin steel blade and the thicker stock, which is often made of wood. The try square is used for checking (that is, "trying," thus the name), for establishing that a cut or joint is true or square. It's also used to mark cutoff lines or as a straightedge to determine whether a board has warped or "cupped."

A try square, as pictured in a post-Civil War tool catalogue.

RAISING THE RAFTERS

The rafter square is designed to take advantage of the geometric laws of the right triangle. For example, the right triangle has, by definition, one ninety-degree angle. The angle at which the blade and tongue of a rafter square meet is also a ninety-degree angle. Thus, if you position your square with one leg level, then the other is always plumb. In building a rectilinear structure, this simple constant has lots of applications.

One is the planning and layout of rafters.

Roof pitch isn't traditionally specified in degrees (as in "This one's a forty-five-degree roof" or "That's a thirty-degree pitch"). Rather, the slant of a roof is specified by a ratio, namely, the relationship between its rise and run.

Whatever the pitch of a roof, it is specified as unit rise (vertical) over unit run (horizontal). The run is always twelve inches; the rise is determined by the builder or architect on the basis of taste (do you prefer the profile of the tall or low roof pitch?) and of practical considerations (a steep roof sheds snow more efficiently but it's more hazardous to work on). So a roof pitch is expressed by such ratios as twelve over twelve or six over twelve – meaning that in any given foot of horizontal distance the roof with a twelve or a six rise will rise twelve or six inches, respectively.

If you know the unit rise and

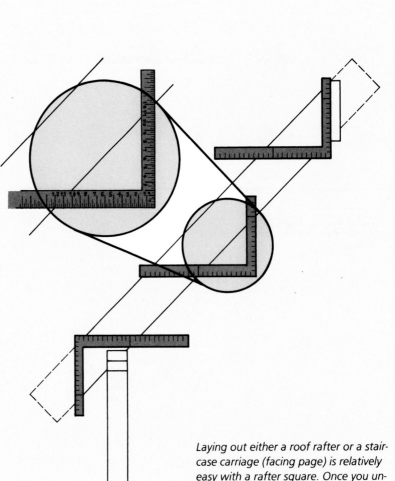

Laying out either a roof rafter or a staircase carriage (facing page) is relatively easy with a rafter square. Once you understand rise and run, it's mostly a matter of marking and cutting.

run of the roof you are laying out, then you can determine the length of the rafter using the rafter tables stamped on the face of the square. For example, if your roof is a twelve over twelve (that is, it has a rather steep forty-five-degree pitch), then the unit length of the rafter is to be found on the face of the square below the twelve-inch mark on its blade. For each foot of rise or run the rafter is 16.97 inches long.

If all this has your head spinning, console yourself with this:

The rafter square is a lot less complicated than the theory that makes it work. That's the beauty of it. To lay out a rafter, in fact, all you have to know is the ratio of the pitch. Then you position your square on the rafter so that the twelve-inch mark aligns with the bottom edge of the rafter; you pivot the square on that point so that the point where the blade and the rafter intersect is the same as the rise of the roof; and, thanks to the magic of ancient geometric figurings, you have your plumb cut.

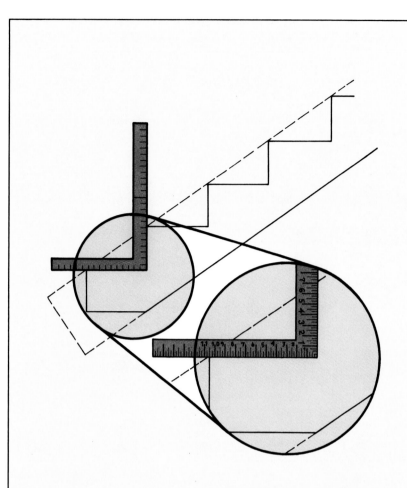

SQUARING THE STAIRS

Laying out a staircase is a task that in some respects resembles rafter layout. Again, the carpenter's square is essential; the rise/run ratio, too, comes into play, applied to the risers and the treads, the boards on the face and top surface of the stairs.

Determining the Rise. The vertical distance between the floors to be linked by the staircase is the principal determinant of the riser and tread dimensions. You divide the height by 7 inches; if, say, the floor-to-floor distance is 8 feet, 10 inches (or 106 inches), then you'll need 15 treads (106 divided by 7 equals 15.14).

Next, you divide the height by the number of treads (15 into 106), producing the exact tread height (7.06 inches).

Determining the Run. Now come the formulas. *The Rise plus the Run should equal approximately 17½ inches.* (Some designers prefer the formula *Two Rise plus the Run should equal between 24 and 25 inches,* but whichever formula you use, your staircase should probably have steps 7 inches or so high and treads 10 inches or so deep.) In our example, 17½ minus 7$\frac{1}{16}$ produces a tread width of 10$\frac{7}{16}$ inches or, to use the alternative formula, we would have a width of between 9$\frac{7}{8}$ inches and 10$\frac{7}{8}$ inches.

Now that you know the rise and run, laying out the carriage (the side boards that support the risers and treads) for the stairs is not unlike rafter layout. Again, the square is positioned on the board, with the blade and tongue calibrations aligned so that the rise and run measurements are at the edge of the carriage. Then you work up the carriage, repeating the process, moving and marking.

You can use the rafter to mark off your plumb cut (where the rafter butts the ridgeboard), the "bird's-mouth" (the angled cut where the rafter bites into the wall), and the tail cut (the rafter's lower end). And a simple gable roof is suddenly within your skills. More complicated roofing designs involving hips and valleys and compound angle cuts are not too difficult. When you buy a new square, it'll come with a booklet that will take you through the various steps in those processes.

Despite signs of years of use and abuse, this rafter square still offers its user the rafter tables . . . up there on the roof or wherever they are needed.

Two speed squares (small and large, top and right), as well as a combination square and try square (bottom left).

One variety of try square is the miter square, which has its blade and stock set at the acute and oblique angles of 45 and 135 degrees. This allows for marking both halves of a miter joint. Also known as a set square, the miter square is a great aid to the cabinet-maker, who repeatedly requires these standard angles.

Try squares come in a range of sizes, with blade lengths varying from two to twenty-four inches, depending upon the age of the tool and the purpose it was intended to serve. Machinist's or engineer's try squares are made entirely of metal and are smaller in scale.

The try square is typically put to use in this way. Lay the tongue flat upon the workpiece, then slide the stock flush to the edge of the wood. Thanks to its thinness, the tongue can then be used to scribe an accurate line on the piece to be cut or shaped. Try squares, both new and old, are often tools of great beauty, with blades of fine steel, iron, or brass, with stocks of rosewood, ebony, or other hardwoods. The blade and stock are sometimes fastened together with decorative rivets.

Speed Square. Sometimes called a "magic square," angle square, or protractor square, this tool functions as a square but is shaped like a triangle. One leg of the triangle has dimensions marked on its face in inches; the other has a raised ridge on the top and bottom to allow it to be butted to the workpiece. The third and longest side of the right triangle, the hypotenuse, has degrees (zero to ninety) marked on it to help in measuring and marking miter cuts.

Made of cast aluminum, the speed square serves most of the same purposes as the try square: You can use it to check a cut or joint for square, to mark cutoff lines, or as a straightedge to identify warped or cupped boards. The magic square is also handy as a cutting guide when using a hand-held circular saw.

The speed square is available in two sizes. The smaller size is seven inches on a side (the hypotenuse is just under ten inches), while the larger version is twelve by twelve by seventeen inches (actually, for sticklers who know the Pythagorean theorem, the precise measurement is 16.97 inches). The smaller magic square fits comfortably into a pocket of most tool belts.

The larger model is especially handy when working on large dimension lumber, two-by-eights and up. Its size makes it handy for laying out framing, when transferring measurements from one wide piece of lumber to another.

Another application for the larger square is in laying out rafters and stairways. An attachment called a layout bar is bolted to the underside of the square, and can be fixed at certain angles (or pitches) for speedy marking of plumb lines or bird's-mouths on rafters or riser and tread cuts on stairs. This handy extra turns the speed square into a sort of bevel gauge (see page 21), with one angle

Almost any square can be used to determine the flatness of a workpiece. The blade of the tool is positioned flush to the surface to be checked. In this case, the workpiece does not fit tightly to the blade of the square, indicating the wood is cupped.

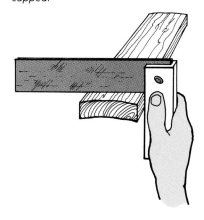

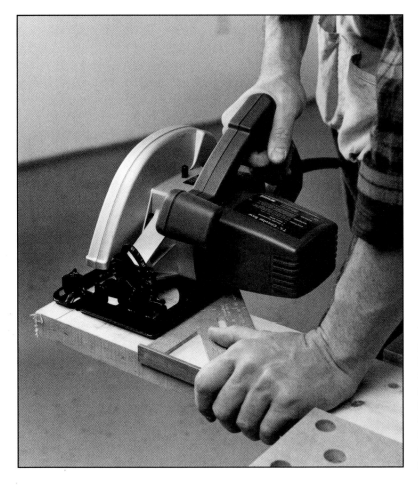

The speed square can be used to mark a board to be cut off . . . and for making sure you cut it square. Position the board securely on a sawhorse or other fixed surface, locate the speed square so that the blade of your hand-held circular saw is aligned with the cut line and its base is flush to the square. Then cut away . . . .

preset so that it can be quickly and accurately marked and replicated.

Like the rafter square, a speed square purchased new will come with an instruction booklet that contains rafter tables and explains a variety of techniques for which the tool can be used.

Combination Square. This tool is essentially an adjustable hand square, with a couple of clever advantages.

It consists of a rigid steel rule, usually twelve inches long (though sometimes combination squares have rules up to twenty-four inches in length), with a headpiece that slides along its length. A knurled nut and set screw are used to fix the headpiece to the rule at any point along its length, depending upon the purpose to be served. The headpiece has both a ninety-degree edge and one that forms a forty-five-degree angle with respect to the rule. The forty-five-degree angled edge accounts for one of the tool's alternate names, the forty-five-degree miter square. It's ideal for marking (and checking) both ninety-degree crosscuts and miter cuts.

The purposes vary: The combination square can be used as a try square, to determine the squareness of a piece of joint; like the speed square, it can also be used as a saw guide. When the head is set at the end of the rule, the combination square can measure heights. It can also be adjusted to measure depths, and some people find it's handiest for marking.

There is a spirit (bubble) level in its handle, so the combination square can be used for leveling. Some models even have a scribe in the handle.

Not all combination squares are created equal. They range in cost from about $15.00 to as much as ten times that price. The most expensive models come equipped with two additional parts: a protractor head, for marking and measuring angles, and a center head, for locating the center of a circular or cylindrical workpiece. But it isn't the added elements that account for the higher price.

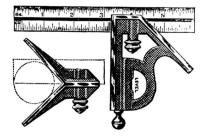

The combination square, along with an optional center head that can find the centers of circular workpieces.

The combination square can be used to mark stock for cuts, as a gauge to measure depth, as a forty-five-degree miter gauge, or as a try square. And it's a ruler, too, of course, with a built-in level and a scribe. The more I use it, the more I appreciate the flexibility of this tool.

The explanation is that the best combination squares are precision tools, useful for accurate work requiring tolerances beyond those needed by most woodworkers. However, if your work involves pattern-making or machine makereadies, for example, a more sophisticated combination square may prove to be a wise (even lifelong) investment. A top-quality square will stand up to lots of abuse without losing accuracy.

THE BEVEL GAUGE

A near relation of the try square, the bevel gauge also consists of a handle or stock with an attached tongue (or blade). In the case of the bevel gauge, however, its purpose is to fabricate or replicate pieces that are *not* square.

In its various forms, this tool is also known as a sliding bevel, angle bevel, bevel square, sliding T-bevel, or adjustable try square. Tongues range from seven inches upward, sometimes to eighteen inches or more. Whatever the length of the blade, the stock is always shorter.

The tongue of the bevel gauge fits into a groove cut into the head of the stock. In most models, a slot cut into the tongue allows further adjustments of the position of tongue and stock.

The tongue is usually made of thin steel and the stock of wood, plastic, or metal. Over the years, many bevel gauges have been made with rosewood or ebony and brass; sometimes, especially in hand-crafted models, the tongue material is also wood.

To put the tool to use, hold the stock against an edge with the tongue stretched across the workpiece. The tongue can be shifted to assume any angle between zero and one hundred and eighty degrees. When the bevel gauge is positioned at the angle you desire, use its locking mechanism (usually a bolt and wing nut, sometimes a lever device) to set the tool at that angle.

I've found the bevel gauge to be one of those wonderful tools that belies its simple design. When used properly, this modest little tool makes certain otherwise difficult tasks easy to do well. For example, to match an existing angle, you set the gauge, then relocate the tool onto the stock from which you want to make the companion piece. Then you're just a line and a cut away from matching the angle exactly. Best of all, there's no geometry or arithmetic, just marking and cutting.

The bevel gauge can be set from a square, protractor, or from an existing piece to be duplicated. It can be used to check the bevel or chamfer on a piece by setting it to match the bevel at one position on the workpiece and then sliding the bevel along its length, with the stock held flush against the piece's face. Where light is visible beneath the blade of the bevel gauge, the chamfer is not true.

If you do any restoration work at all, or cut oddball angles, buy a bevel square. I think you'll be surprised how often it proves its worth.

"Measure twice, cut once. . ." may be an aged aphorism your Industrial Arts teacher used to use. Oft repeated or not, it's good advice. Double-checking your measures and markings will save you double-cutting time and again.

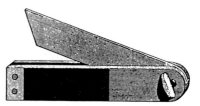

The bevel gauge, with its wooden stock and metal blade.

The bevel gauge is at its most useful when copying an angle is the task at hand. In this case, the gauge is set on the angle cut to be duplicated, then moved to the new stock (below) for marking and cutting.

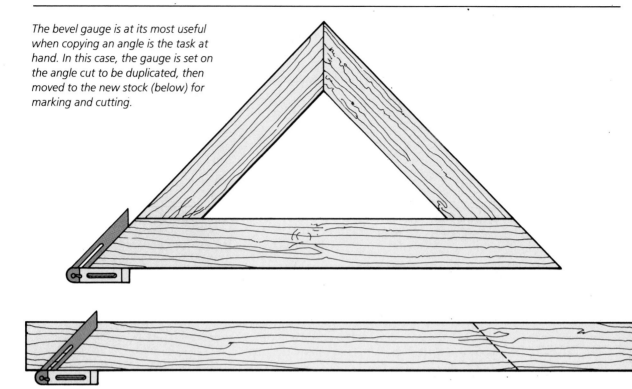

The level vial, complete with bubble and incised hairlines.

LEVELS

In making or repairing small rectangular objects, a square is invaluable in helping insure the joints are tight and the overall shape is true and square. But for a fixed structure, the scale of a mere square, even a framing square, doesn't permit it to provide all the answers.

Enter the level and its partner, the plumb (see page 27). These tools are used to establish true vertical and true horizontal.

The key element in a level is the sealed glass or plastic tube containing water, alcohol, chloroform, or some other clear liquid. The tube or vial is slightly curved and has two parallel lines drawn at its center. The vial is nearly filled, leaving an all-important air bubble. The vial is then precisely mounted in the body of the level.

No matter what size the level, its function depends upon that tiny air pocket in the vial. Since the specific gravity of the fluid is greater than that of the air, the bubble always rises to the highest point in the vial. When the frame of the tool is precisely level, the bubble will be aligned between the two hairlines at the center of the vial.

The bubble tube or vial can be mounted in a variety of instruments. Some are fixed permanently in place at the time of manufacture, others are adjustable or replaceable. The most common kinds of levels are described on the following pages.

THE PLUMB SQUARE

The genius, said Plato, has the shortest biography. Well, whoever it was that devised this device left behind only a remarkably clever tool.

Known to tool collectors as a plumb square or plumb level, it can actually be used as a plumb bob or a level. In some configurations, it can even be used as a square. Its unknown inventor must have died well before the birth of Christ, since it is believed that the ancient Egyptians used a version of this tool.

The plumb square comes in various configurations (shaped like an **L**, an **A**, an inverted **T**, and sometimes an **I**, as in a traditional level or even just a plane board held vertically). But the key element is a string-mounted plumb at the top of the tool, whatever its shape.

The **A**-shaped and the inverted **T** versions are designed so that their bases will be level when the plumb aligns with the center line; the **L**-shaped configuration and the plumb board are intended to help establish true verticality.

More convenient tools have come to be used in place of the plumb level or plumb square, but you still have to admire the good sense of the tool's creator.

Whoever he was.

A handsome maple plumb level (left) and an oak plumb square, both dating from the nineteenth century.

Carpenter's Levels. These levels come in many sizes, as two-, four-, six-, and eight-foot models are commonly available. For the tasks most of us address, one each of the two-foot and four-foot varieties will be sufficient.

Two-foot levels consisting of a wooden body and one or more bubble tubes are generally called carpenter's levels. Typically, such levels are about three inches high and an inch or so deep.

Two-foot and four-foot models alike usually have three bubble vials, one at each end mounted transversely for establishing true vertical, and one mounted at the center along the length of the level for horizontal leveling. For generations, carpenter's levels have been made of handsome (and very stable) woods like rosewood, ebony, and mahogany.

Mason's levels are usually four feet or longer.

Two things to keep in mind: the longer the level, the greater the accuracy – and that when working in cramped quarters, an overlong level is useless. So having a nine-inch torpedo level in your kit is probably a good idea. There are smaller ones, too, as short as an inch in length.

For odd jobs around the house, the two-foot length is easily stored, and used. The four-foot level is handiest for cabinet installation.

Vials are replaceable in many new models. Some levels also have a vial set at a forty-five-degree angle to the length of the tool. This allows you to determine proper position for braces and other angled pieces.

Torpedo Level. Typically nine inches long and tapered at the ends, this variety is sometimes known as a canoe or boat-shaped level. The body of the level contains two or three spirit tubes. The torpedo level is handiest when working in tight quarters. It's small enough to be

A pile-up of levels, from bottom to top: a four-foot aluminum level; a mahogany carpenter's level; another aluminum level, two feet long; a rosewood torpedo level; and a line level hung from a chalk line.

put to use in spaces that are too cramped for longer levels. The torpedo level will also fit comfortably into a pants pocket.

Line Level. Not much larger than the vial it contains, the line level is designed to be hung from a taut string stretched between the two points to be leveled with one another. Hooks at either end of the line level's body attach to the line at roughly the midpoint of the reach. As with other levels, when the bubble is centered between the vertical markings on the vial, the line to which the level is attached is true.

Line levels are used by masons, but carpenters, too, often find them handy when framing a new floor or ceiling, or in squaring off an old ceiling. Lining up concrete piers or fence posts, or checking the pitch of a driveway or gutter are other tasks that can be done conveniently with the line level.

Note that a sagging string will almost guarantee a misleading reading, so be sure to keep the string taut. Despite this precaution, however, you should keep in mind that even the tightest of strings sags perceptibly, which means a line level has limited accuracy. The line level should not be used where precision is all-important, but in foundation work and rough carpentry, it's a handy tool indeed.

Water Level. This level consists of a length of flexible plastic tubing or hose (typically, three-eighth-inch outside diameter, a quarter inch inside). At the ends of the tubing are rigid plastic cylinders set on bases that hold the cylinders upright. Water is contained within the device, usually with a few drops of food coloring added to make the water levels easier to read. On commercially available models, calibrations are printed on the cylinders.

Rather than relying on a single bubble, this clever device relies on Pascal's law which, in its simplest terms, states that water always seeks its own level. In practice, then, you set the two cylinders atop the two surfaces you want leveled with one another; the connecting tube can assume whatever position it will as long as it is below the level of the water-filled cylinders. If the surfaces are the same height, the water level in the two cylinders will be level; when the cylinders are not level with one another, the water in the device will be in the high zone at one end and the low zone at the other.

Levels must be handled with care. The vials can be broken with careless use; rough handling can also cause the precisely located vials to be shifted out of position. Dropping a level just once can throw the bubble out of alignment permanently.

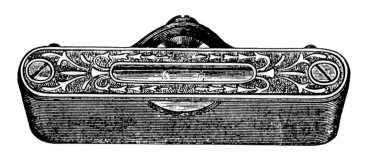

A Victorian ornamented pocket level.

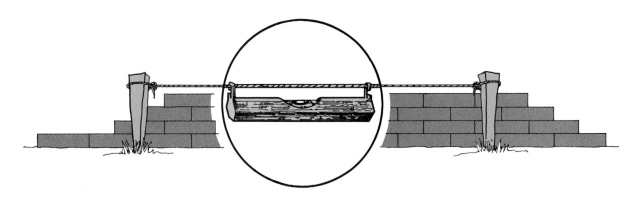

The line level isn't much more than a level vial with hangers, but this small-scale tool is a surprisingly handy construction aid.

The water level is often used by foundation contractors, but also by carpenters, landscapers, plumbers, and other tradesmen. Locating a dropped ceiling, for example, is made simpler by using a water level. Lining up footings for a deck (or the decking itself) is another task often tackled more easily using a water level than with a carpenter's level or even a line level.

One key advantage of the tool is that it can be of virtually any size, giving its user the ability to level objects that are many feet apart. The length of the hose between the cylinders can be only a few feet (in leveling a pool table, for example) or a hundred or more feet in leveling the foundation of a building. The nature of the water level also allows objects that are separated by some obstacle – a tree, a structure, or another obstruction – to be leveled.

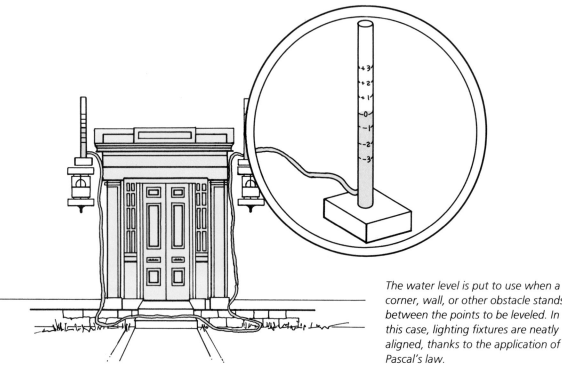

The water level is put to use when a corner, wall, or other obstacle stands between the points to be leveled. In this case, lighting fixtures are neatly aligned, thanks to the application of Pascal's law.

The calibrations on the cylinders also allow objects to be positioned out-of-level, such as porches or gutters that require a specified slope in order for water to drain or run off. A well-made water level should be accurate to approximately one-sixteenth of an inch.

THE PLUMB BOB

The plumb bob or plumb line employs the law of gravity to establish what is "plumb" (that is, what is exactly vertical, or true). You don't have to have aced high school physics to understand that a

When using any level, make sure the surface being leveled is clean of debris and dust . . . a small pebble or scrap of wood beneath one end of the level (especially a short level) can produce a significant error.

From left to right, four plumb bobs: an antique brass one in a teardrop shape, two modern plumbs of steel and chrome, respectively, and a chalk box doubling as a plumb. Any and all will do the job nicely.

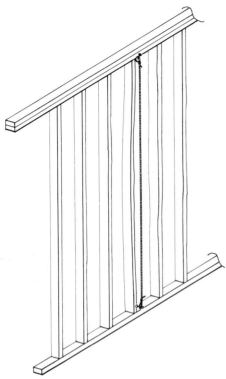

Strings are always straight . . . So if you're wondering whether that wall is true, just run a line from end to end of that last joist you nailed in place. . . .

string suspended with a weight at the bottom will be both vertical and perpendicular to any level plane through which it passes. In a sense, the plumb bob is the vertical equivalent of the line level.

I doubt that you'll be surprised to learn that this tool, too, has ancient origins. Evidence suggests that Egyptian architects used plumb bobs to establish verticals in constructing the pyramids. (It's also thought that, in tandem, they used flooded ditches to determine levels.)

The plumb consists of a specially designed weight and coarse string made of twisted cotton or nylon threads. (Masons prefer nylon because it stands up better over time to the dampness that comes with the trade.) At one end of the string the weight is affixed. Precisely machined and balanced bobs have pointed tips, and can be made of brass, steel, or other materials, including plastic.

To use the tool, the string is fixed at the point to be plumbed. The weight, or bob, is then allowed to swing freely; when it stops, the point of the bob is precisely below the point at which the string is fixed above. (Note that the line must be hanging free to get an accurate reading.)

The plumb bob is useful in establishing vertical for a wall in construction or a doorjamb when hanging a door. A spirit level will also accomplish those tasks, but some jobs are much more easily done using a plumb bob. For example, you can locate fixtures or decorations in relation to an object or surface below (or above) using the plumb line. Once it is hung and still, the top and bottom points can be marked and used as guides. The plumb line in one place can be

When staking out a foundation, batter boards with strings stretched between indicate the wall location. A line level is used to level off the strings, then the plumb, suspended at the intersecting corner points, is used to transfer the corner points to the grade below.

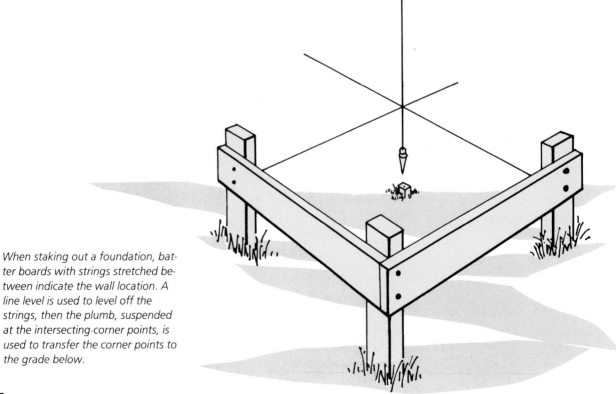

used to sight an object in another – a pipe, for example – for plumb. Surveyors sometimes use plumb bobs for lining up points or transferring them. Excavation and foundation contractors rely upon the plumb line, and in constructing a chimney the plumb bob can indicate whether a flue is running true vertical or veering off plumb.

Some bobs have pointed tips that can be bent by repeated use or abuse; if the point on yours is bent or out of alignment, replace it.

Plumb bobs may weigh as little as an ounce or as much as several pounds, depending upon the application. For most home toolboxes, I recommend having a single bob that weighs a few ounces. As is so often the case, it isn't how fancy the tool is, but how well you use it.

THE TRANSIT LEVEL

The practice of what is known as plane surveying (determining the position of buildings, boundaries, and topographical features as if they were located on a flat surface) has a long history, dating back to the ancient Egyptians. In the United States, a couple of early American all-stars, George Washington and Thomas Jefferson, were both trained surveyors.

The transit level is to plane surveying what the hammer is to nailing. It's an optical instrument (essentially a telescope) mounted on a

Periodically, you should check each of your levels for accuracy. To do so, find a flat, level surface and position the level on it. If the surface is not exactly level, shim one end of the level until the bubble reads true level. Then flop the tool, reversing the position of the ends. If the bubble no longer reads level, the level itself must be adjusted as it is out of true.

This nineteenth-century transit suggests something of the tool's constituent parts: There's a plumb, a spirit level, and a lens, as simple and refined as you could wish.

tripod along with a built-in spirit level. In combination with tape rules and calibrated rods, the transit compass, as it is also known, allows its user to determine the relative position of points, lines, and objects. Such determinations are useful in executing maps or plans – and, in some cases, construction.

A transit level is a precision instrument. It is calibrated to indicate not only true horizontal but also to provide a reading of the angle of inclination in degrees, minutes, and seconds. In the hands of a professional, a transit level is a varied and flexible instrument capable of many tasks, but some of its most basic applications are easy to master. As a result, this tool can be invaluable to anyone planning to build a new structure.

The tool works like this. The transit itself is leveled using the spirit level. The telescope then can be pivoted on a horizontal axis to point in any direction. With the help of an assistant who positions the graduated rod, the transit operator can then sight the transit on the rod and determine the relative height of the grade or the object on which the rod is located.

The transit level, thus, is invaluable for excavation and foundation work, as well as for landscaping. Some framing contractors, especially timber framers, also find it very useful when sighting in on flooring or ceiling surfaces to ascertain level.

There are remarkable antique transits to be found in collections and shops. I've seen some amazingly sophisticated new models in the hands of professionals that feature a variety of bells and whistles few homeowners could ever make use of, including computer chips and laser beams that extend the reading of the level to one hundred feet or more. But there are also some very practical new models to be bought for about $200.

A basic setup should consist of the transit level itself, a tripod base, a calibrated rod, and a windup tape measure, perhaps one hundred feet or more in length. (A powdered wig and wooden teeth are strictly optional.)

The transit can be the mason's best friend, making asymmetrical and non-uniform materials like stone easy to align in situations where level and plumb are critical.

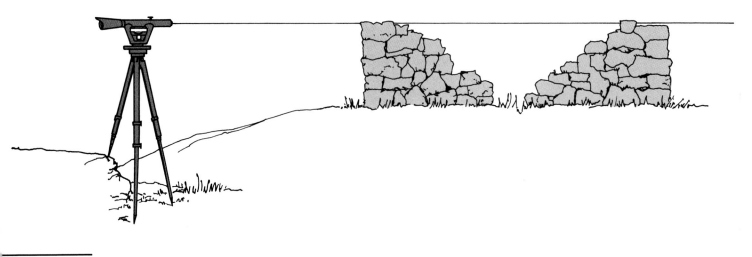

THE ON-SITE LEVEL LENGTHENER

One level plus one straight board and two loops of electrical tape equals one homemade level lengthener.

All right, let's say you're raising a stud wall of eight or nine feet and the longest level you have on hand is two feet. You know full well that the dimension lumber you're using is full of bows and warps – it always is. And you also know that an error of less than a sixteenth of an inch within the two-foot span of your level can multiply to a quarter-inch headache over the full height of the wall.

The problem, then, is establishing plumb (or level) over distances much greater than the length of your level.

The solution? The on-site level lengthener.

Sort through your woodpile and find a straight piece of stock (sight down its length, as you would the barrel of a gun). Cut it to the approximate length you're trying to plumb or level. Then tape your two-foot level (electrical tape will do as it's thin; duct tape probably won't because it is thick enough to add to the board a margin of error you don't need). And *Voilà!* A longer level is born.

(Check it before you use it, though, in case the milling on the piece was less than perfect. To check it, find a level surface with your level, then turn the level end-for-end.

Does it still read level? If not, you'll need to shim the level where it's mounted to the lengthener, perhaps with building paper or cardboard, until the bubble is dead center.)

You can get fancy, too, and fabricate a more permanent model. If you do, you should probably use a very stable wood that won't warp, or a piece of three-quarter-inch plywood, perhaps with solid wood edges glued to it.

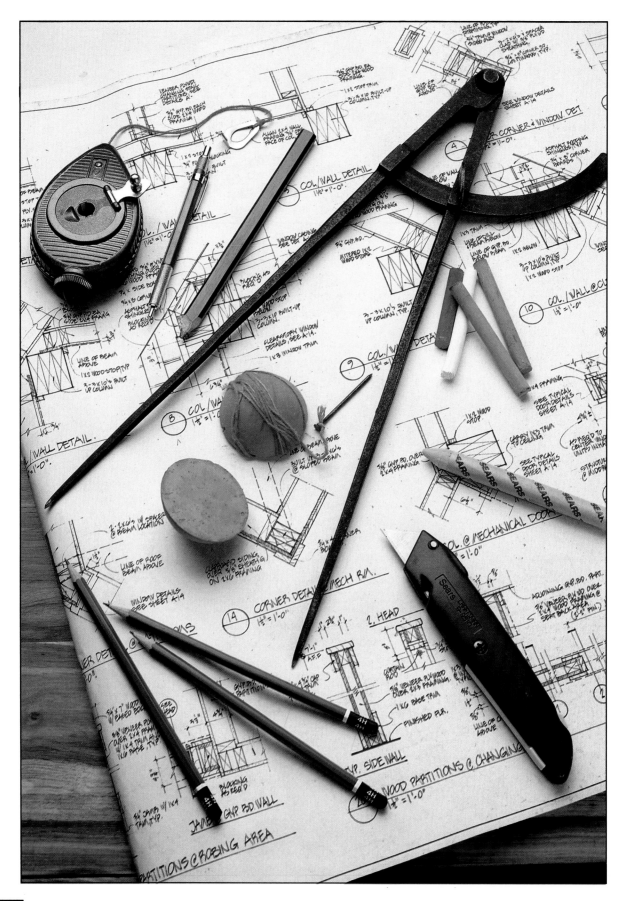

Chapter 3.
Making Your Mark

Y̲ou may think it's strange to devote a whole chapter, even a short one, to pencils and other marking devices. Surely anyone who can write his or her name can make a simple cut mark on a board?

Not so fast, I've been told by cabinetmakers of distinction. Seconded, mumble the finish carpenters whose joints are tight and true. You see, not all lines are created equal. What suffices nicely in cutoff work on two-by-tens is wildly inaccurate when making dovetails on a jewelry box.

Keep in mind, a fine line can mark the difference between first-class workmanship and the merely average. A genuinely sloppy look can result from a few finish cuts that are only tiny fractions of an inch off.

So here's the range of implements you might wish to have at hand to make your marks.

Pencils. Most framers I know use soft lead pencils, preferably the so-called carpenter's pencil. It's rectangular in section so it won't roll away and is easy to sharpen with a utility or pocketknife. Its point is also less likely to break off than that of a typical desk pencil because the graphite at the core of the carpenter's pencil is a broad, flattened strip. The dark lead reads well against the rough surfaces of dimension lumber and in less-than-perfect lighting conditions.

For work in a cabinet shop or other, more precise work, I favor a hard, sharp lead pencil. Drafting pencils work well for more accurate work and are available for a few cents at art supply stores. They come with lead cores of varying hardness. Softer pencils with H and HB leads are good for sketching but they aren't much help in the workshop. Harder leads – at least 2H and preferably 4H – are good choices for marking off.

Whatever kind of pencil you're using, keep it sharpened. For a fine point, keep a piece of sandpaper within reach. A twirl of the pencil tip on a piece of fine sandpaper will restore the point almost instantly.

Chalks and Other Markers. For marking rough layout on plywood or large pieces, chalk works well. It can be rubbed off later (or sooner, if the layout is changed) and is easy to see.

Other kinds of markers and crayons are commercially available, too, though many are indelible and can bleed through paint or

Surrounding the antique pair of scribes are (clockwise from top left) a chalk box, drafting pencil, carpenter's pencil, colored chalks, a crayon marker, utility knife, 4H drafting pencils, and two hemispheres of colored chalks.

A scribing or scratch awl, with wooden handle and steel shaft.

CHOOSING YOUR WEAPON

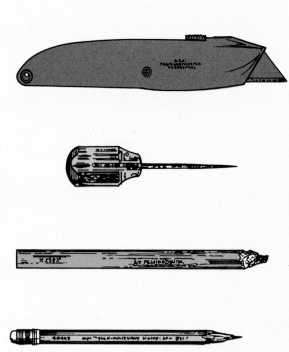

Your marker of choice may be a pencil or an awl, but keep in mind that pencil lines can be broad and inaccurate if the point is anything but perfectly sharp, and awl lines can be a bit fuzzy (especially when the tool is drawn across the grain). For straight lines, then, to be drawn on smooth surfaces where tiny fractions of an inch matter, a sharp knife blade works best.

There are numerous purpose-made marking knives, some of them crafted from fine woods and steel. But if pure practicality is your bottom line, you'll find a standard utility knife works well. In the shop when making cabinets, a razor-sharp X-acto knife with a smaller blade may work best.

The score line a sharp blade puts in the wood also cuts the fibers and reduces the risk of the grain tearing out when sawing or chiseling to the line. And to make it easier to see the lines on the workpiece, you may want to run the tip of a 4H pencil through the line you scored with the blade.

The layout stick is the cabinetmaker's equivalent of a story pole (see page 10), and it's a time-saver when you're cutting many workpieces to the same size.

Start with a piece of one-by-four or other planed stock you have handy. Cut a board to the precise length of the workpiece you'll need, then use it to mark the other pieces you need of that size. The layout stick will save you not only time but trouble (the time required to measure each piece, the trouble involved when you discover you have mismeasured one or two in a big stack). And it increases the likelihood that you'll get uniform pieces.

You can also mark on the layout stick using your try or magic square the various other lengths required for the job. This helps insure your cuts are uniform. But make sure you cut the layout stock to the longest dimension you'll need.

wallpaper. Use them with care when working what are eventually to be finished surfaces.

SCRIBERS AND AWLS

Pencils are not always the answer: A soft lead pencil with a dull tip produces a line roughly a sixteenth of an inch wide. In some kinds of woodworking, a sixteenth of an inch to one side or the other of the desired point produces shoddy workmanship.

I've found a scratch awl another option for marking workpieces. Such marking awls, which are sometimes called scribing awls or prickers, are commercially available. Make sure the point is very sharp so that it scratches into the grain.

While scratch awls are often used for marking straight lines, I think you'll agree that they are invaluable for locating the center of a hole. The indentation the awl leaves also serves as a starter point for a drill bit or wood screw.

Remember, the eye never lies. Whenever you make a cut mark, take a second look after the measuring and marking tools have been removed from the workpiece. Does it look right? Is it square or true?

Sometimes your eye can be fooled: A plumb line adjacent to one that is not true may not look right. But more often than not, if a line looks amiss, it probably is.

They look like a compass or a pair of dividers; in fact, they're called a pair of scribes. This tool is used to mark irregular cuts when matching one surface to an irregular one. For example, wallboard or a molding that is to be fitted around stone or brickwork or another uneven surface can be scribed and then cut to fit.

Before the chalk box and its ground chalk in reds and blues and yellows, there was just a reel. Before chalk, charcoal was the marking medium, and had to be applied to the string by hand. Later, the string was drawn across a hemisphere of solid chalk which many hardware stores still carry. However, the modern chalk box is a good deal easier to use. Note that the early Pennsylvania winder pictured here features mortise-and-tenon joinery.

THE CHALK BOX

I've admired this deceptively simple tool since I first saw my father use it decades ago. It is used to mark straight lines on a surface and, like so many tools that seem positively elegant in their simplicity, the chalk box as we know it today has been around for many, many generations. It's also known as a chalk line and snap line.

Its chief advantages, then and now, are that it can mark lines on rough surfaces (where pencils or other markers would be difficult to use) and it will make long, straight lines beyond the reach of any standard straightedge. Lines of more than twenty feet become less and less accurate as the distance increases.

The chalk box consists of a string with a hook on its end and a convenient case into which the line is reeled when not in use. Cotton string is generally preferred because its natural fibers retain the chalk well, don't stretch, and leave a neat line. The metal or plastic case has a crank for retracting the line and contains a reservoir of powdered chalk (usually red, blue, white, or yellow in color) that can be purchased in plastic containers for refilling.

When the line is pulled from the chalk box, chalk adheres to the fibers of the string; a gasket at the mouth of the chalk box insures the coating is consistent.

The chalk-covered line is then stretched between points on a plane, often using the hook at one end to hold the string in place. A small nail tacked in position also works well if you're working alone and the clip seems unwilling to stay put.

The opposite end of the line is pulled tight, and the string pressed against the surface to be marked. The line between the points is then lifted off the surface slightly, and allowed to snap back. The result is a line – in chalk – connecting the points.

The chalk box itself is designed and weighted so that it can act as an oversize plumb bob (see *The Plumb Bob,* page 27), allowing it to be used to snap a plumbed line when needed.

Tilers and wallpaperers find chalk lines handy since centerlines or start-finish lines can easily be snapped to act as guides for the application of their materials to fixed surfaces.

The line itself varies in length; some models come with as few as twenty or so feet, others with lengths of one hundred feet. If you find you use the chalk box often and for different tasks, you may want to have two on hand, each filled with a different colored chalk. That can make distinguishing lines on a wall or grid easier.

While we're talking chalk, if the line you are snapping is more than eight or ten feet long, pull the line taut, and have your helper come to its mid-point and pinch the line to the surface being marked. Then snap the line twice, once on either side. This will make for a more accurate line with less "drift" at the center.

With one end fixed in place, the string is pinched taut at the other. The line is then lifted at any point in between and allowed to snap back. A line of chalk is thus deposited on the workpiece.

CONTENTS

CUTTING AND DRILLING TOOLS

Building houses, making furniture, or fixing just about anything requires cutting, shaping, and fastening bits and pieces together. In Part III I'll discuss the tools used for shaping, and in Part IV we'll discuss fastening tools and techniques. But in this section my subject is the devices used to cut materials to size and those used to cut holes in them.

Given the elemental need for shelter, cutting tools were necessarily among the first tools to be devised by humankind after our ancestors abandoned their caves. On our continent, for example, Stone Age Indians shaped flint and other stones into implements for cutting and shaping, mounting them on handles. More than a few primitive hatchets survive in museums. Despite the excitable imaginations of small boys, many fewer were used for scalping than for cutting wood.

Drills and blades, whether saw blades or knife blades or snips, remain basic to any tool kit, whether you are building new or doing a restoration job. In our day, though, no single saw (or knife) will suffice to fulfill the range of needs for any but the most elementary tasks. The well-equipped toolbox today may contain more than a dozen saws, not to mention various knives and other cutters. Drills come in fewer configurations, but can accommodate a wide range of bits and drills to perform a variety of tasks.

Some of the tools described in these chapters were designed for precision work, others for rougher cutting and drilling. Certain of them cut wood, others metal, glass, and plastic. Many rely on the power of the human hand, while electricity drives the blades and drills of others.

The challenge is to identify the right tool for the job, and to use it accurately and safely.

Yours truly, sawyer in action, in proper position

Chapter 4.
A Symphony of Saws

Like people and plants, saws come in all sorts of shapes and sizes. By strict definition, a saw is simply a strip of metal with points ("teeth") cut along one edge. However, in conversation, we usually use the term *saw* to refer not only to the blade but to the framework that contains it and even to the motors that drive power saws.

Different saws are designed to perform different tasks, with varying degrees of accuracy and speed. Some are larger or smaller than others, some with blades that cut in a circular motion, others that cut in an up-and-down, reciprocating movement.

I'd like to be able to tell you exactly what you need, but the fact is that *you* have to identify which saws you need to have at hand. To do so, you must consider your requirements, your budget, and your particular tastes. Chances are you'll want to have both power saws and handsaws (see *Power or Precision: Handsaws Versus Power Saws*, page 42) and crosscut and ripsaws (see *Sawteeth: Their Kinds and Cuts*, page 46).

In making your selection, you'll also need to think about such practical considerations as weight, balance, and comfort. A nineteen-pound worm-drive circular saw may be too much for you to handle safely. On the other hand, a twenty-four-teeth-per-inch Japanese dozuki saw may be too fragile for the rough-and-ready woodworker.

I recommend that, if possible, you heft the saw before you buy it. Better yet, use a friend's to make a few cuts. Is it balanced? Does it feel as if it belongs in your hand? Does it look sturdy and well made? Ask yourself, "What will I use this saw for?"

Only you can know what are your basic needs; very likely, too, your needs will change as your skills improve and you take on more challenges. A basic yet comprehensive toolbox might include a crosscut handsaw; coping saw; hacksaw; saber saw; hand-held circular saw; backsaw and miter box.

Don't forget that, as tough as these tools may appear, you need to take proper care of them. Which also means using each of them safely (see *Safe Sawing* and *Protecting Yourself,* pages 58 and 66).

The saw family is one of multiple generations, as the varied ages of the tools pictured here suggest. Atop the mantel are (left to right) a hacksaw, saber saw, circular saw, and reciprocating saw; hanging above are fret, coping, bow, gentleman's, and dovetail saws. Surrounding the table saw are (moving clockwise, from top left) a handsaw, stair saw, Japanese folding saw and ryoba, compound miter saw, flush saw, drawknife, and miter box with backsaw.

POWER OR PRECISION: HANDSAWS VERSUS POWER SAWS

Two centuries ago, the average carpenter had no choices: The muscles in his arm were his sole source of power for his tools. In the nineteenth century, steam power came into common use in factories, but even the best-equipped builders and craftsmen still were left with no alternative to hand power beyond the reach of their belt drives. It wasn't until well into our century that power tools became portable and the province of the homeowner.

Even so, the debate goes on. Which is better? We know, in general, that power tools are faster, but does a router do a better job than a hand plane? Most purists would argue it does not. Certainly, there are some jobs that only a purpose-made handsaw, in skilled hands, can accomplish. Cutting dovetails, for example, or even coping a simple molding cannot be done as well with lots of watts as with one wrist.

So which is it to be – power or hand tools? The bottom line is that, unless you have no access to electric current, there's no reason to make an absolute choice. As usual, the point is to pick the right tool for the right task, and to use it well.

There's a simple rule of thumb that may be helpful. The more precise the work is, the more likely a hand tool will do it as well or better than one powered by electricity. So cut all your two-by-fours with a portable circular saw, since such framing members are usually hidden behind later surfaces and the tolerances are low (who cares if it's a sixteenth or so off?). But you may wish to do at least some of your fine-finish cut work with fine-toothed handsaws. You'll save yourself time both ways: in cutting the two-by stock and in the sanding and scraping time in the finer work.

THE HANDSAW

Many of the saws discussed in this chapter can be described as handsaws: They are the hand-held cutting tools that require the user to provide the power. However, the term *handsaw* brings to mind for most of us the generic carpenter's tool like the one my father had in his toolbox.

The handsaw I have in mind here has a blade roughly two feet long that tapers from the heel (at the handle) to its far end, the toe. Perhaps its most common application is on-site cutoff work: It's quicker to grab your handsaw and cut off a two-by-four or two than it is to set

The handsaw family, including the backsaws at left, the handsaws at right, and a coping saw and fretsaw at bottom. Beneath the standard backsaw are a gentleman's saw and a tenon saw. Note that the middle of the three handsaws has a slight sway or "skew" in its back, a traditional indication of a finely made saw.

up a power saw to do the job. The handsaw's depth of cut and narrow profile make it a flexible and useful tool for many tasks.

At the broad end of the handsaw is a closed handle that you approach as if to shake hands. The flat blade is usually steel and will flex from side to side (unlike the family of backsaws that have an added support along the back or "backbone" of the blade; see *The Backsaw*, page 45). Some high-quality handsaws have a slight sway at the back; they are lighter and better balanced. More expensive saws also are taper-ground, meaning the blade is thinner at the toothed edge than at the back, adding balance (by lowering the blade's center of gravity) and reducing the friction between the wood being cut and the body of the blade.

The handsaw handle is most often made of wood, though plastic handles are found even on good-quality saws. Wooden handles are likely to be beech or another close-grained hardwood. In some models, in particular those of a certain age, the handle may be carved not only for a comfortable grip but for ornament as well.

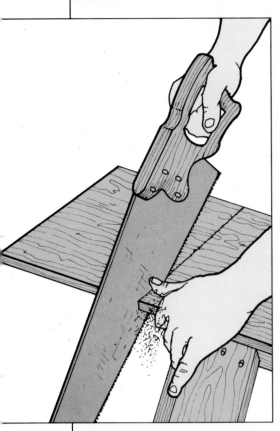

Use your thumb in starting a cut to guide the saw.

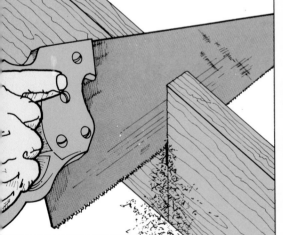

kerf [kurf] n. *The cut made by a saw in a piece of wood; or, the width of that cut. E.g. "A matter-of-fact place is a sawmill.... Its great problem is how to minimize the 'kerf,' the kerf being the track of the saw." From W.J. Gordon's* Foundry, *1890.*

PUTTING A HANDSAW TO USE

In some old-fashioned corner of my mind, I believe that a carpenter isn't a carpenter until he or she can make a straight handsaw cut without strain or complaint. Can you?

Rest the piece to be cut on a pair of sawhorses or on another sturdy surface. The wood must be high enough that the toe of the saw will not strike the ground at the bottom of the cutting stroke.

Your stance is important, with your left knee or foot weighing down the piece. Use a vice if the piece is too short to be held in position with your hand and leg.

Grip the board next to the cut line with your left hand. The right hand will wield the saw, with your index finger extended toward the end of the saw, as if to point out the direction of the cut.

To start cutting, position the blade to the waste side of the line (if you cut directly atop the line, you will shorten the piece by half the width of the blade). Now, draw the saw blade upward, using the side of your thumb to guide its teeth to the cut line. One or two short strokes should establish a slight indentation that will aid in keeping the saw on line.

Now the real cutting can begin, as the teeth on all but Japanese-made saws like the dozuki (see page 55) are shaped to cut on the downstroke. Watch the line, not the saw blade. And blow away the sawdust frequently so you won't veer off the line because the sawdust has obscured it.

Never push hard or force the handsaw. Too much pressure will reduce the accuracy of your cuts and succeed only in tiring your arm. Apply no pressure on the return stroke.

Your stroke should be regular and your arm should stroke up and down like a reciprocating piston with forearm and saw aligned. Think of the saw as an extension of your right arm. As you grow comfortable with it, exert more pressure on the downstroke; the return stroke does no cutting, so it's a restful return of the saw to the top of the cycle. When ripping a board, the strokes should be long and easy, using virtually the entire saw blade.

Keep in mind that saw speed isn't necessarily a virtue: When you try to race across a piece, you'll probably get off line, or you'll wear yourself out. A comfortable, steady stroke cuts surprisingly quickly.

When you near the end of the cut, you may need to support the waste to prevent its weight from binding the saw.

If your saw complains, making screeching noises or requiring additional pressure, the blade is probably being bent, twisted, or pinched.

With a little practice, you will master making straight cuts with a handsaw.

Some handsaws are designed for cutting across the grain (crosscut saws), others for cutting with the grain (ripsaws). The sawteeth in each case are ground differently (see *Sawteeth: Their Kinds and Cuts*, page 46). The ripsaw blade is also slightly longer than that of the crosscut saw (typically, twenty-six inches versus twenty-two or twenty-four inches).

With so many options available, handsaws are no longer an essential in every woodworker's toolbox. For my money, though, the convenience and practicality of these tools recommend them for an immense variety of uses (not least finishing off cuts started by portable circular saws where the cut stops at midboard: A few easy strokes of the handsaw will square off the kerf).

A ten- or twelve-teeth-per-inch crosscut saw of twenty-two inches in length is sure to be of use; if necessary, it can also rip a board, though not quite so efficiently as a purpose-made ripsaw can. For a more complete range of tools, you may opt for a ripsaw with five and a half teeth per inch. Don't use the ripsaw for crosscutting; it's hard on the saw, and can ruin the piece of wood, too.

THE BACKSAW

Like the word *handsaw*, the name *backsaw* is something of a catchall term. In general, a backsaw is a handsaw with a broad flat blade that has a reinforced back edge that insures the blade remains straight during cutting. The blade is usually of high-grade steel, the handle of wood (or, occasionally, plastic), and the back of steel or brass. Most backsaws have crosscut teeth.

The backsaw's blades are shorter than the handsaw's (sixteen inches is one common size) and narrower (typically, three or four inches wide). The combination of the smaller blade and the brass or steel reinforcement results in added control. I find the added weight of the spine (especially in more expensive brass-backed models) gives a more definite feel to the saw, and means that making a cut requires less pressure, which enhances accuracy.

Backsaws can be used for simple cutoff work or to perform numerous exacting tasks, from cutting small joints to dovetails. Backsaws of smaller sizes are generally used for such purposes, including the tenon saw, dovetail saw, and the so-called gentleman's saw.

Tenon Saw. In England, woodworkers call what we know as the backsaw a tenon saw. Typically, a saw sold here as a tenon saw has a blade twelve to fourteen inches long with fifteen teeth per inch. The broad blade allows cuts roughly three inches in depth. Some tenon saws have rip teeth, as they were originally designed for cutting tenons out of end grain, which means cutting with rather than across the grain.

SAWTEETH: THEIR KINDS AND CUTS

Muscles or electricity are required to power a saw, but the sawteeth really do the cutting, reducing the fibers of the material that is being cut to dust. Different classes of saws are manufactured to accomplish different purposes, and the configuration of the teeth on the cutting edge of the saw (whether it's a hand- or power saw, a circular saw, or a reciprocating saw) are designed and ground for specific uses.

In comparing handsaws, one of the first distinctions you'll notice is the number of teeth per inch. A handsaw with, say, eight teeth per inch will saw more quickly than one with twelve teeth per inch. However, the coarser teeth will also leave a rougher cut surface. Finer cutting saws, in general, make a neater cut but do so more slowly.

The nomenclature of blade-making can get unnecessarily complicated, but a couple of technical terms are useful. There is an easy logic, so saw talk needn't be confusing.

The sawteeth on a saw blade work by making two grooves in the material being cut. The sawdust is pushed out of the resulting kerf by the bevels on the teeth. In handsaws (and some circular saw blades) the teeth are alternately bent (or "set") beyond the plane of the blade itself, meaning that the cut made by the teeth is wider than the body of the blade.

Another tooth term worth knowing is *gullet*. Several names for parts of the teeth are self-explanatory, like face, back, and point. But the trough between teeth is called the gullet.

Gullet

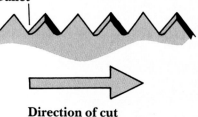

Direction of cut

Crosscut teeth

Rip teeth

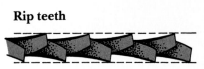

Blade set

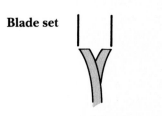

HANDSAW TEETH. The basic kinds of teeth on handsaws are these:

Crosscut. The knifelike teeth on a crosscut saw are angled at about seventy degrees to the length of the blade. Typically, there are ten or twelve beveled points per inch. Other kinds of handsaws, like Japanese saws and backsaws, generally have more teeth per inch.

Rip. Ripsaw blades are designed to cut parallel to the grain, so ripsaw teeth are square, ground perpendicular to the length of the blade. Five or six points per inch are usual.

Think of the distinction this way: Crosscut teeth are shaped like knives, to cut across the grain; ripsaw teeth are more like chisels, so that they can chop through the wood along the grain.

Handsaws can be resharpened. Files and other accessories are sold to assist in that task. However, saw-sharpening requires practice and precision, so it may be better left to the pros.

CIRCULAR SAW BLADES. Because of the speed at which the blades spin and the fact that they are ground onto a round blade, circular sawteeth differ somewhat from those on handsaws. The same rule of thumb regarding number of teeth holds true (the more teeth, the finer the cut) but because circular saws are sold in a variety of diameters (ranging up to ten, twelve, and even fifteen inches for large miter and radial arm saws), teeth-per-inch comparisons are not applicable. Rather, you need to compare the number of teeth on a given blade to those on another of the same diameter. Thus, a seven-and-a-quarter-inch blade might have anywhere from sixteen teeth to two hundred, depending upon its quality, kind, and use.

The common circular blades are these:

Combination. Most circular saw blades sold today are combination blades. Designed to cut hard or soft wood, either with or across the grain, the combination blade features both rip and crosscut teeth with deep gullets between them.

Not all combination blades are the same, as some so-called master combination blades have deeper gullets and others have shallower gullets. "Expansion grooves" are cut into the body of some saws to dissipate heat. Some blades have set teeth, while others are termed hollow-ground, meaning the body of the blade is thinner than at the edge; a cut made with a hollow-ground blade looks as if it were planed (hence the other name of planer blades for hollow-ground blades). A fine combination seven-and-a-quarter-inch blade has forty teeth; coarser general-purpose blades have fewer teeth, sometimes as few as sixteen.

Rip and Crosscut Blades. These blades are designed to cut with the grain and across the grain, respectively. As with handsaw blades, rip and crosscut teeth are ground differently: Rip teeth cut parallel with the grain, crosscut teeth at an angle. Rip teeth are generally larger and crosscut teeth finer.

Plywood and Veneer Blades. These fine-toothed crosscut blades will cut all sorts of woods, but are specifically designed for cutting plywood. A minimum of splintering of

The differing saw blades illustrated below are each drawn both in profile and top view.

Combination blade

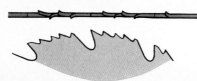

Rip blade

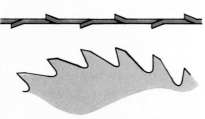

Crosscut blade

Carbide-tipped blade

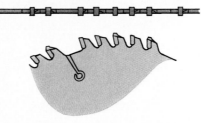

the surface veneer occurs because of the set and the sheer number of the sharpened teeth. In a seven-and-a-quarter-inch blade, two hundred teeth are usual.

Carbide Blades. Carbide or tungsten-carbide blades are not actually different types of blade; their names refer to the materials used in the hardened tips that have been attached to their teeth. They outlast traditional steel blades and though they are more expensive to purchase, generally prove more economical over the long run.

Carbide blades can be bought in a confusing variety of tooth configurations. The different kinds are identified by the way the carbide tips are ground. For example, the "flat top" is for ripping, the "triple chip" for ripping hardwood, the "alternate-top bevel" for cutoff work, and on and on. A thirty-six or forty-toothed ATP (alternate top bevel) will perform the widest range of cutting tasks.

When buying circular saw blades, select tooth configurations that are best suited to your needs. Be aware, too, that the arbor on your saw (the shaft that passes through the center hole on the blade) is not always the same, so buy the one that fits your specific tool. Five-eighths of an inch is the most common arbor size in portable circular saws.

As with handsaws, some circular saw blades can be reset and resharpened. Again, a professional can probably do it faster and better than you can and at a reasonable price.

BACKSAWING

The technique of backsawing is somewhat different from that of sawing with a handsaw. The fundamental distinction is that the backsaw's cutting edge isn't angled to the workpiece; rather, you hold the backsaw so that its cutting edge is parallel to the board.

Starting the Cut. Begin by positioning the wood to be cut on a flat, steady surface. Grip the saw as you would a handsaw, with your index finger pointed along its length.

Position your saw, as always, to the waste side of your mark, and tilt the blade up slightly, perhaps ten degrees. Guiding with your finger, begin the cut with a firm but patient push stroke.

Cutting Through. As you saw, gradually level the blade so that you cut a kerf across the board of approximately even depth, perhaps an eighth of an inch. With this kerf line established, saw the board at a steady, measured pace.

Your forearm, wrist, hand, and the backsaw should be aligned; the cutting motion should be pistonlike, moving back and forth on a horizontal line. Use almost the entire blade, keeping the cutting edge parallel to the workpiece. Stop shy of the last few teeth at the heel and toe of the saw to prevent the blade from jamming.

Cutting Wooden Elements in Place. The backsaw is also handy for cutting wooden elements that are still in place, like cutting out a piece of baseboard or other trim molding. You will have to adjust your stroke to each job, shortening and slowing as necessary.

The backsaw put to use in situ to cut a chair rail.

Dovetail Saw. This small backsaw is designed specifically to do what its name suggests. Typically, dovetail saws have blades of about ten inches in length with fourteen to twenty teeth per inch. Most dovetail saws can cut to a depth of roughly one and a half inches.

Gentleman's Saw. This backsaw is the smallest of the breed. Traditionally a tool of the hobbyist "gentlemen" of an earlier era, the gent's saw has a blade six or eight inches long, and very fine teeth (eighteen teeth per inch is common). Great for cutting dovetails or model work, the gentleman's saw probably is more at home in the workshop than at the work-site.

Backsaws of several different sizes are also available with special hardened teeth for making cuts in plastics or brass and with offset handles that allow cutting flush with a surface.

You won't find this one at your local hardware store. It's called a stairbuilder's saw and dates from the eighteenth century. The shaped wooden handle was fitted with a handmade blade, which is attached in this saw with a handwrought nail.

Stair saws were used to cut the sides of the grooves on stair carriages (the rest of the groove would have been chiseled out, then the stair treads and risers fitted in). Probably made in England, this antique tool was also known in its day as a grooving, trenching, and notching saw.

Miter Box Backsaw. Backsaws have traditionally been used in miter boxes, too (see *The Miter Box,* below). Such saws are usually larger than standard backsaws, with blades up to twenty-six inches in length. Crosscut teeth are standard.

THE MITER BOX

Making a clean right-angle cut doesn't take the hand of a craftsman, but miter cuts are different. I've done them and you probably have, too; if so, you probably agree that even standard forty-five-degree cuts are difficult to line up perfectly and not worth attempting freehand. Out-of-the-ordinary angles are even trickier, but you needn't abandon any notions of making such cuts, since there are lots of devices available to assure that forty-five-degree or other angle cuts are true.

The miter box is one such tool. In one or another of its guises, the miter box has been in common use for more than three centuries. At its simplest, it is a troughlike wooden box, open at the ends, with slots in the sides. A handsaw (often a backsaw) fits into the slots which act as guides to keep the saw on line, making miter cuts accurately and quickly.

Metal and plastic miter boxes are available, too, some even adjustable for compound miters (angle cuts that are more or less than ninety degrees from the vertical as well as the horizontal plane of the stock). The simpler wooden boxes have a limited number of guides cut into the sides (forty-five, ninety, and one hundred and thirty-five degrees at a minimum), but more expensive models adjust in quite

You have to admit, the miter box hasn't changed all that much since this model was marketed before World War I. And it was hardly a new idea even then.

precise increments, allowing you to cut almost any angle. Top-of-the-line models have bearings for smoother sawing and grips to hold fast the workpiece that is being cut. Many models come with a built-in or matching saw, either a backsaw or a purpose-made frame saw with interchangeable blades.

Miter boxes (or their powerful brethren, miter saws, see page 72) are invaluable for molding work, frame-making, and other tasks requiring tight angle-cut joints. If you can use a handsaw, you can use a miter box; it's really that easy.

I see many fewer professionals carrying their miter boxes to the job these days than I used to only a few years ago (thanks to the power miter saw). But many traditional woodworkers, professional and amateur alike, still swear by the feel, control, and even the familiar reassuring sound of the backsaw at work in the miter box.

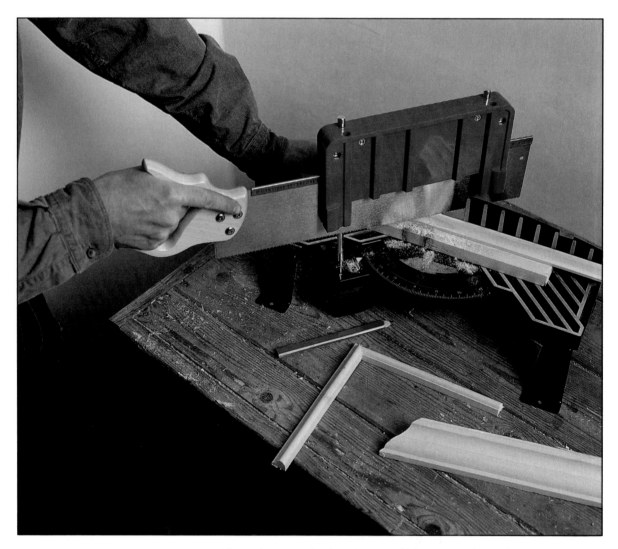

When using your miter box, it's a good idea to raise the workpiece on a piece of scrap to protect the base of the miter box.

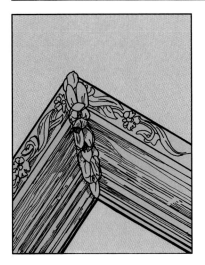
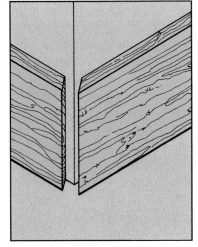
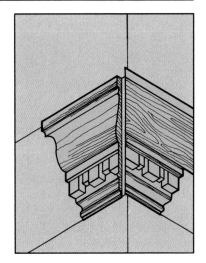

miter [my-ter] n. *An oblique surface shaped on a piece of wood or other material so as to butt against an oblique surface on another piece to be joined with it; a matching angle cut.*

Whether the molding is simple or ornate, a miter is a miter is a miter.

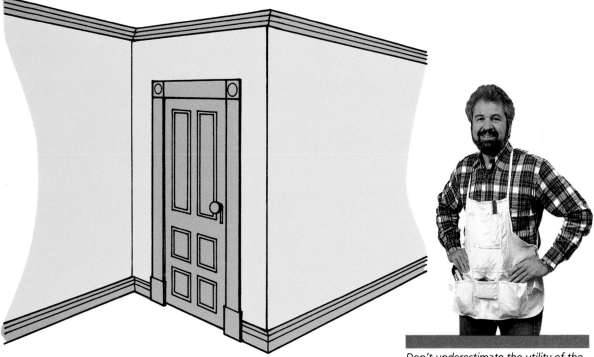

An inside *corner is the place your second-grade teacher sent the bad boys to stand in when they misbehaved (left); an* outside *corner juts into a room.*

Don't underestimate the utility of the miter box for making ninety-degree cuts. When your workpiece has to be cut perfectly square, the miter box is good insurance.

THE COPING SAW

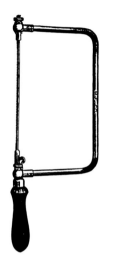

Coping is a process by which one piece with an irregular surface is fitted to another. In practice, most of us encounter coping in cutting trim work, especially cornice and baseboard moldings.

Only the coping saw can give the tight inside corner joints that make your work look professional. Corners that aren't coped gap and look sloppy; they're a telltale sign of unskilled carpentry. The coping saw and its cousin the fretsaw (see below) perform other tasks, too, as both are designed to cut along most any curve at a range of angles.

The lightweight coping saw has a hardwood handle affixed to a **U**-shaped steel frame. The frame holds a very thin blade between the arms of the **U**. A threaded bolt connects the frame and the blade to the handle. Turning the handle tightens (or loosens) the tension on the blade. Holders at either end of the blade can be pivoted so the angle of cut can be adjusted.

The standard blade on most contemporary models is six and three-quarter inches; ten-, fifteen-, and twenty-teeth-per-inch blades are available. The depth of the throat varies, but approximately five inches is usual.

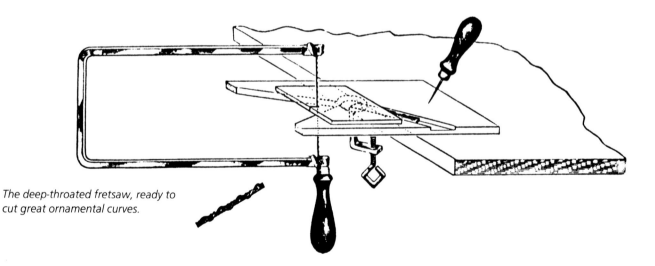

The deep-throated fretsaw, ready to cut great ornamental curves.

Fretsaw. Also called a scroll saw, the fretsaw has a frame with a much deeper throat. The blade of a fretsaw usually has very fine teeth, typically twenty to thirty per inch. It is used to cut shapes deeper within a board, panel, or sheet of plywood, and given its thin, toothy blade it can cut tight, fine curves. Blades with forty teeth per inch for cutting metal are also available.

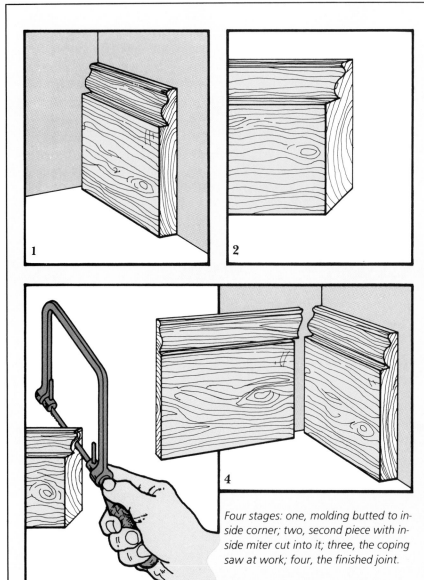

Four stages: one, molding butted to inside corner; two, second piece with inside miter cut into it; three, the coping saw at work; four, the finished joint.

COPING AN INSIDE CORNER

Many, many years ago some very clever person devised this technique. Even today, there's a wonderful simplicity to coping a corner that leaves me wondering, "Now, how did they ever figure this would work?"

Fitting a molding into an inside corner is a four-step process. First, identify the piece that is to run along the length of wall that is the most obvious. Cut its end off so that it butts neatly into the corner. In most instances, a simple chop cut will do. Tack the piece in place.

Next, cut the second piece using a miter box or power miter saw. Cut it at a forty-five degree angle, leaving the end with an inside miter. This means that the portion of the molding that stands proud of the wall will be shorter than the side that is to be nailed to the wall.

Finally, cope along the cut line on the face of the mitered molding, sawing perpendicular to the length of the piece. You may find it fits better if you cheat slightly, cutting at a slight angle toward the rear of the piece.

Fit the coped piece in place. If your cut is neat, the coped molding will perfectly match the contour of the first piece of molding.

This coping technique may sound harder than it actually is. If you feel hesitant about trying it, you'll need to get bold and go for it when you are doing cornice or other moldings with curved profiles. Simple miter cuts of such moldings almost never align neatly. But get your confidence and sawing skills up first by practicing on cove, quarter round, or other simple moldings.

JAPANESE SAWS

These saws are distinguished by more than their country of origin. The shape of each saw is distinctive, as is the configuration of their teeth (each tooth is typically cut in a diamond shape that has come to be known as Japanese style). They are even used in ways that contrast with how saws of American or European origin are used. (Let it be noted, however, that saws that work on the same principle have long been utilized by Eastern European craftsmen.)

Despite the initial strangeness of these saws, many American woodworkers, I've observed, have not only come to admire their design but to prefer them for some jobs.

The key difference from most Western handsaws and backsaws is in technique. Japanese-made handsaws cut on the *pull* stroke. To someone who has been push-sawing for a good many years, the feel of cutting on what has always been the return stroke can seem odd indeed, at least at first. You may be surprised, though, that with a minimum of practice the pull-saw technique comes to feel quite natural.

Five saws from the Japanese toolbox: the ryoba (top); a dozuki (right); a keyhole saw; and two folding saws.

One reason is that the basic motion remains familiar, still a reciprocating push-and-pull. More to the point, the approach will also come to seem quite logical, since by pulling the saw blade toward you, you are better able to watch the progress of the blade as you cut. I certainly won't argue that these saws are for everybody, but you can't be sure until you've made a cut or two with one.

As with Western handsaws and backsaws, there are different Japanese saws for different purposes. Four that may come in handy are the *dozuki, ryoba,* keyhole, and folding saw.

Dozuki. The dozuki is the equivalent of a back or tenon saw. The supported blade is approximately ten inches long with fine teeth, usually with more than twenty teeth per inch. As with all Japanese saws, its kerf is very narrow, and it cuts quite rapidly.

This saw is useful in finish work (like cutting moldings) as well as one-repetition cutoff work (when you need one oddball length of, say, one-by-four, it's easier to cut it quickly with a dozuki than to set up a power saw and sawhorse). Once you grow accustomed to having a dozuki at hand, you will come to rely on it for countless spur-of-the-moment jobs.

Ryoba. While the dozuki clearly belongs to the backsaw family, the ryoba really has no Western equivalent. At first sight, it more nearly resembles a weapon than a tool, but it's actually a clever combination saw.

The ryoba has two sets of teeth on opposite sides of its blade. One set is for crosscutting, the other for ripping, with ten to fourteen and five to seven teeth per inch, respectively. If you have a toolbox in which your on-site tools are stored conveniently after each use, this is a very handy tool. But keep in mind that it's also a fragile one that is never the same again after it's been stepped on.

Keyhole Saw. A Japanese-style keyhole saw is also available. It, too, has a finer blade than its American counterpart and cuts on the pull stroke. It's handiest for cutting holes with very small radii, some even smaller than the saber saw can conveniently cut.

Folding Saw. Japanese folding saws are probably the handiest of the Japanese saws on site. Several different configurations are sold (dozukis with back supports, others without), but all are useful to have at hand, especially for one-shot tasks. After use, the blade folds safely into its handle like an oversized jackknife, and the whole tool is small and light enough to be carried in a back pocket.

The teeth on such folding saws are generally a bit coarser than on dozuki dovetail saws (usually about eighteen per inch), but they are fine enough for trim work. The blade length varies from model to

Another imported saw (this one from France) has an occasional use, in this case in the repair of a salvaged door. When I had filled the old mail slot, two holes remained. I filled them with dowels, then cut them flush to the rail of the door. With a coat of paint, the door looks like new.

model, but nine inches is common. Quite inexpensive mass-production models are beginning to arrive on the market, so these are becoming very affordable tools.

THE HACKSAW

Even woodworkers have an occasional need to cut metal. From time to time, a nail, a bolt, a pipe, or some other metal element appears that needs to be cut out or cut to size. Enter the hacksaw, a tool that belongs in every toolbox.

The hacksaw consists of a bow-shaped steel or aluminum frame that adjusts to hold replaceable blades of eight to sixteen inches. There is a pistol-grip handle of plastic, wood, or metal at one end; at the other, a wing nut and bolt adjust the tension on the blade.

Blades are available not only in different lengths but with varying teeth sizes. Finer teeth are usually set in a wavy pattern; the twenty-four-teeth-per-inch blades are best for cutting angle iron, heavy pipe, brass, or copper, while the thirty-two-teeth-per-inch blades are suitable for cutting sheet metal or thin-wall tubing. Coarser teeth (fourteen or eighteen teeth per inch) are usually set in a raker pattern, with the teeth set to protrude alternately from one side of the blade to the other. Used for thicker, tougher metals like steel, blades with raker teeth can clear chips that would clog finer-patterned teeth.

Like most saws, the hacksaw cuts on the push stroke. However, on the return stroke the hacksaw should be lifted slightly to prevent the teeth from dulling.

Keep the blade on your hacksaw finger-tight, but don't tighten it with a wrench or pliers. Too much tension will break the blade almost every time when cutting.

The hacksaw, circa 1887. Little has changed except for the handle which today more nearly resembles a pistol's grip.

THE BOW SAW

One reason for the fascination of antique tools is their visual appeal. For many people, the bow saw has just such an attraction; to my eye, even its shape looks tried-and-true, as handsome as it is utilitarian.

The bow saw is of ancient design; the hacksaw and coping saws are its diminutive and distant contemporary cousins. More than likely, the bow saw was devised to utilize to best advantage a small amount of an expensive material, such as iron and, later, steel. Thus, the substantial wooden elements of the saw provide a framework for holding the metal blade in tension. A woodsman or toolmaker could easily shape these of beech, birch, cherry, or other hardwood, and would

The metal piece to be cut should be secured in a vise, as you will require both hands on the saw to get the cut started and to cut most efficiently.

Position one hand on the handle (pointing the index finger along the frame of the saw) with the other at the front of the saw gripping the bow frame. This allows you to guide and to add force.

Cut in a steady rhythm. Take care not to wander off line. If you do, and then try to twist the blade to compensate, the brittle hacksaw blade may break.

have to purchase only the long, thin metal blade.

The ends of the blade attach to the cheeks, as the wooden members perpendicular to the blade are called. Running parallel to the blade across the center of the bow saw is a stretcher. Atop the cheeks is a cord and winding stick that is turned to tighten or loosen the blade. The closer the upper ends of the cheeks are drawn together, the tighter becomes the tension on the blade.

The bow saw can be used for a variety of tasks, both on site and in the shop. In some European countries, the bow saw is a standard woodworker's tool; in others it is rarely found in the workshop but is often used in the forest. The explanation is more a matter of tradition than of function.

As with any tool, the bow saw takes a bit of practice to master. The larger models require two hands (some users prefer a two-handed grip that distantly resembles that used on a golf-club handle, others like a front-and-back grip similar to that used when hacksawing). A well-balanced smaller bow saw can be comfortably used one-handed. The blade length may range from as little as fifteen to as much as forty inches.

The bow saw is sometimes called a frame saw, although some frame saws are not bow saws. The broader category of frame saws includes those that have two blades (one each at the top and bottom, flanking a wooden stretcher) and some with single blades at the center. Some frame saws have larger blades and are intended for cutoff work; others have thinner blades that can be turned in the frame so that the tool can be used like an oversized coping or fretsaw.

Not everyone needs a bow saw, of course, but if looks are part of the appeal tools have for you, few tools are more impressive than a handsome bow saw.

The Tubular Bow Saw. *A very durable and practical variety of the bow saw is made of metal tubing. Also called a log saw, buck saw, or forester's saw, the tubular bow saw is a very handy tool for limbing branches from a tree, cutting up firewood, or doing rough cutoff work on-site. As you can tell, these once belonged to Rip Van Winkle, who hung up his saws and promptly fell asleep.*

Made of beech, this delicately shaped bow saw probably dates from the late nineteenth century. The blade is twenty-two inches long, the frame fourteen inches high.

SAFE SAWING

Every time you use a power saw you put your very own flesh and blood at risk. I've worked with more contractors than I like to think about who have lost fingers or sustained other injuries thanks to the powerful tools of the trade. According to the U.S. Consumer Product Safety Commission, in 1991 alone, nearly twelve thousand people required emergency-room treatment for circular saw-related injuries.

I've observed that two kinds of sawyers are the most likely to get hurt. The most obvious is the raw rookie, the person who uses a powerful cutting tool in ignorance. Ironically, the other class of workers in danger are the veterans who use their tools constantly, especially to perform repetitious tasks. Using the saw seems so natural, so automatic as to be second nature; then the

worker loses concentration – and an accident happens.

Never take a tool for granted, no matter how familiar with it you may be. Just about any circular saw, whether it's a portable, chop box, or table saw, can take off a fingertip – or more – in a second. Reciprocating saws require careful use, too.

The good news is that most accidents are preventable if these and other cutting tools are treated with respect and care. Employ the following strategies for avoiding mishaps.

Establish a Pattern. The first time and every time you use a power tool, do so from a balanced, comfortable stance. Once the workpiece is marked, locate it securely on a sawhorse, bench, or tabletop. Position the tool, too, so that your cutting stroke is easy and logical. Avoid awkward positioning.

Plan, Pause, and Then Power Up. Once you are in position,

mentally cut the piece. Are there any obstructions to the blade (that means in the piece itself, like old nails) or beneath the piece (like the top of your work surface)? Will the saw blade bind? Will the waste fall safely out of the way? Once the piece is cut, will either end be unbalanced and fall awkwardly, sending you or your saw for a ride? If you're using a portable power tool, where will you put it after the cut has been made?

I suggest you make it a habit to pause one moment more, each time you make a cut. Ask yourself three more little questions – even if you're making a cut identical to one you made a minute ago. First, are you wearing your safety glasses? Second, is the blade clear? And, third, are both of your hands safely positioned?

Keep Your Work-Site Neat. Too much sawdust, carelessly strewn chunks of wood, piles of stock, or snaking power cords are all threats to the

THE HAND-HELD CIRCULAR SAW

The circular saw was invented in England at the turn of the nineteenth century, though there is considerable disagreement on precisely when and by whom the tool was devised. Whenever and wherever it happened, the innovation was a great step forward. Among many advantages of the circular saw is its simple efficiency. Unlike the reciprocating saw, which cuts only half the time (each cutting stroke is followed by a return stroke), the circular saw is ready to cut whenever its blade is in motion.

With the possible exception of the electric drill, the hand-held circular saw is the power tool most often found in the average homeowner's tool chest. It is easy to use, affordable, and astonisinghly flexible and practical. The portable circular saw has other names, too, including the Skilsaw (a proprietary trade name) and electric handsaw.

sawyer. A minor stumble with a spinning saw blade at hand can be disastrous.

Use Only Sharp Blades. A dull blade is an invitation to trouble and leads to unnecessary wear and tear on your equipment. With a dull blade, you'll find yourself forcing the cut. Before replacing blades, always disconnect the saw from its power source.

Wear Your Protective Equipment. Always wear your safety glasses – a scratched cornea, or worse, is never more than one tiny airborne sliver away. Other protective gear may be appropriate, too (see *Protecting Yourself,* page 66).

Maintain Your Equipment. Check to be sure that the blade guard is functioning properly. In the case of a portable circular saw, the spring-loaded lower guard should pivot back into the blade housing as you cut, then automatically return to position after the cut. If the guard doesn't

work, set it aside to get repaired and use another saw until it comes back in safe condition again.

Unless the tool is double-insulated, it should be equipped with a three-prong grounded plug. Do not remove the third prong. Three-pronged plugs should be plugged into a matching electrical receptacle or into adapters used with the ground wires properly attached.

Some woodworkers complain that blade guards on table saws obstruct their vision. On the other hand, surveys suggest (no surprise here) that accidents are much less frequent on a properly protected table saw. Use the guards you have; install one if there isn't one.

The switch location on table and radial arm saws and other fixed power tools is important. It should be within reach; switches that can be turned off without letting go of the workpiece, like foot-

operated models, are a sensible precaution.

Don't forget periodically to inspect your power cords, because a cord in poor condition can be an electric shock just waiting to happen. In general, maintain your tools properly, whether it's lubricating your worm-saw or cleaning the accumulated sawdust out of the table-saw housing.

Remember, Safety Saves Time. If all these preparations sound time-consuming, keep in mind that injuries are expensive, both in emergency-room bills and in lost time. You will also find that a little planning for safety often produces other efficiencies. The better organized you are and the more you make every operation a logical routine, the less time you spend looking for tools, randomly moving stock, and rushing into costly mistakes.

Don't forget that most circular saw blades have a kerf an eighth of an inch thick—so if you cut to the wrong side of the line, your piece will be an eighth of an inch short.

The portable circular saw is designed to cut lumber and boards to size. Various models require different-sized blades, among them blade diameters of six and a half inches and eight and a quarter inches; the most popular by far, however, are the seven-and-a-quarter-inch models.

Most portable circular saws have electric motors with two or more horsepower that turn the blade at about five thousand revolutions per minute; capacities and revolutions per minute vary from model to model. The motor is protected in a housing, the blade by a fixed guard on top and a retractable guard below. There is a handle on top, and a sole plate or shoe on the bottom. Some models come with an adjustable T-guide.

A typical circular saw weighs between nine and twelve pounds. Most contemporary models feature insulated, rigid plastic casings, with steel soles and guards.

The vertical angle of cut can be adjusted from its standard ninety degrees to forty-five degrees, or to any angle in between. The depth of cut can be adjusted, too. A typical seven-and-a-quarter-inch circular saw will cut to a depth of two and a quarter inches at ninety degrees. At a forty-five-degree angle, the saw will cut through a two-by-four on one pass, a thickness of one and a half inches.

These saws can also be fitted with masonry or other specialty blades for cutting other materials. Blades with a wide range of teeth configurations for cutting wood are also available, though a combination blade, which crosscuts and rips, may suffice for most or all of your needs (see *Sawteeth: Their Kinds and Cuts,* page 46).

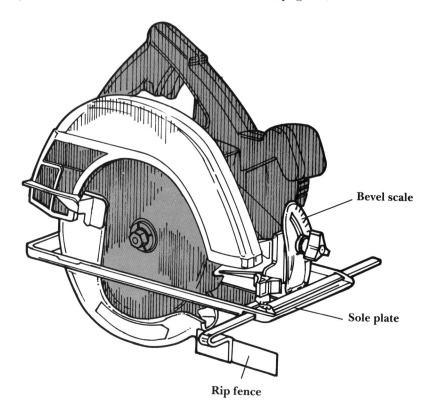

Bevel scale

Sole plate

Rip fence

In addition to the common seven-and-a-quarter-inch saw, other sizes are available. On one extreme, there's a three-and-three-eighths-inch saw that uses a rechargeable battery. This saw is expensive, however, and has significant built-in limitations. For example, its depth of cut is only eleven-sixteenths of an inch when sawing a forty-five-degree bevel. And the saw runs out of power pretty quickly (ripping four lengths of half-inch plywood is the present maximum per charge). For some applications, however, the convenience and light weight of this little saw may make it very handy. At the other end of the spectrum, there are giant models designed to be used by timber framers, but they are unwieldy and of little use to most woodworkers.

Worm-Drive Circular Saw. One heavy-duty variety of the portable circular saw is the worm-drive saw. Most circular saws are direct-drive, meaning that the shaft to which the blade is attached is part of the electric motor's rotor. In a worm-drive saw, however, the motor drives the blade from the rear.

The worm-drive mechanism that connects the motor to the saw arbor or shaft consists of two gears. One is cylindrical in shape and threaded like a screw. This is the "worm gear" attached to the armature of the motor, which in turn drives a wheel-shaped gear called the worm wheel. The worm wheel is attached directly to the arbor shaft onto which the saw blade is fastened.

The advantage of the worm-drive saw is that it delivers the high revolutions of the engine to the saw blade at a much reduced rate of speed. This means that the torque (rotational force) is much greater, making tasks like cutting double thicknesses of dimensional lumber or several sheets of plywood much easier. The saw just keeps on cutting without the complaints or stalling you would get from most sidewinder (that is, traditional configuration) circular saws under such circumstances. When forced, a worm-drive saw is much less likely to kick back than a sidewinder saw.

Many experienced framing carpenters prefer worm-drive saws. The worm-drives are heavier (some weigh twice as much as direct-drive models) but the added power more than compensates. They are a bit more convenient for right-handers because the blade is to the left of the motor, and you can see the cutting edge without leaning over the saw.

A worm-drive circular saw is not an appropriate tool for the occasional user, not least because it is significantly more expensive than sidewinder saws. But it's a real workhorse designed for long, hard use. So, for building that big barn you've been thinking about . . . it just might be the answer.

MAKING A SAWHORSE

The sawhorse is an indispensable piece of work-site furniture. It's part workbench, part scaffold, and now and again functions nicely as a place to rest your weary frame. I know one carpenter who swears he is a better problem-solver when he puts his butt down on a sawhorse and scratches his head.

The sawhorse laid out here also doubles as a tool carrier, with a built-in tool tray. It's simple but sturdy, and can be made in about an hour with scrap materials. Reproducing this design will also enable you to put your carpenter's square and miter square to good use.

The Legs. Position your carpenter's square on a length of one-by-four stock. The heel of the square should hang off one edge by four inches. Mark the miter cuts across the face of the twenty-four-inch legs.

Don't get your saw out quite yet: The legs must be cut at a compound angle in order to sit flush to the sawhorse top and flat to the floor. Turn the leg stock onto its side, and reposition the carpenter's square, this time with a five-and-a-quarter-inch overhang.

Now you have your saw lines. You can make your cuts with a handsaw or a portable circular saw. If you use the latter, set the angle of the cut by fixing your miter gauge at the angle marked across the thickness of the stock. Set the saw using the miter gauge (after having unplugged the tool first, of course).

The Top. The top is made from a piece of two-by-six lumber. Two-by-four stock will do, too, though the wider lumber will result in a sawhorse that's easier to use because of its greater surface area.

For reasons of strength, the legs in our sawhorse are set into notches or "gains" in the side of the top. These are laid out using a square, four inches in from each end of the forty-four-inch-long top piece.

The layout gets a bit complicated here because the legs come in at two angles, splayed out to the sides and ends. Use your miter gauge to transfer the bevel from the end cuts on the legs to the side notches.

That will give you one angle of splay. For the other, mark the top of each notch to be cut at a three-quarter-inch depth and the bottom of each to three-eighths. The gains are best cut in a series of cuts with a handsaw, taking care that each kerf extends only to the depth lines marked. A chisel and mallet can be employed to clear away the waste.

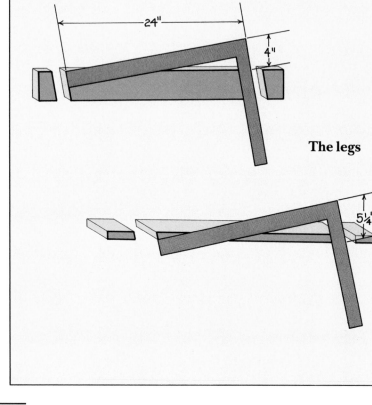

The legs

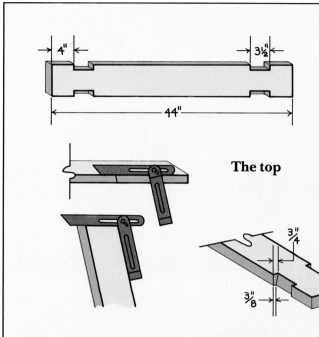

The top

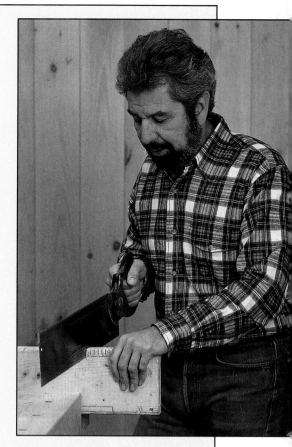

To make the notches for the legs, cut a series of three-eighth-inch kerfs. Be careful to cut only to the layout lines at three-quarters of an inch on the top and three-eighths beneath.

The Gussets and the Shelf. The tool tray and end pieces can be made from three-quarter-inch plywood or one-by-ten stock. Bevel cuts aren't necessary: Simply square-cut the stock to the dimensions indicated on the drawing.

The gussets

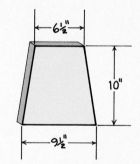

Assembly. The sawhorse can be put together with sheetrock screws or nails, though I favor ringed siding nails for extra strength. First, attach the legs to the top. Next, position the leg and top assembly upside down on a bench, and locate the gussets and tray. Tack them in place with finishing nails first, to be sure the sawhorse sits square; stand the horse upright and inspect it *before* you bury the nails.

Braces of one-by-two furring should be cut to fit along the sides of the tray and beneath it, on the inside of each pair of legs.

The assembled sawhorse

The end product: A sturdy sawhorse, ready to ride off to the work-site.

The shelf

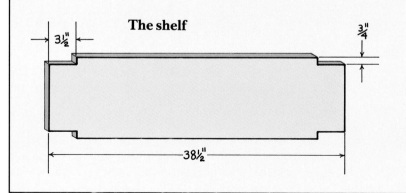

CUTTING STRAIGHT LINES WITH A CIRCULAR SAW

Despite its name, the portable circular saw (or any circular saw, for that matter) cuts only straight lines. Its name actually refers to the shape of its blade. To put it to use, follow this procedure.

Set the Depth of Cut. First, adjust the distance the blade protrudes from the sole of the saw. The saw should cut only slightly (perhaps a quarter inch) through the workpiece, for reasons of both safety and efficiency.

Cut with the Good Side Down. The blade in a circular saw rotates so that the teeth come from the lower side and cut up into the workpiece, which means that any splintering that occurs will be on the top of the piece. Thus, on finish work, you should mark the back of the piece to be cut: That way, the good side will have the smoother edge.

Align with the Line. Position the workpiece on a sawhorse or a stable work surface. Now, rest the front of the saw base on the workpiece, aligning the cutting guide at the front of the sole with the line to be cut. Crosscutting is difficult to do accurately, so use a guide like a speed square or combination square to insure a straight cut.

When preparing to cut, bring the saw to full speed before bringing the blade in contact with the wood. Advance the saw smoothly: If you push too

hard, the blade may jam (if it does, back off slightly, then advance again at a more measured rate). The sound the saw makes is your best indication of a proper pace.

Making an Angle Cut. To cut on an angle, the adjustable sole of the circular saw is shifted to the desired pitch. The depth of cut may need to be adjusted as well.

Pocket Cuts. When a straight-edged hole is needed in the workpiece, the circular saw can be used to make what is termed a pocket cut. Adjust

Here's the pocket-cut position. Take care with this one – it's tricky. And do not try to cut in reverse with the saw once it is through the board. Doing so puts you at risk because the circular saw is likely to accelerate suddenly, given the direction the blade spins, if you try to guide it backwards.

the depth of cut so that the saw will cut no more than a quarter inch beyond the thickness of the wood. Angle the saw on the toe of its shoe immediately above a line to be cut.

Power up to full speed, then gradually lower the saw. Wait until its sole is flush to the sur-

When cutting miters, square ends, or making long cuts in plywood, you can insure straighter cuts by clamping a piece of scrap wood to the workpiece to function as a straightedge saw guide.

face of the material being cut before advancing the saw.

Repeat the procedure for each line to be cut; a handsaw or saber saw will be required to clean out the waste from the corners.

And don't forget: Wear your protective equipment, plan your cuts carefully, position the workpiece with care, and be conscious of your safety at every step (see *Safe Sawing*, page 58).

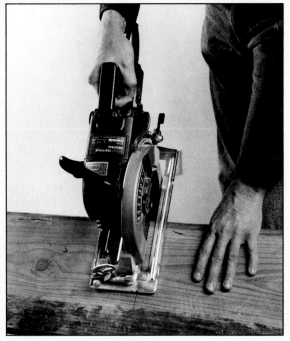

One way to compensate for the added weight of the worm-drive saw is to use gravity to advantage. Whenever possible, cut from above the work, letting the saw run downhill. The added torque of a worm-drive prevents the extra speed from stalling the saw.

PROTECTING YOURSELF

I've never known why, but a traditional nickname for the catcher's gear in baseball is "the tools of ignorance." I like to think that a less ironic name for the implements pictured here would be "the tools of intelligence." Surrounding the bright yellow and blue carving gloves are headphone-style ear protectors, a full-face shield, goggles, plastic gloves, ear plugs, a disposable mask, a pair of safety glasses, and a respirator. To use these is just plain smart.

Insurance agents have a favorite inside joke they use when a baby is born. Unlike most people, they don't say to the new parents, "Hey, congratulations! How's the new baby?"

Rather, they like to ask, "So how's your little beneficiary?" Well, borrowing a bit from our insurance agent friends, if you don't use proper protective devices for your own sake, wear them for the sake of your beneficiaries. Accidents do happen, even to the most careful and experienced woodworkers. Some are minor, like the little scrapes and slivers that seem endemic when working with wood. Many are more serious. Not a few can be prevented by properly protecting yourself and by following appropriate safety procedures (see also *Safe Sawing*, page 58).

The following are relatively inexpensive, easy-to-use devices

that can help you protect your eyes, ears, lungs, and hands from some of the dangers of the workplace.

Eye Protection. Eye injuries are all too common, and almost all are preventable. Always wear safety glasses when you're cutting, nailing, chiseling masonry, using a power tool, or performing any task that can produce airborne debris.

If your safety glasses are uncomfortable, try another design. There are a number of different types on sale for only a few dollars.

The most common variety resembles regular eyeglasses. Find a pair that has protective mesh or other material at the sides of the eyes, as well as lenses made of safety glass or an impact-resistant plastic like polycarbonate.

Goggles are another option. (So what if they look funny? Kareem got into the Hall of Fame despite them, didn't he? *And* with his eyesight intact.) They will fit over normal eyeglasses, and can be purchased with ventilating louvers to reduce fogging. Goggles are a good choice if you'll be working with chemicals or lots of dust.

Full-face shields restrict vision the least, but cost a bit more. They're probably the best choice for those who frequently operate large machinery, like saws and presses, from a standing position. They're less practical for the worker who is always climbing ladders, working in crawl spaces, or doing a different sort of task every time the toolbox gets opened.

For welding, a specially designed welder's mask or

goggles are required. Dark lenses protect the eyes from the intense light, heat, and weld spatter.

Ear Protection. Does it drive you crazy to have to repeat yourself time and again for someone who's always saying, "What?" or "Huh?" If you don't protect your ears from the screams and screeches and bangs and clangs of tool use, one day soon you'll probably be a what'd-you-sayer, too.

Again, various designs are suited to different tasks and different people. There are hearing protectors that resemble old-fashioned ear-muffs, which are highly effective at blocking out extremely loud machinery; others of the same design block out less sound and allow the wearer to converse with coworkers or others nearby. Most models feature foam-filled plastic cups that fit over the ears and a padded strap, usually sprung, that is adjustable to fit your head.

Another choice are plugs that fit at the opening of the ear canal. Commercially available designs include simple rubber plugs that are inserted and close out sound uniformly, though not as efficiently as ear-muff protectors.

Another type that serves many woodworkers is a combination filter-plug device made of plastic and aluminum. At its heart is a metal filter that blocks out high-decibel machine sounds but that allows voices to be heard; the filter is encased in plastic that has small ribs to hold the plug in place in the ear canal.

Lung Protection. When working with any material that produces airborne particles, a protective mask is in order. For those with allergies such masks are especially necessary, but even if you don't feel an immediate discomfort, always wear a mask when sanding, working with insulation or dusty materials, or spray painting.

Here, too, there are simple devices and more complex and expensive variations. For as little as a few cents, disposable masks with elastic straps can be purchased. They are preshaped to fit over the nose and mouth, and some designs have a thin strip of metal that a little finger pressure will shape to fit snugly over your nose. For a one-day job of insulating the attic, this is a suitable, inexpensive solution.

These masks will not provide adequate protection from fumes, but filtered respirators will. When varnishing woodwork, stripping paint, or doing other tasks that involve fumes and large quantities of fine dust, purchase a twin-cartridge respirator.

The filters in the respirator will need to be changed occasionally, both because they get dirty over time (accumulating particulate matter, for example) and because different filters serve different needs. Paper filters are best for dusty applications or when spray painting. Charcoal cartridges are suitable for working with chemicals or other tasks that involve fumes. When the paper becomes clogged (and

breathing more difficult) or when you begin to smell the vapors, change the filters.

Gloves. For most jobs, gloves are likely to be more of a hindrance than a help. On cold days when you're working outside, however, gloves may be welcome. If you find that they limit your dexterity, try cutting off the fingers for the index finger and thumb. That way you can still feel textures, grasp nails, and utilize the tactile sense of your fingertips.

There are purpose-made gloves that have important uses. Carver's gloves can help protect you from cuts and gashes; plastic or rubber gloves are necessary when working with certain chemicals (always read labels carefully when using finishes, paint removers, solvents, poisons, or other chemicals, and follow the advice found there). When working with fiberglass insulation, always wear gloves. If you don't, you may end up covered with tiny slivers of fiberglass which, at the very least, make for itchy fingers.

Other Clothing. In general, pants (rather than shorts), sturdy shoes or work boots, and shirts of practical, comfortable design are appropriate. Your clothing should be loose-fitting, but not so baggy that the material could be caught by a spinning blade and pull your flesh into it. Wear short sleeves or roll up longer sleeves. Rings, watches, and neckties are potential hazards. Long hair should be tied back or contained within a cap.

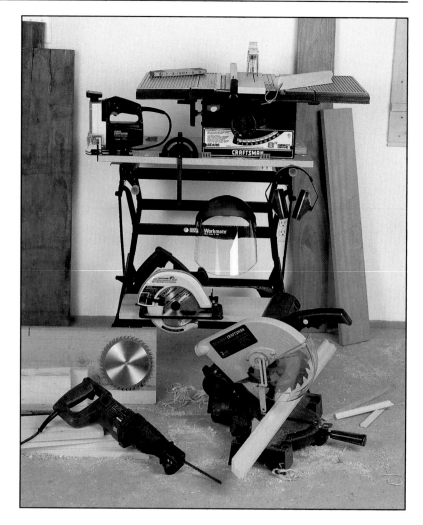

With a tip of the cap to Thomas Edison, here are some electric power tools, including a miter box and reciprocating saw (foreground), a portable circular saw (center), and a saber and portable table saw (top). My compliments to Ben Franklin and his kite, too.

A precursor of the saber saw, the power scroll saw of the nineteenth century made possible the architectural decorations we know today as "gingerbread." The graceful, curvilinear barge boards and rake boards that adorn Carpenter Gothic and other Victorian-style houses were the carpenters' way of expressing their delight at the flexibility of the (then) new and wonderful tool.

THE SABER SAW

A rule of thumb in the tool world is that the smaller the blade, the greater the variety of cuts. One tool that demonstrates the truth of the axiom is the saber saw.

This versatile power tool, which is also called a power jigsaw or power scroll saw, is used most often with short thin blades to cut curves and openings in boards or panels. The hand-held saber saw has only limited power, however, so using it to cut through heavy lumber or to make long cuts is very time-consuming. While saber saws can be purchased in a range of sizes and power ratings, a one-quarter horsepower saw with a three-quarter-inch stroke will suffice for most jobs. Saber saws with variable speed controls are handy for some kinds of cuts.

The saber saw can be fitted with a variety of blades for different purposes. Varying in length from about three to six inches, saber-saw blades are manufactured with a smooth knife edge (for cutting materials like linoleum and leather), as well as with teeth. Blades with as few as six or seven teeth per inch can be purchased for quick and dirty cuts on wood; an eight-teeth-per-inch blade is often used for plaster or wallboard. Those with ten or more teeth per inch are suited to cutting certain metals and more exacting woodworking. Blades with even finer teeth are used to cut some metals (twenty-four per inch) or for finish scrollwork (twenty per inch). Carbide- and tungsten-carbide tipped blades are also available and last longer.

A trigger switch in the handle of the saber saw controls the action of the saw; in variable-speed models, the range is from a slow starter speed to a high speed for cutting soft materials. As with other saws, use a slow to medium rate of speed when cutting metals.

Never force a saber saw, no matter how slowly it seems to be cutting. The usual result of too much pressure is not faster cutting but a broken blade.

SAWING WITH A SABER SAW

In comparison to the hand-held circular saw, the saber saw is simpler and safer. Still, care and caution in its use are appropriate.

To make a simple cut from the edge of a board, position the saw with the front of its shoe aligned with the line to be cut. The saw cuts on the upstroke, so the board being cut should be face down. Make sure the workpiece is balanced or fastened so that it will not slide about while you're cutting – and so that the saw line isn't on top of any surface you don't want to cut. The saw can be used freehand or with a guide.

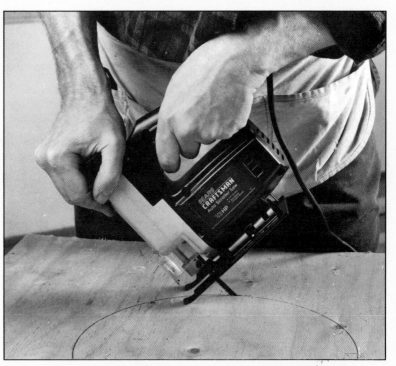

Hold the saber saw firmly when making a plunge cut: It'll try to dance out of your hand.

Most saber saws can be tilted on their bases, allowing for miter cuts. Making a miter cut is much the same, though keep in mind that a miter cut involves cutting through more stock, so it will take longer. Allow the saw to set the pace, and don't force the blade.

Plunge Cut. If you are cutting into the middle of a piece, you may wish to drill a starter hole (as with the saber saw's hand-powered brother, the keyhole saw). However, a bit of practice – and a nearly new short, stiff blade – can save a step by making a plunge cut using the saber saw itself.

Tip the saber saw forward on the tip of its base, positioning the blade over the hole to be cut. Depress the trigger of the saw, and gradually tip the base of the saw (and the blade) downward to the surface to be cut.

When the blade strikes the surface, it will jump, but a steady hand, a little patience, and some gentle pressure will eventually plunge the blade through the workpiece.

THE KEYHOLE SAW

Not many years ago, I used to see keyhole saws in use almost daily; now, for many carpenters, keyhole saws have been relegated to the category of rarely used tools. The responsibility for this lies with the saber saw, which will perform most of the tasks for which the keyhole saw has traditionally been used – and does all the work with virtually no elbow grease required.

Nevertheless, the inexpensive and convenient keyhole saw has a place in the fully equipped carpenter's toolbox.

These days, the keyhole saw is sometimes called a compass saw although a few years back the standard keyhole saw had a narrower blade (and could cut quite fine arcs) while the compass saw's larger blade had coarser teeth and was better suited to curves with larger radii. Smaller keyhole saws were commonplace in years past, in part because they were traditionally made from the broken blades of larger saws. When they broke, the fractured blade would be chopped down and fitted to a suitable handle.

Despite the traditional names, what is sold today interchangeably as a keyhole or compass saw is a bit large for cutting keyholes. Still, the keyhole saw can be used to cut holes for large-diameter pipes, vents, plug or switch boxes, and other purposes. They are used away

A nineteenth-century compass saw, with a beech handle and an interchangeable blade.

When cutting into the interior of a panel or board, a starter hole is drilled within the area to be cut out. Then the keyhole saw is inserted through the hole.

from the edge of a board, panel, or sheet of plywood, or for cutting in tight places where an ordinary handsaw could not be used.

The keyhole saw and its near relation the wallboard saw have wooden handles and thin, tapering steel blades. The teeth are usually coarse, in the eight- to ten-teeth-per-inch range. Blade length varies (some are as short as five inches) but can be up to twelve or fifteen inches long. Some models are designed to use replaceable or interchangeable blades and are sometimes sold as utility saw sets. The handle comes complete with several blades, one of which may be designed to cut metal. The narrower the blade, the tighter the curve it can cut; finer blades are preferable for cutting plywood.

THE RECIPROCATING SAW

On different days, the average home craftsman wears different hats: plumber, electrician, carpenter, tiler, plasterer, whatever. On demolition day, this is the tool for you. The reciprocating saw is a larger, more powerful version of the saber saw. Though it is designed for cutting on the horizontal (with the blade moving backward and forward, unlike the saber saw's up-and-down stroke), the reciprocating saw can be used at all sorts of angles for demolition and rough-cut purposes. It isn't a high precision tool, though rough scrollwork

On-site demolition is the strong suit of this muscular saw.

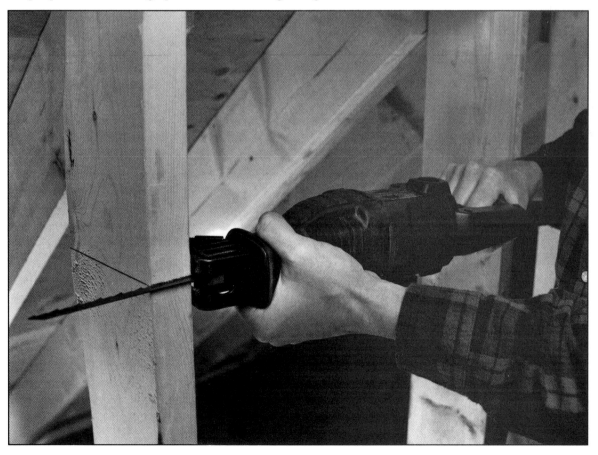

can be done with it. More often, the reciprocating saw is used for its brute strength, to saw through walls or ceilings, creating openings for windows, plumbing lines, or other purposes.

The reciprocating saw, which is sometimes referred to by the proprietary name Sawsall, is a powerful tool and must be used with care. Two hands are needed for proper control, one at the pistol grip where the on-off trigger is located, the other on the body of the saw to stabilize it while cutting. Some models come with variable speed controls, which make for more efficient cutting through various materials. Remember, metal-cutting is done at slower speeds, but softer materials like wood can be cut at a higher rate.

Blades for cutting wood, plywood, metal, plastic, and other materials are sold. They are available in various lengths ranging from about four inches (for scroll cutting) to as long as nine or even twelve inches (for rough cutting of wood). Metal-cutting blades are also sold that can cut through nails, bar and angle stock, and metal tubing.

Cordless reciprocating saws are also being introduced, though they are less powerful and less flexible. On a work-site with no electricity (or in an awkward position where a power cord would be in the way), the cordless models can make good sense.

THE MITER SAW

Only in recent years has this versatile and accurate tool come to be something of a fixture, not only in the workplace but in many home workshops as well.

The motorized miter saw or "chop box," as it is commonly called, is a cross between a miter box and a portable circular saw. The saw blade and motor are mounted on an arm that hinges on an elbow fixed at the rear of the saw. When the blade is lowered in a chopping motion, the blade cuts through the workpiece, passing through a slot in the base. The rear is designed so that it acts as a fence, allowing you to position the wood at a preset angle to the blade.

The motor and blade can be pivoted with respect to the base, allowing for miter cuts. Some miter saws are designed so that the blade turns on two axes to cut compound miters (angle cuts that are more or less than ninety degrees from the vertical as well as on the horizontal plane of the stock).

The size of the blade of the miter saw determines the maximum cut width the saw will make. Some miter saws use eight-inch blades, others ten- or even fifteen-inch blades. Most eight-inch models will crosscut at a ninety-degree angle up to a two-by-six of dimension lumber, but a ten-inch miter saw is considerably more flexible in cutting larger miters. A ten-inch model is sufficient for most finishing jobs.

Back in the days of the backsaw and miter box, you had to cut your workpiece just right the first time. One of the signal advantages of the miter saw is its ability to trim minute amounts of wood – so the piece that almost fits becomes a perfect fit.

Miter saws are useful for cutting moldings and frames and making almost any cut that requires angles of more or less than ninety degrees. High-quality honed blades and high blade speed mean that a miter saw's cuts are remarkably accurate – as exact as any but the most precise of workers will get out of a miter box. In addition, the power miter saw allows you to shave minute amounts of material from a workpiece, which just isn't possible even with the stiffest and sharpest of backsaws in a miter box.

Yet the popularity of the miter saw is probably better explained by the fact that it is less expensive than and almost as versatile a tool as the radial arm saw. This means the miter saw is very useful for cutoff work. If you're framing a wall, you can set up a miter saw table with a stop on it and cut a hundred studs with absolute accuracy much more quickly than you could marking and cutting with a portable circular saw. Cutting plumb cuts on rafters, too, is easy (though, again, the size of the blade is a limiting factor in relation to the width of stock that can be cut).

THE PORTABLE TABLE SAW

Last but hardly least in the on-site sawyer's repertoire comes the table saw. In my opinion, for the finish carpenter who has a modicum of skills a table saw is probably the most essential tool. It rips and crosscuts; it miters and cuts compound angles, rabbets, and tenons. It can also function as a shaper and a sander, when equipped with appropriate blades.

(I would note here, however, that not all carpenters agree with the placement of the table saw in this paramount position; some favor the radial arm saw instead. For the purposes of this volume, I've opted for the portable table saw, in part because of its reasonable cost, light weight, and ease of use. In the companion volume to follow, *Bob Vila's Workshop*, I'll talk at length about the versatile radial arm saw.)

For on-site work, a portable table saw is more practical than larger, heavier table saws. Portable table saws are often made largely of aluminum for ease of transport. They consist of a box that contains the motor, controls, and blade mechanics, along with a tabletop through which the blade protrudes.

A table saw it is, though it's hardly portable and isn't driven in the way most of our electric saws are today. Notice the crank on the front side of the saw and the treadle beneath. What we have here is a state-of-the-art (circa 1899, that is) hand- and foot-powered table saw.

Portable table saws, which are occasionally referred to as bench table saws, do not come with built-in stands, but leg sets can be purchased separately or fabricated without much difficulty. Portable table saws can also be used on top of sawhorses, workbenches, or other level surfaces at the work-site.

Like the larger iron table saws designed for shop use, portable table saws adjust for different cuts. The blade can be raised and lowered for cutting stock of various thicknesses (a table saw with a ten-inch blade can cut stock slightly more than three inches thick when the blade is fully extended). The blade can also be tilted to make bevel cuts.

The cutting surface on portable table saws is smaller than on shop models (roughly one and a half by two feet square, rather than approximately two feet by three and a half feet). This is perhaps the greatest single disadvantage of a portable table saw: A larger tabletop makes the tool safer and easier to use, offering more support and stability for the workpiece while sawing. However, a portable sawhorse or similar device of the same height as the table can be bought or made, and it can be positioned to support either boards or lumber.

Essential accessories for any table saw are a miter gauge and a ripping fence, both of which help guide the workpiece safely past the blade. The miter fence, as it is also called, is a pushing device for making crosscuts. The miter gauge adjusts to any angle you wish to cut, and slides along the tabletop in either of two parallel grooves that run the length of the working surface on either side of the blade. The rip fence is clamped in place, also parallel to the blade, and allows boards to be ripped evenly to the selected width.

Blade guards are also standard on all new saws. If you have a durable old table saw (the good ones can last many, many years) that has no guard, you should consider installing appropriate guards. These should include at least a metal or plastic covering over the blade itself, and if you do any ripping, a splitter. The splitter is a fin-shaped piece of steel as thick at its widest point as the width of the saw kerf. Situated beyond the saw blade, the splitter separates the wood to prevent the stock from binding on the blade. Most new saws also have anti-kickback fingers, metal grippers that help prevent the workpiece from being propelled backwards and hitting the sawyer.

Use the guards. Period. There are already more than enough carpenters and cabinetmakers, professional and amateur, with incomplete sets of digits thanks to the power saws of the world.

Circular saw blades, including three with carbide tips, one for plywood (center, right) and a masonry blade (bottom).

TABLE-SAW TECHNIQUES

Your table saw can perform a remarkable number of tasks. There are probably enough to fill an entire chapter, especially when additional equipment like dados and molding cutters are added to the tool repertoire. But the several basic table-saw techniques we'll discuss here are those you are most likely to need at the work-site, including cutoff work (that is, crosscutting boards at a ninety-degree angle) and miter sawing (angle cutting); ripsawing; resawing; and rabbeting.

Crosscutting and Miter Sawing. Preset the miter fence to the angle desired, whether it's a square cut (in which case the miter setting will be zero degrees) or a reading you got using your miter gauge to match an existing surface. Once the miter fence is set to the desired angle, the workpiece is held flush to the face of the gauge with one hand, while the other balances the piece. Only after you are in position should you turn on the saw. Then push the gauge and workpiece together toward the blade.

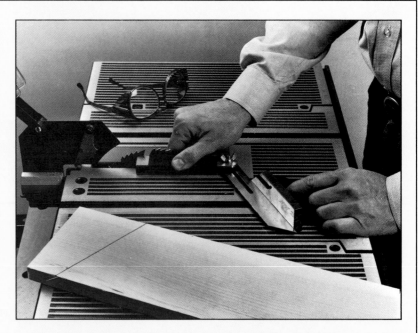

Set the saw's miter fence using your miter gauge (top). Then use the fence to guide your cut, pushing with the right hand and stabilizing the piece with the other.

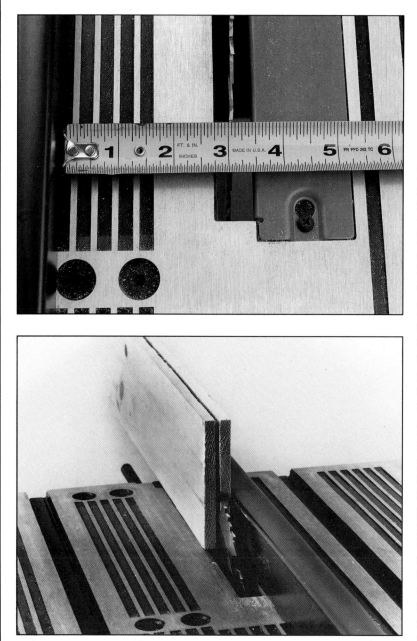

A board being resawn, on its second pass through. Keep in mind that you can only resaw a board that is less than twice the maximum cutting height of your blade.

To position the rip fence on your table saw, run your tape from the fence to a tooth that is set in the direction of the fence (note that other teeth are set right as well as left in the picture). Then turn the blade away from you, and measure again to be sure the fence is parallel. This procedure should always be done with the saw unplugged.

Ripsawing. Position the rip fence parallel to the blade, measuring the distance from the fence to a tooth that is bent (set) from the near side of the blade. Once the fence is in place, tighten its built-in clamp to fix it in position.

How wide will the piece be after it is ripped? The narrower the piece, the greater the need for a push stick to power the piece through – and to keep your fingers away from – the blade.

Resawing. If you require a board thinner than the stock you have on hand, resawing may be your answer. Resawing is essentially a two-step ripping process. You begin by presetting the rip fence to the thickness you desire; then you run the workpiece through the saw on its edge. Now, turn the piece over and run it back through, so that the blade will make a matching cut that reaches to the first kerf.

Cutting a rabbet on a table saw is a two-step process. First, you cut a kerf at the width and depth of the rabbet required. Second, you reset the saw and cut out the waste to complete the rabbeting.

Rabbeting. Especially in restoration work, some moldings need to be rabbeted – that is, a deep lip or "rabbet" is cut onto their edge. Rabbet joints, new or old, are stronger than simple butt joints. Making rabbet cuts for such joinery is simple on a table saw.

Two cuts are required. To make the first one, you must set the height of the saw blade to cut the piece to the depth of the rabbet; then you need to set up the fence so that the cut will be the appropriate distance from the edge of the stock. Make the cut as you would any rip cut.

To make the second cut, you need to reset the blade height and the fence so that a cut made perpendicular to the first will create the desired rabbeted edge. This cut is made with the board turned ninety degrees so that it is perpendicular to the tabletop.

Set up, cut with care, and a rabbet appears – not quite by magic.

Thinking Ahead. Make it a habit, before you turn on your saw, to think about the cut to be made. Are you wearing your eye protection? What about your ears?

And where are your hands with respect to the blade? If the workpiece is short and doesn't require two hands to balance it, put the unneeded hand behind your back or otherwise locate it out of the way.

After the cut, where will the waste fall? And what about the

piece you want? Will it be balanced, or do you need to locate a sawhorse or other support to keep it level?

Are you cutting with the good side up? The table saw is the reverse of the portable circular saw, as its blade cuts on the downward rotation, meaning that any splintering will occur to the underside of the workpiece.

Where appropriate, use a featherboard and push stick.

Stay in Line. As with any saw cut, keep in mind which side of the line you wish to cut. The kerf on a typical table saw is an eighth of an inch wide, so cutting to the wrong side of the line will result in a significant error.

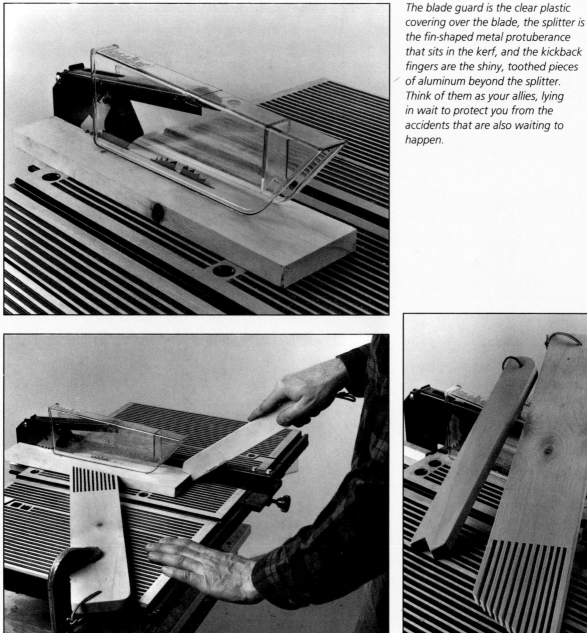

The blade guard is the clear plastic covering over the blade, the splitter is the fin-shaped metal protuberance that sits in the kerf, and the kickback fingers are the shiny, toothed pieces of aluminum beyond the splitter. Think of them as your allies, lying in wait to protect you from the accidents that are also waiting to happen.

The featherboard, along with the rip fence, makes accurate, safe ripping of boards easier. It is positioned to brace the workpiece against the fence, and will both hold the work in line while the saw is cutting and help prevent kickback.

You can buy factory-made featherboards of space-age plastic with clever clamping devices, but if you have a C-clamp at hand, you can make one out of scrap wood for a few cents. Just miter the end of a wide board (a one-by-four will do), then make a series of closely spaced rip cuts in the end grain, leaving fingers that are about the width of the saw kerf. The cuts make the board flexible. Then, after positioning the rip fence, clamp the featherboard in place as shown here. Use a featherboard and push stick in resawing operations for added accuracy and safety.

At left is the push stick, at center the featherboard. The push stick allows you to keep your fingers farther from the blade of a table saw... and, let's hope, out of harm's way.

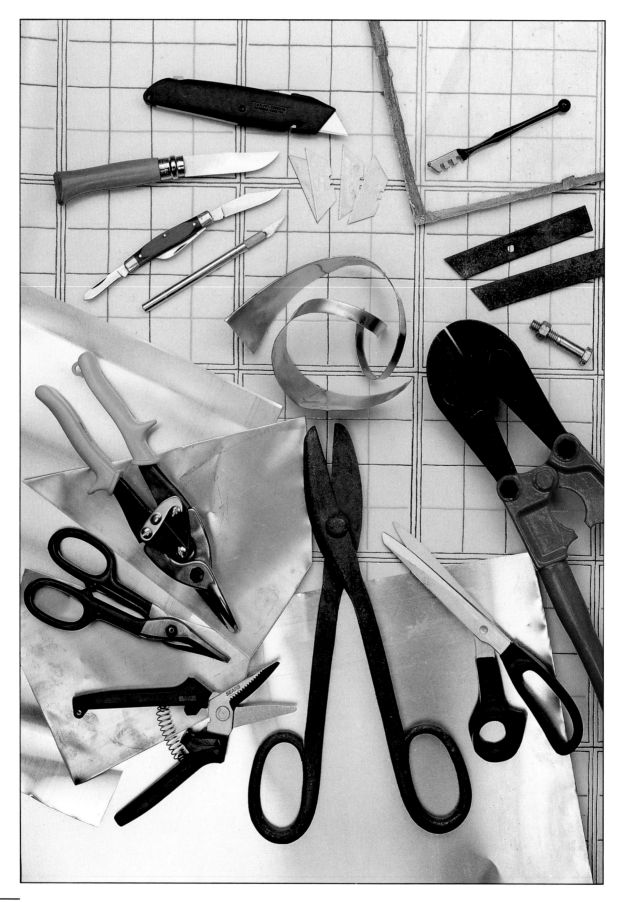

Chapter 5.
Other Essential Cutting Tools

In the previous chapter, we looked at dozens of saws. Each featured a toothed blade that chewed its way through wood, metal, or other materials, chopping through fiber by fiber. Some saws cut cleanly, others in a rougher way, but each saw hacks its way through, mincing some of the material into dust as it goes.

In the pages that follow, we'll consider cutting tools that slice and shave and snip, with smooth, honed, and toothless edges. Neither sawdust nor fragments are produced in the process; rather, these tools sever the material, cleaving it into parts.

As usual, I'll describe a range of tools. We'll talk about the light and compact pocketknife, the familiar scissors, and the utility knife. Cutting glass is a technique covered here, as are tougher tasks, like cutting steel and iron with the heavy and bulky bolt cutters.

Each of these tools has its place in the toolbox. Some, I think you'll agree, have an everyday place in the kitchen and the desk, too, for the miscellaneous tasks that offer themselves now and again.

Although the antique snips (bottom, center) were handmade by a blacksmith, they look much like modern versions. Moving around clockwise are utility, duckbill, and aviation snips; a pencil-handled razor knife, two pocketknives, and a utility knife; a glass cutter, bolt cutters, and a pair of scissors.

POCKETKNIVES

A pocketknife is, simply, a knife with one or more blades that fold into its handle, of a size that will fit conveniently into one's pocket. Whether the one you favor is called a jackknife, folding knife, pocketknife, Swiss Army knife, or whatever, they're all related.

In my opinion, some sort of pocketknife belongs in your pocket most all the time. A good pocketknife comes in handy when you need to remove one or two screws – and your tool kit and screwdrivers are not at hand. Or for whittling a point on a stick or for trimming off an edge of this or that. I've never known an electrician who didn't have a jackknife in his or her pocket. And, I must admit, over the years, I've seen a few folks open a bottle or two at the end of the working day with a pocketknife.

The variety that will serve you best depends upon the kind of work you do, but almost certainly there's a model out there that will prove its worth again and again.

Here's a two-blade pocketknife, complete with "cocoa" handle and so-called spear-blade. This knife and line cut date from 1865, but some pocketknives are made today in almost the same style.

Army Knives. No doubt the most versatile models are those that have come to be known by the generic name of Swiss Army knives. Some

Here are three tools that will fit comfortably in your trouser pocket. The Swiss Army knife at center offers the most blades, but the jackknife and folding knife (right) also have a multitude of uses.

THE DRAWKNIFE

This two-handed tool was basic to the tool kit of wheelwrights, cabinetmakers, carpenters, coopers, and other woodworkers for centuries. One early example survives from 100 A.D. and is thought to have been used by a Viking shipwright.

Used for chamfering or rough shaping of large wooden elements, the drawknife can quickly create curved or straight contours. This tool can put the points on fence posts and give shape in short order to pegs, wedges, and tool handles. Once given its approximate form, the workpiece can then be more finely shaped with a plane, spokeshave, or carving tools – though, in experienced hands, the drawknife can also put on such finishing touches as chamfers.

The drawknife consists of a pair of wooden handles flanking a steel blade. The blade is beveled along its front edge so that in section it resembles the profile of a chisel. The ends of the blade are bent and shaped into what are known as tangs, projecting tongues that, in this case, run perpendicular to the blade.

Wooden handles are mounted on the tangs, and the tool is used in a two-handed pulling motion. The angle of your wrists controls the depth of the cut. The drawknife is used to shave wood *with* the grain.

The drawknife is to be found in a variety of blade configurations. Most have flat blades, with the bevel on the top, front edge. Blade widths range from roughly three inches to a foot or more. Some blades are straight, others curved. Specialty drawknives are also available, including inshaves (with sharply curved blades for barking trees and hollowing and scooping) and scorps (a one-hand draw inshave for finer work).

The drawknife: In this case, one made in 1911 with a steel blade and beech handles.

are actually made in Switzerland according to Swiss Army specifications, but there are probably more knockoff models on the market featuring the Swiss Army cross than there are troops in the Swiss Army. Not to mention the countless other models that don't feature the familiar red plastic casing but do feature a similar range of implements within.

So-called Army knives and their relations have two knife blades, usually one that's two and a half inches long and roughly half an inch wide with another about half that size. There are at least two other blades on most models, typically a pair of screwdrivers. One is small enough to be usable on Phillips-head screws with another, larger one for slot-headed screws. Both these blades have additional uses, as the smaller driver typically has a hook on its edge that can function as a can opener, while a bottle opener is found at the base of the larger driver.

From there, the variations are almost endless, as the options include a toothpick, tweezers, scissors, a tiny saw, an awl, another Phillips-head screwdriver, a file, and even a corkscrew. The bigger the knife, the more cumbersome it gets, however, meaning both a big bulge in the pocket and added weight. Perhaps more important,

The drawknife is no longer found in every woodworker's toolbox. But this tool is still sold by antique tool dealers and new woodworking tool dealers alike. While you may well be able to accomplish what you need to without a drawknife, more than a few woodworkers today – including some timber framers and Windsor chairmakers, for example – like to have them at hand. If one or another of your occasional labors involves sculpting large stock into shapes with curves and bends, the drawknife will prove invaluable.

This drawknife was a gift from a contractor friend. As you can see, it does a nice job of shaping heavy stock.

When the blade on your utility knife shows the slightest sign of getting dull, replace it. The blades are inexpensive, and a dull utility knife is an invitation to accidents. And always stow the knife with its blade retracted.

knives equipped with many of the optional blades are also cumbersome in the hand, making them less convenient to use to remove a single screw or score one cut line. I favor a simpler, more basic knife than the top-of-the-line, gee-whiz-it'll-do-anything model.

Make sure when you purchase one of these knives, whether it was made in Switzerland or not, that the steel is stainless and that the knife looks well made. No rivets or joints should be visible and the blades should be honed sharp.

Folding Knife. By folding knife I mean simply a knife with one blade that folds into its handle. Again, there are more varieties of folding knife than there are rainy days in a rain forest, so surely there's one for you. The good ones have fine steel blades and hardwood handles; some are handsome, almost art tools, others more workmanlike.

If you're in the market for a folding knife, I'd suggest that a suitable one should have a locking mechanism, one that holds the blade rigidly in position, preferably both when the edge is stored away and when it's open and ready to use. Various models have locking rings, set screws, and spring devices.

Examine the blade carefully, too: It should be of fine, stainless steel, and the edge should be precisely honed. The handle should fit comfortably in your hand. If it's too small or too large or feels awkward, keep on looking until you find one that fits.

THE UTILITY KNIFE

This is truly a tool of a thousand uses. The thinness of its blade means it can be used for precise marking on cutoff work (see page 34). The razor-sharp edge can cut through plastic, wood, and other fibers; it can be used to score soft metals. The utility knife is invaluable for tasks like hanging wallboard, trimming wallpaper, cutting cardboard or plastic sheets or ceiling tiles, and dozens of other jobs.

As handy as the tool is, the utility knife must be handled with respect. Its design and manufacture allow for this, as the blade retracts into the body of the tool. A flick of your thumb on the button built into the top of the case slides the blade in and out.

Given its thin, sharp edge, the blade is fragile. Since utility knife blades dull quickly and are breakable, the tool is designed to accept replacement blades easily. On the side of the case is a screw that, when loosened, allows the case to be opened. Inside is a cavity for storage of new blades, as well as the sliding mechanism that allows the blade to be withdrawn when the utility knife is not in use.

The sharp and pointed blade can also cut the user with ease, so the blade should always be retracted when it is not in use. Spare blades should be stored in a safe place, and the tool should always be stowed out of the reach of children.

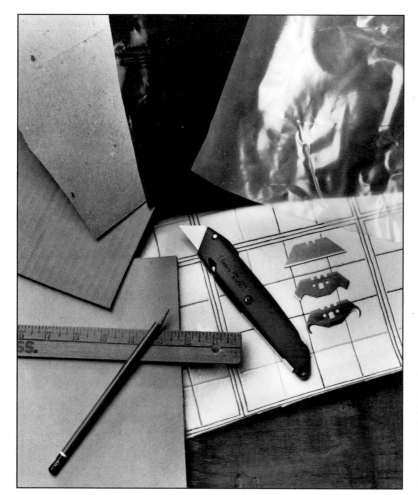

The utility knife is an invaluable tool for cutting wallboard, cardboard, paper, plastic, and many other materials. While the straight blade is used most often, the scoring blade (center) and linoleum hooked blade (bottom) have their specific applications, too.

This tool is sometimes referred to as a razor knife and (especially in England) as a shop knife or trimming knife. The standard blade has a straight cutting edge, but some models will accept other blades, some with hooked or curved blades. The hooked blade is especially useful for cutting linoleum because the blade is sharpened on the inside curve, which makes it less likely to slide out of a cut. Blades with the edge on a convex curve are useful for making cuts along lines that aren't straight, such as when cutting to match a scribed line.

One variation on the standard utility knife is a thinner, lighter model that uses a blade that is scored so that sections of it can be snapped off. With such knives, when the end of the blade dulls, the blade is advanced out of the casing, the old tip is broken off, and a fresh edge is then usable. Such models have the advantage of making a new, sharp edge available in a second, as against the disadvantage of a shorter cutting edge and, on some models, the fact that withdrawing the blade into the handle is more time-consuming than on traditional utility knives.

Snap-off blade models are best suited to uses where new blades are required very frequently; for most purposes, the traditional utility knife is easier and safer to use.

SNIPS

When I see a pair of giant snips, I think of Laurel and Hardy. Snips do look a lot like scissors, but they tend to be large enough to make great props for a comedy routine. Maybe a Three Stooges skit is more like it: The scene would benefit from some of their inimitable sound effects.

Some pairs of snips are enormous, some are smaller, but all consist of a pair of blades that pivot at a center point. They are put to use like scissors, too, in cutting operations that slice through thin layers of material.

Snips are, by definition, metal-cutting tools. Compared to scissors, snips have disproportionately long handles, which provide added leverage when cutting metal. Some snips have ring-shaped handles enabling the tool to be held like scissors; others have straight handles. At times, snips are used one-handed, at others both hands may be required, depending upon the weight of the tool and the gauge of the material to be cut.

Snips are indispensable for a variety of jobs. For example, in cutting flashing (metal used to seal off roof joints and angles to prevent leaks), using snips can make accurate cuts of the aluminum or copper a simple matter.

These tin snips look big enough to cut through the armor on a battleship, but they're perfect for working with tin. The length of the handles and the weight of the tool add leverage, making for smooth, effortless cutting.

Before making your cut, mark the copper or other metal carefully. Position the blades of the snips flush to the outside of the cut line (remember that, unlike saws, snips do not remove material when cutting, but slice along the cut). Be sure the blades are perpendicular to the workpiece; otherwise, the metal may twist in the jaws of the snips, and you will do more bending of the material than cutting.

As with the hacksaw, you should use as much of the length of the blade as possible, starting close to the joint of the jaw and stopping just short of the end of the blades. This will make your cut line smoother. Gently roll the waste side of the material away from the snips as you cut.

Snips are manufactured with blades that have straight cutting edges or curved ones. Tight, concave cuts are made easily using hawk's-bill snips, tools with blades in a crescentlike curve. More gradual curves are cut with blades that are curved more gently.

Unless you need to cut sheet metal frequently, the chances are that a single, smaller pair of snips will fill your occasional needs. One option I favor is a design called compound leverage snips. The advantage of their double-hinged design is that the force required for cutting is less, which also means it is easier to make accurate cuts with them. Compound leverage snips, which are also known as aviation snips (because they were developed for use in the manufacture of aircraft), can be purchased with blades designed for right-hand, left-hand, or straight cuts.

Another option is a pair of duckbill snips. Though unsuitable for cutting sheet metal of heavier gauges, duckbill snips are ideal for cutting screening, light-duty sheet metal, and wire. Because their blades are relatively narrow, duckbill snips can also be used for cutting gentle curves.

Whatever kinds of snips you use, never try to force them to cut materials that are heavier or harder than they are designed to cut. If you do, the blades will dull rapidly.

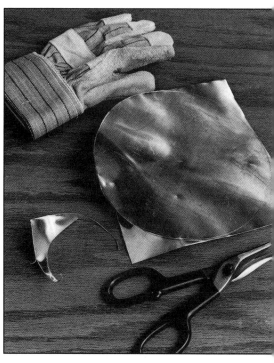

Even if you don't have snips with curved blades, making a cut with a gentle curve can still be done with straight-bladed snips. Prepare the workpiece by making rough tangent cuts around the curve. Cut to the final shape in a counterclockwise direction. Dispose of the narrow trimmings with care as they may have extremely sharp edges.

A word to the wise: When cutting sheet metal, always wear tear-resistant gloves. No matter how callused your hands and how careful your approach, sheet metal is forever ready to cut or tear the skin.

THE GLASS CUTTER

The glass cutter is a clever tool about the size of a pencil. Its handle, whether made of wood, metal, or plastic, acts essentially as a holder for the cutter itself, which is either a small wheel or a chip of industrial-grade diamond.

The glass cutter doesn't truly cut glass – at least not in the sense that snips or knives or bolt cutters do. Rather, the glass cutter scores the surface of a piece of glass, much as a utility knife or scribing awl is used to score a piece of wood when marking it for cutting. Given the brittle nature of glass, however, a score on its surface can, given some appropriately applied pressure, result in a neat break along the score line.

Cutting glass takes a little practice. Before you try making any precise final cuts, it's a good idea to experiment a bit on a few pieces of scrap glass. Needless to say, always handle glass with respect: It's sharp, delicate, and inclined to cut its handlers. Wearing gloves is a sensible precaution, too.

To cut a piece of glass, begin by cleaning it. Remove all grit, dust, or other material from both the side to be scored and the underside.

SHEARS

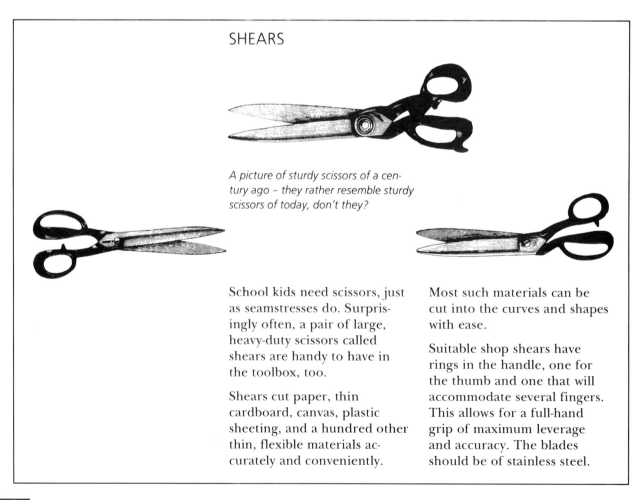

A picture of sturdy scissors of a century ago – they rather resemble sturdy scissors of today, don't they?

School kids need scissors, just as seamstresses do. Surprisingly often, a pair of large, heavy-duty scissors called shears are handy to have in the toolbox, too.

Shears cut paper, thin cardboard, canvas, plastic sheeting, and a hundred other thin, flexible materials accurately and conveniently.

Most such materials can be cut into the curves and shapes with ease.

Suitable shop shears have rings in the handle, one for the thumb and one that will accommodate several fingers. This allows for a full-hand grip of maximum leverage and accuracy. The blades should be of stainless steel.

Any grease on the surface will interfere with the cutting wheel, so be sure to wipe off any slickness with a clean rag. Use a solvent like paint thinner if necessary.

Next, lay the glass down on a layer of fabric or a few sheets of newspaper. That padding should be, in turn, atop a flat cutting board (a piece of scrap plywood or chipboard on a bench top works nicely). Measure and mark the glass where you wish to cut.

This circa 1915 line drawing suggests that this particular tool hasn't changed a great deal for a good long time.

It's mostly a matter of scoring the glass (above) and then snapping it carefully in two (below).

Position a T square or wooden straightedge along the line to be cut. Butt the side of the glass cutter to the straightedge, and pull it gently but firmly along the line. Don't put too much pressure on the glass (especially at the edges where the score line begins and ends because too much pressure can cause the glass to chip). Don't go back for a second stroke: score it only once in a smooth, even motion. You should hear a crackling, grinding sound as you do so. A drop of machine or cutting oil on the cutter will increase the chances of an even cut.

After scoring the glass, put a dowel, wood slat, or perhaps a pencil beneath the glass along the score line. Press down upon the glass, with one palm outspread on each side of the line. The glass should snap neatly along the line.

Any sliver or chips that remain beyond the line can be trimmed off with pliers or with the nibbling slots found on the heads of some glass cutters. Don't be surprised if your first cut isn't perfect. That's why a few practice cuts are a good idea.

In order to make accurate, square cuts, a T square is invaluable. There are purpose-made glazier's T squares available in a variety of lengths. You may wish to purchase one if a good deal of glass cutting looms in your future, or use a simple wood drafting square. For one or two cuts, however, a wooden straightedge (preferably one with a beveled edge) will do.

Keep in mind that you should mark your glass for cutting approximately an eighth of an inch smaller on each dimension than the frame into which it is to fit. Cutting glass is imprecise work; going back to shave off a sixteenth of an inch is next to impossible.

BOLT CUTTERS

I like to think of the bolt cutters this way: They are to the glass cutter what the chain saw is to the gentleman's pocketknife, the heavy, brutal cutter versus the fine blade that looks just too light for utility.

Bolt cutters are anything but light, being made of steel with alloy jaws. They have long handles for added leverage. Two sets of pivots produce a compound cutting action, which makes slicing through solid bolts, nails, or rods remarkably easy.

Bolt cutters come in a range of sizes, from fourteen inches to three and a half feet in length. The longer the tool is, the larger the reach of its jaws (and the larger the diameter of material it will cut). A

Bolt cutters cut bolts, of course, but also chains, nails, bars, and other metal stock – and with surprising ease.

fourteen-inch bolt cutter will cut a quarter-inch diameter bolt, a two-foot bolt cutter cuts up to three-eighths of an inch, and on up to a five-eighths diameter cut for forty-two-inch cutters. For most people, a twenty-four-inch bolt cutter is a good investment, sufficient for many uses.

Bolt cutters will cut steel up to medium hardness, so most chains, bolts, nails, and rods can be cut with them. However, hardened steel like that used in quality padlocks may resist even the power of the bolt cutter's jaws. The jaws do wear out over time, but replacement heads can be bought and easily installed.

When using the bolt cutter, position the rod or bolt to be cut as deeply into the jaws of the tool as possible. Position your hands near the end of the handles and squeeze them together firmly but gently. Wear goggles or a face shield, as cutoff pieces occasionally become airborne and dangerous.

Bolt cutters are not essential in every toolbox, but when demolition work requires cutting out old reinforcements, eliminating lag screws, or chopping off large nails, the bolt cutters seem less a luxury than a necessity.

Chapter 6.
Drills and Drilling

Boring holes is basic to building almost anything. Strange as it may sound, a timber-frame house without holes would fall down, since the wooden pins that hold it together are positioned in carefully placed holes. Any house, new or old, without holes would have no electricity, no plumbing, not even doorknobs. A house without holes is, well, no house at all.

Holes have always been essential to houses (and to chairs and tables and any other construct that is assembled out of various pieces). I don't mean to suggest, however, that the drilling devices we use today have remained unchanged over the centuries. Far from it, in fact, as electrically powered drills are now the rule; in quite recent years, cordless, battery-powered models have come very much into vogue, even to dominate some kinds of drilling tasks.

Yet, for the tradition-bound woodworker, there'll always be a place for the tried-and-true bit and brace. That cranklike device with its screw-shaped bits will always remain, at least for some of us, a symbol of the process of learning to use tools. Using a brace and bit requires a sense of balance and some strength; using a brace and bit can, over time, help teach the user something of the blend of physical and mental skills that constitutes tool sense.

In the meantime drills – of whatever sort – are indispensable for countless jobs and projects.

Drills old and new, manual and electric. Above the giant auger is a hand brace, while moving clockwise downward are a half-inch drill, a primitive Archimedes' drill, a push drill, a cordless three-eighths-inch drill, another (corded) three-eighths-inch drill, and a hand drill. Interspersed are a set of spade bits, some twist drills, a set of French gimlets (at front, left), a hole saw, and a pair of safety glasses. Don't forget the latter.

THE ELECTRIC DRILL

The electric drill is about as versatile as a tool can get. It drills holes of many kinds, of course, but it can sand and grind, too, as well as drive screws. And it can stir paint or plaster. Not too many years ago, drills with specialty attachments were commonly used as routers and even saws, but other purpose-made tools have now, for the most part, taken the place of such attachments.

Power drills are manufactured in a number of sizes. The large are distinguished from the small on the basis of chuck capacity.

The chuck is the set of jaws that grips the drill or bit which does the actual cutting. In the familiar, pistol-shaped drill, the chuck is located where the barrel of the gun would be. A specially made key with a beveled gear on its end is used to tighten or loosen the chuck

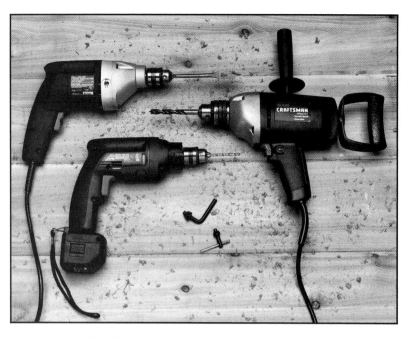

A squad of power drills, together adequate for just about any drilling or driving task you will come across. There's a three-eighths-inch cordless drill (bottom left), a half-inch drill (right), and a three-eighths-inch corded drill.

in most models. The size of the chuck denotes the largest diameter drill it will accommodate.

Keyless chucks are available, both on new drills and to retrofit others. If you've ever invested frustrating minutes in attempting to find a missing chuck key, you'll understand the inspiration that no doubt led to the invention. The keyless chuck is larger than the traditional chuck, and its size and molded shape can be gripped securely in your hand to tighten the bit in the chuck.

Many drills come with a locking button that, when the trigger is depressed, locks it in place for continuous running. The trigger lock is released by pulling the trigger again.

While smaller and larger capacity drills are available, the great majority of needs are served by either a three-eighths-inch drill or a half-inch drill. The cordless three-eighths drill is another popular option. The well-equipped toolbox might well contain all three, but to my way of thinking no homeowner is properly equipped without at least a basic, three-eighths model.

Three-Eighths-Inch Drill. This size drill is affordable, small enough to be hefted comfortably in one hand, and practical for a great many uses. Most models of this chuck size have a pistol grip and trigger control.

For a few extra dollars, most manufacturers offer two very useful options. One is trigger-controlled variable speed, the other a switch that reverses the direction in which the drill turns. Both are well worth the modest additional cost.

Being able to vary the speed makes it easier to start holes, drive screws, and drill metal (metal is drilled and cut at slow to medium speeds). The reversibility option can help reverse drills out of holes and remove screws.

A wide range of electric drills are available with more or less power (one-half horsepower is about average) and with various maximum speeds (most models top out at between twelve hundred and twenty-five hundred revolutions per minute).

Half-Inch Drill. This is a more powerful model, typically with a three-quarter horsepower motor. Half-inch drills are available in pistol-grip configurations, but for some of the demanding drilling to which the half-inch drill is well suited, a bulkier configuration that features a closed handle at the rear and an auxiliary grip on the side of the drill's body is probably the most generally useful. The added handholds allow you not only to steady the tool as it drills, but to apply additional pressure while drilling. Working two-handed will also help insure that if the drill becomes caught in the work the drill won't twist itself out of your grip.

Most half-inch drills are designed to turn at fewer revolutions per minute, but have more power. That makes them indispensable for drilling large diameter holes through dimension lumber and timber (for utility lines), in mixing plaster or joint compound, or for other heavy-duty tasks.

Cordless Drill. These tools are convenient: There's no cord trailing you up the ladder or circling your feet, threatening to trip you up. They can be used almost anywhere, even miles from the nearest electrical outlet. For some tasks, they're just about essential.

With the good news, though, there's a bit of bad news, too. Cordless drills are heavier than corded drills, because the power source is a rechargeable battery that adds weight. Most designs are well balanced, but if you're accustomed to using a traditional drill, the added weight will feel strange in your hand, at least at first.

Cordless drills also have less power available to them, so for some drilling and driving jobs the built-in clutch on most models will, from time to time, alert you to the limited power of the cordless drill (the bit will stop turning and you'll hear the clutch clicking). Newer models have improved torque, but raw power just isn't the forte of the cordless drill.

Remember that the cordless drill works only as long as its battery is charged. The charge will last a surprisingly long time (many days, given only occasional use), and professionals keep a spare battery on hand. Most models recharge in approximately an hour.

Cordless drills are usually reversible; some have the same variable speed control as corded models, which functions by depressing the trigger gently for low speeds, harder for higher ones. Some models have just one or two speeds (roughly five hundred revolutions per minutes and twelve hundred revolutions per minute are typical) and a speed-control switch.

With a suitable mixing bit, a half-inch drill will mix plaster, paint, or even small batches of concrete. The result will be both a saving in time and, equally important, a more consistent blending of the ingredients.

DRILLS AND BITS

An electric drill without bits is like a bow without arrows. And the better the bit (or arrow, I suppose) the better the results.

Like the assortment of sawblades in the last chapter, drill bits come in lots of flavors, with one or another that's suited to drill through just about anything. Depending upon your individual needs, you'll probably want to have several different types on hand, but a good starter set of drill bits should include at least a small index (perhaps ten drills) of twist drills and a set of spade bits (perhaps six pieces).

selves do no drilling, but clear the debris from the hole to prevent the drill from binding or being slowed by the waste.

The tips on most twist drills are ground at a fifty-nine-degree angle to the shaft so that they will cut metal efficiently; naturally, they'll cut wood, too. Carbon steel bits are ground specifically for drilling wood and should not be used to cut metal. Twist drills are commonly sold in sizes ranging from a sixteenth of an inch up to half-inch diameters. Most twist drills larger than a quarter inch have reduced shanks of a quarter inch.

range between a quarter inch in diameter to one and a half inches.

Brad point drill

Brad Point Drills. Designed specifically for cutting wood, brad point drills are a cross between spade bits and twist drills. The shaft of the drill resembles the twist drill, with fluted chip channels spiraling around the shaft. Most of the cutting is done at the lips of the channels, but the hole is actually started with a smaller diameter brad point (or spur) that leads the shaft into the hole. Two other spurs at the outer edge of the drill help keep the drill on line. The channels are usually cut deeper on brad point drills than on twist drills, in order to clean out the wood debris.

Spade bit

Spade Bits. These bits look like their name suggests: Each steel shaft terminates in a spade-shaped blade. The spade is flat, with a sharp point at the center. The point acts as a guide, centering the hole and leading the way, but the bulk of the drilling is actually done by the honed cutting edge at the shoulder of the spade.

Don't try to cut metal with this one. Spade bits are for wood, plywood, and some plastics, and cut quickly with surprising precision. Use them only at high speeds, so as to prevent the bit from catching in the workpiece and the drill from trying to wrench itself from your grasp. Spade bits are found in the

Twist drill

Twist Drills. No, Chubby Checker didn't invent this one. In fact, a fellow by the name of Morse did, so sometimes you'll hear machine-shop types refer to a twist drill as a Morse drill.

A twist drill has a cylindrical steel shank and a pointed tip. A pair of helical flutes (sometimes called chip channels) run along some two-thirds of its length, twisted around the shank like the stripes on a barber's pole.

The cutting edge (called the lip) is at the tip where the mouths of the flutes meet the workpiece. The flutes them-

Countersink drill

Countersink Drills. Specially made bits are sold that drill pilot holes for wood screws. These drills have profiles to match the shape of the screws: The holes they drill taper gradually along the length of the screw, then enlarge, allowing the heads of the screws to be set (countersunk) into the wood.

Some countersink drills can be purchased with adjustable stop collars that can be set to halt the drill's progress at a fixed depth. Another variety of drill, called a plug cutter, can also be purchased. It is used to cut small plugs from the same wood; the plugs can then be inserted into the screw holes after the screws have been sunk in order to camouflage their presence.

Hole saw

Hole Saws. Given its name, this one requires a bit of explanation. The hole saw bit consists of two parts, the mandrel and the blade. The mandrel is a shaft to which the blade is attached; the mandrel is gripped by the chuck of the drill like the shaft of any other bit. The blade of the hole saw is a hollow cylinder with teeth on its top edge.

Hole saws handle the work in the gray area between the smaller holes best made with twist or spade bits (those roughly an inch in diameter and smaller) and larger ones (three or four inches and up) that are sawn most easily with a saber saw (see page 68). Hole saws cut wood, plastics, and a variety of metals, including iron, steel, and aluminum. Hole saws are invaluable when installing piping, tubing, conduit, and cables.

Forstner bit

Forstner Bits. These clever bits drill holes with virtually flat bottoms. Rather than having a steeply ground tip that is followed by angled cutting edges, the Forstner bit is guided by the rim. Channels in the drill clear the hole of chips and dust. The resulting hole has a virtually flat bottom, marred only by a $1/32$-inch hole at center where the starter spur of the drill is located.

Forstner bits are relatively expensive, and they aren't necessary for most jobs. However, they are essential for others, like mounting hinges that must be recessed into a round hole that extends only partway through the door stile. (If you were to use a spade bit for the same purpose, its point would probably protrude through to the other side, marring the surface.)

Masonry bit

Masonry Bits. These are designed for drilling concrete, brick, stone, plaster, and other masonry materials that would quickly dull or fracture most drills. A masonry bit has an enlarged tip of tungsten carbide that is attached to a steel shaft.

These bits are used to cut relatively small holes (typically three-quarter-inch or less) in masonry, either to run cables or piping through, or for mounting plugs or shields for attaching shelves or other materials to the masonry.

Masonry bits should be driven at relatively slow speeds to prevent them from overheating. Periodically withdraw the bit from the hole as you drill, to remove loose dust and debris.

Other Drills. As you can see from the drills already listed, there is an impressive array of bits and drills available. Among other options are corner drills (they resemble spade bits, but the sides as well as the face of the drill are sharpened); glass drills; and mixing bits, large and small, for paint, plaster, and other liquids.

When cutting metal, you'll find your drill bits tend to overheat unless you provide cooling lubrication. When drilling iron or steel, a few drops of machine oil will do; for aluminum, kerosene is best.

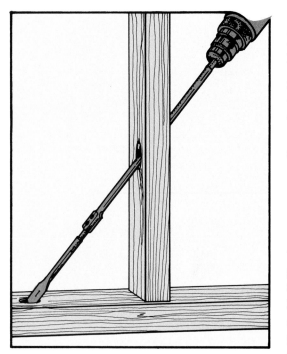

Use an extension bit for deep or hard-to-reach holes. One end of the extension bit is gripped by the chuck, while two set screws in the other hold fast to the drill bit.

Other Options. For making holes in concrete, a variation of the power drill called a rotary hammer is available. It delivers its power in a hammering motion as it drills, using specially designed percussion bits. Some models hammer out tens of thousands of strokes per minute. Another purpose-made drill is an impact wrench, which is used for tightening (or loosening) nuts and bolts. The impact wrench is a standard in auto shops.

Electric screwdrivers for drywall and other work are also available (see *Power Drivers,* page 143).

BRACES AND HAND DRILLS

If you think it's time to teach your son or daughter about working with wood, a drill brace and a few auger bits might just be a suitable gift for his or her toolbox. The elegant simplicity of a brace seems to appeal to woodworkers of all ages and eras: Its crankshaft shape challenges us to put it to use, coordinating the rotation of the handle and the pressure applied to the head to help drive the drill. It's also relatively safe, easy to use, and produces very satisfactory results: The sound of crunching wood, a small pile of chips, and a regular hole.

The brace is no toy, don't get me wrong. Many a sophisticated cabinetmaker today relies upon the brace daily; but for most of us, the electric drill in one or another of its incarnations has now taken the place of the traditional brace.

I'm as fond of antique tools as most people, but when it comes to power tools my affections tend toward modernity. For one thing, saws and drills of a certain age aren't double-insulated as new tools are, meaning that you are at greater risk of electric shock.

If your drill has a chrome or metal housing, make sure the cord has a grounded, three-pronged plug. Use an adaptor if necessary. If the plug has just two prongs, never use the tool outdoors or in damp locations. And perhaps you should think seriously about retiring it to a place of honor on a top shelf somewhere.

DRILLING SKILLS

Drilling isn't difficult and, at least in comparison to sawing, it isn't particularly dangerous. Still, skilled drillers drill with care.

Fixing the Workpiece. Place the workpiece in a clamp or vice. This leaves both hands free to manage the drill, and will prevent the piece from moving as you drill.

Locating the Hole. When drilling metal or using a twist drill on wood, you'll need to establish a precise center point for the hole to be drilled. A punch or, in the case of wood or sheet metal, a nail can be used to make a tiny hollow to start the hole. A pilot hole drilled with a smaller drill may be necessary if you're drilling a large hole in metal or hardwood.

Drilling the Hole. Place the drill bit on the center point indentation. Begin drilling at a slow speed to be sure the bit doesn't wander away from the center point.

Never force the drill; the machine will slow or groan if you do. Too much pressure is more likely to dull or break the bit than to quicken the drilling process.

Slow to medium speeds suit metal and masonry drilling; fast speeds will help you race through wood.

Monitor the progress of the drill as it proceeds through the workpiece. If the drill ap-

Braces use bits called augers. They resemble large-scale brad-point bits, with helical flutes that clear the hole of debris. The tip has threads like a screw for starting the hole on center.

Braces are still manufactured and are often to be found in secondhand and even antique shops. Some follow the traditional design, others have a ratchet that allows the tool to function even when a full sweep of the crank isn't possible. There are purpose-made braces for cutting at right angles (joist braces) and at forty-five-degree angles (corner braces).

Hand drills, too, come in different configurations. They are used for cutting smaller holes (the blade can cut holes of an inch or more in diameter, while the hand drill typically cuts holes of roughly a quarter inch or smaller).

Auger bit

For generations, the hand drill was standard issue to carpenters and other tradesmen. This particular model is called a breast drill after the manner in which it is used. It's efficient and tough, but now very much superseded by the electric drill.

pears to lug or jams, withdraw the drill partway, allowing the bit to clear the debris from the hole.

As the bit approaches the far side, drill more slowly. When a drill bit breaks through the far side rapidly – or if you are applying considerable weight to the drill – the edges of the exit hole will probably be ragged, leaving burrs if the material is metal or tearing out large chips from the wood. Sometimes, too, a workpiece that isn't properly fixed in place will spin on the drill as it passes through the far side. Finish off the hole gently for safe, smooth work.

Place a piece of wood beneath the workpiece you are drilling. This will prevent tear-out.

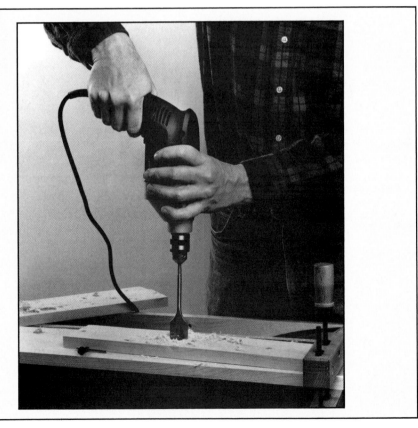

Standard brace

Ratchet brace

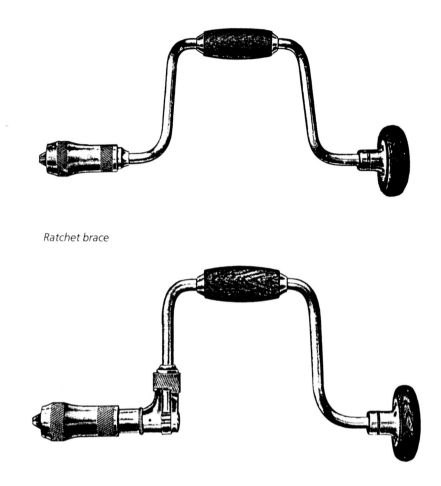

Corner brace

Over the years, the brace was redesigned and improved again and again. One of the innovations was the addition of a ratchet, which allowed the user to employ the drill even when working in a confined space that made a full sweep of the crank impossible. A variation on the standard brace was the corner brace, which also enabled the driller to make holes in awkward spots, particularly those close to and aligned with framing members that, again, would have prevented a full sweep of the crank on a standard brace.

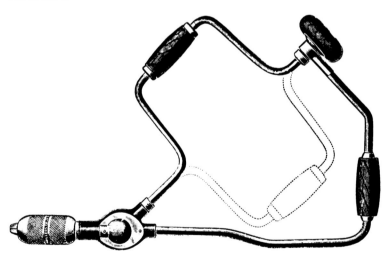

THE POCKET PUSH DRILL

Some two centuries before the birth of Christ, a Greek mathematician named Archimedes explained the principles behind buoyancy and the lever. Thanks to another of his discoveries, the Archimedes' spiral, a small and very portable hand drill bears his name to this day.

Well, sometimes it does. It has been improved upon a bit over the years, and as a result is known by other, newer names as well, among them Yankee drill, spiral ratchet drill, and push drill. Whatever its name, the basic operating principle is much the same as the one Archimedes discovered.

The drill is simple to use. An index of drill points (as the bits for the push drill are sometimes called) is conveniently built into the handle of the drill, so one of them is selected and inserted into the chuck. Drill points have straight flutes along their length.

The point is then positioned where the hole is to be, and the handle of the drill pushed in the direction of the workpiece. The spiral cut onto the shaft of the push drill causes the drill point to turn; when the pressure on the handle is released, the drill will spring back, ready for another cycle.

The portable push drill is handiest for making a few holes in wood (though it can be used to drill some metals, plastics, and other materials). The usual selection of drill points ranges from approximately a sixteenth to a quarter inch. The push drill is at its most convenient in cramped quarters, or when only a handful of holes are required. The setup is almost instantaneous, and this hand drill can easily be carried in a tool pouch.

The Archimedes' drill is put to use by sliding the handle on the screw shaft up and down. With its threaded inside, the traveling handle, as it is called, causes the stem to rotate. Bits for this primitive model had to be sharpened on both sides because the shaft turned in both directions as the traveler was moved reciprocally on the shaft.

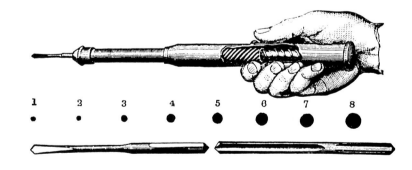

Electric drills do more than drill. Along with performing sanding and grinding chores, they will also willingly drive screws. Inexpensive slotted, Phillips-head or other screw bits can be purchased. They can prove to be major time-savers if you have lots of screws to drive.

CONTENTS

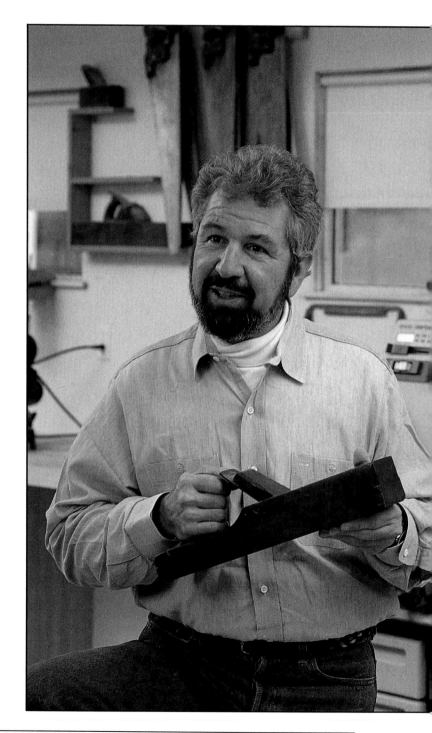

SHAPING
TOOLS

Men of wisdom have observed repeatedly over the years that the experience of hunting changes as a man ages. At first, the shooting of the gun alone provides a raw thrill. That in itself is enough.

After some years, they say, the excitement is less a matter of loud noises and blood lust, and more a matter of skill, of tracking the animal, of one's feel for the woods, for the sounds and smells of a natural world that humankind once inhabited rather than dominated.

For me, sawing is not unlike shooting: Quick, powerful exertions of energy. Which makes shaping more like the chase, requiring more practice and patience for mastery. The same quiet diligence that typifies the hunter tracking is to be seen in a gifted woodworker shaping and smoothing with chisel and plane. The continuing challenge is there, too, because no two pieces of wood are the same and, like every crafty animal, each piece of work has a personality to be probed and challenged.

In the two chapters that follow, I'll talk about the tools for shaping, chisels and scrapers in the first, planes and sanders in the second. These are tools that require skill and care to use, but they repay the effort. Rather than merely assembling parts, the worker who masters the chisel and plane enters a sculptural realm, one that requires both finesse and a gentle touch.

An old jack plane, for joining and smoothing.

Chapter 7.
Chisels and Scrapers

Iknow capable woodworkers who have only occasional use for chisels and never use scrapers. On the other hand, more than a few cabinetmakers, timber framers, and other craftspeople might well nominate the chisel for the Most Valuable Tool team.

This paradox is mostly a matter of the joinery employed by the woodworker. Simple butt joints and even lap joints can be cut with saws. They require straight-cut edges, and are glued, nailed, or screwed together, all of which is quite adequate for a vast array of construction activities.

For those who rely upon mortise-and-tenon joinery, however, saws don't provide all the answers. The mouthlike slots (mortises) into which the tenons fit are essentially square-cornered holes in the workpieces. They may be large or small, depending upon the stock being used and the purpose of the joint, but most require shaping with a chisel. Mortise-and-tenon joinery is but one kind of woodwork for which chisels are invaluable, as wood chisels are used for rough shaping, paring, trimming, and even chopping small wood elements to size.

Not all chisels are wood chisels, either, for cold chisels are used to cut sheet metals, chain stock, rivets, or to do other rough-cut metalwork.

Scrapers, like chisels, are used for shaping, but they remove only small amounts of material. In cabinetwork, they are used in place of sanders, especially when smoothing the surface of hardwoods. More

Welcome to the wonderful world of chisels and scrapers. Surrounding the giant timber-framer's chisel, called a slick, are an array of scrapers (foreground), numerous wood chisels, and a couple of cold chisels (center, rear).

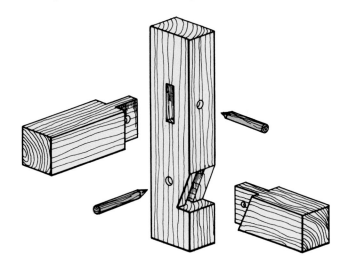

Back in the days when metal components were expensive, the all-wood mortise-and-tenon joint was economical. Today, when high-quality hardwoods and skilled labor are at a premium, such sturdy and enduring joints are no longer common in house construction, though a small renaissance is under way, particularly in the northeast.

often, however, scrapers are used to remove old paint, caulk, wallpaper, or other matter from surfaces being refinished. They are tools for the novice and the expert alike.

WOOD CHISELS

Suppose you borrowed H. G. Well's time machine and traveled back into history a few centuries or even a millennium. Suppose, too, that you got stuck there.

The chances are that you wouldn't be able to find work as a handyman. The tools you knew back home in the twentieth century evolved over the centuries, assuming forms almost unrecognizable from those you would observe in the toolboxes of the distant past. But the chisel – well, *there* you might find a familiar shape and feel.

Stone chisels were used by Neolithic man; bronze chisels were cast in stone by his descendants. From the time of the Romans of classical antiquity up through the nineteenth century, chisels were made of iron, eventually with a thick layer of steel heat-welded onto the working surface. But whenever and wherever your time machine delivers you, you'll probably find chisels of recognizable form that were intended to be used for shaping much as we use chisels today.

Despite the chisel's continuity through time, not all wood chisels are the same (we'll talk about cold chisels for cutting metal next).

A variety of chisels and mallets, including all-metal carpenter's chisels (left), beveled chisels with boxwood handles (right), and an all-purpose butt chisel (front).

They come in various sizes, and their blades and handles are made differently, depending upon the purposes for which they are intended. In general, chisels are used to trim off unwanted wood while shaping or, in joinery, to give the elements of a joint their final form by shaving off waste.

Most chisels are divisible into two classes: Tang chisels, in which a portion of the blade, called the tang, fits into the handle; and socket chisels, in which a portion of the handle fits into the blade. In theory, socket chisels are to be used with a mallet; tang chisels are not struck, but pushed and guided by muscle power. But in practice these lines are blurred.

There are subdivisions within these two classes, too, most of them named for the uses to which the various tools are put. These names are often omitted or used incorrectly, however, and the confusion is made worse by the variety of trades that use chisels, many of which have their own tool terminology. To a shipwright, for example, the preferred firmer chisel was called a registered chisel; the violin maker uses a purfling chisel. If you were making a gun, you'd probably be glad to have a gunstocker's chisel. You see, a chisel is not a chisel, despite the natural tendency of the uninitiated to think so.

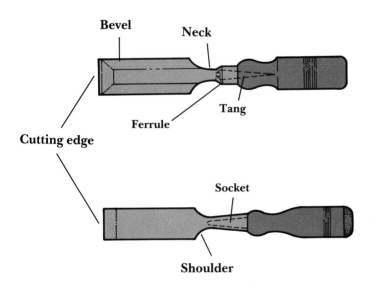

The two main chisel designs: A tang chisel (top) and socket chisel.

Firmer Chisels. These are all-purpose wood chisels. The name evolved from the French verb *former,* meaning to form or to shape. It will come as no surprise, then, that this tool is used most often for shaping a workpiece, for cutting away the unnecessary wood to produce the rough form you want. The blade of the firmer chisel is flat, with parallel sides, and typically about four inches long.

The handle may be hardwood or plastic and is intended to stand up to the abuse delivered by a mallet. Don't interpret the word mallet to mean any old hammer you have at hand, by the way. Mallets are indeed hammers that are made of wood, but the tools are not interchangeable. When a hammer is used to drive a chisel, the life expectancy of the chisel's handle plummets. Some of the impact-resistant plastic handles on new chisels will stand up to metal hammers, but using a wooden mallet is always a good practice.

If I had to limit my toolbox to a single type of chisel, the firmer chisels would be my choice. These chisels come in blade widths ranging from a sixteenth to three inches, but for most purposes a set of four chisels of a quarter-inch, half-inch, three-quarter-inch, and one-inch widths will be quite adequate.

Heavy-duty firmer chisels, often with hooped handles (in which a metal reinforcement ring encircles the end of the handle) are called framing chisels. They are generally longer, sometimes with blades ten inches long and overall lengths of as much as twenty inches.

Paring Chisels. Paring chisels have thinner, lighter blades than firmer chisels, and tend to be longer than most firmer chisels (seven inches or so is usual). The handle is often of a different kind, too, because a paring chisel is *not* designed to be struck with a mallet. Rather, the paring chisel is used for finer work, shaving and paring the workpiece, powered solely by the muscles of the hand and arm.

So many paring chisels on the market today have beveled edges that maker and suppliers have begun to identify paring chisels as bevel-edge chisels. They are available in eighth-inch to two-inch widths.

Mortising Chisels. Used for cutting deep mortises, these chisels are designed for use with a mallet. Their blades are thicker to prevent bending when levering out waste.

Three rules for chiseling: First, chisel with the grain whenever possible. Second, when using a mallet to drive the chisel in rough shaping, use the chisel bevel edge down. Third, for finishing and paring work, drive the chisel with your hand, and hold the tool with the flat side (back) against the work.

Cranked-Neck Chisels. *These are paring chisels with a difference. The cranked neck on the blade allows the offset handle to clear the work surface, while keeping the blade absolutely flat on the workpiece. That's a very convenient attribute, especially when working in the interior of a workpiece.*

Butt Chisels. The butt chisel is essentially a shorter version of the firmer chisel. It is designed for use in hard-to-reach or cramped applications.

Solid Steel Wood Chisels. These durable chisels will stand up to mallets and hammers alike. In fact, they are perfect for use at a work-site, as you can afford to be less concerned about their exposure to the elements and careful storage.

These probably aren't the best tools for precise work, but for construction purposes, they are handy and somewhat less expensive. They are sold in various sizes, typically in quarter-inch, half-inch, three-quarter-inch, and one-inch widths.

Other Chisels. There are other kinds of wood chisels, too, including corner chisels, carving chisels, and turning chisels, the latter designed to be used with a lathe. Those tools will be discussed in this book's companion volume, *Bob Vila's Workshop.*

A bevel-edge socket chisel.

Never use your chisels for opening paint cans or for prying up nailheads. Inspect any workpiece you wish to shape before employing your chisel: The chisel blade should never be at risk of contacting any metal. The delicate edge of a chisel can be marred by as tiny an item as a staple, and a dull chisel is almost worse than no chisel at all.

MAKING A MORTISE

Chisels are useful for lots of jobs, but only the chisel can make mortises of almost any size for almost any purpose. Whether the mortise is for a mortise-and-tenon joint or a shallow indentation for a door hinge, the technique is similar. Here are a few tips on how to shape a mortise properly.

Finding the Feel. As with any new tool, practice is required with chisels. Good ones are balanced and fit in the hand as if they belong there, but it takes a while to be able to use them confidently.

And to use them safely. Good chisels are sharp indeed and always ready to send you off to the emergency room for a few stitches. Ask any veteran woodworker. These are not toys, but must be used with care and preparation.

Never push and strike a chisel in the direction of your hands or body; always work away from yourself, with both hands *behind* the cutting edge of the chisel at all times. Assume a comfortable, balanced stance, gripping the chisel comfortably but securely in your hands. Good lighting is also important.

Getting Ready. Any chiselwork is only as good as the marks you make to guide you. Lay out your mortise precisely, using a square and a sharp marker. Fix the workpiece in place so that it, and the sharp chisel in your hand, won't suddenly jerk dangerously when you're applying pressure.

Chiselwork consists of laying out the cut lines (1), roughing out the waste within the mortise (2), and then paring to the edges of the mortise (3).

Work from the Waste. Don't begin at the cut line, but start within the waste area. Rough out the inside first, removing as much of the waste as possible. If you're using a firmer chisel, wield the mallet gently: You will soon find that exact work requires lots of little taps rather than big bangs.

Paring to Perfection. Once you have trimmed the waste to within about an eighth inch of the edge of the mortise, trim to the line. Take only small amounts of wood at a time, as paring too much can cause the wood to split beyond the edge of your layout lines. The thinner the shavings, the better your end result is likely to be.

Err on the side of taking too little waste, and try fitting the hinge or tenon for which the mortise is intended. If it's too small or too shallow, repeat the process again. Start with the waste, then pare to the edge.

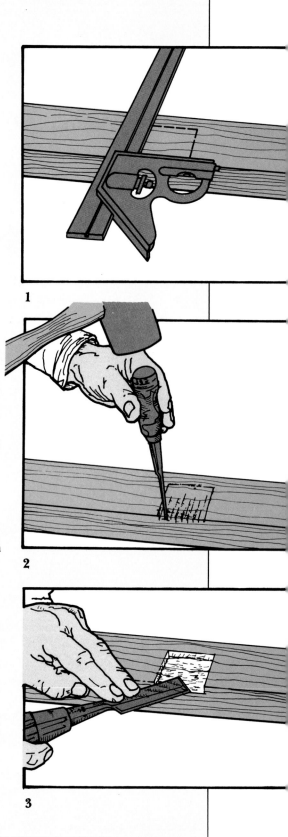

1

2

3

COLD, MASONRY, AND BRICK CHISELS

Cold chisels aren't for cold weather; they're for cutting cold, hard metal. A cold chisel will cut any metal that is softer than the material from which the chisel itself is made. Made of hardened steel, cold chisels have a beveled cutting edge and an octagonally shaped handle. The cold chisel has a flat cutting edge, but related chisels are wedge-shaped (cape chisel), half-round, diamond-shaped, or round.

Cold chisels are used to cut rivets, to split nuts or bolts that refuse to come loose, or to break castings. They can also be used to cut sheet metal. The metal chisels with edges in other shapes have other applications, such as grooving or shaping corners.

Don't use a cold chisel to cut masonry; there are specially made tools for that purpose.

To use a cold chisel, select a hammer of suitable weight, usually a ball peen or club hammer. The bigger the chisel, the heavier the hammer that is needed, because a large chisel will absorb much of the force of a light hammer blow and do little or no cutting.

Find your safety glasses or goggles, too, and wear them whenever you are cutting with a cold chisel. Shrapnel-like chips are an occupational hazard.

Grasp the handle of the chisel, making a fist around its handle with your thumb and forefinger an inch or so from the top. Hold it securely but not tightly. A too-rigid grip will transfer much of the force from the hammer blows to your hand and arm, leaving them ringing with the shock of the blow.

Surrounding the antique pointed chisel (it looks rather like a railroad spike) are two cold chisels (foreground), a brick chisel (right), and an all-purpose mason's chisel (rear). That's a ball peen hammer in the foreground and a club hammer standing on its head.

KEEPING YOUR CHISELS SHARP

I know you've heard it before, but it's true: Sharp tools are safer tools. The chisel is a perfect case in point. A dull chisel requires more force to drive; the greater the force applied, the greater the likelihood it'll slip or skid out of the cavity you are shaping and cut you instead of the wood. Dull chisels also tend to crush rather than cut wood, so the work done with a dull chisel is noticeably inferior.

Keeping your wood chisels sharp is not difficult. Unless you use them frequently, you don't even need to sharpen them more than once or twice a year, or perhaps even less. But that does assume they are kept in proper storage: Protect their edges, and they will require fewer sharpenings.

Sharpening stones can be purchased in a surprising variety of sizes and shapes (including square, conical, triangular, and rectangular) in order to sharpen chisels, plane irons, and cutting edges of all descriptions.

The Wet- Versus Water-Stone Debate. When I was a boy, there was an ongoing argument in my elementary school between the Ford followers and the Chevy devotees. The discussion was not characterized by the expression of high-minded views; it was usually a matter of one side insisting, "Fords are better" and the other countering, "No way, Chevys are the best." Needless to say, the dispute has yet to be resolved.

A similar perennial argument goes on among the honing and sharpening crowd. There battle lines are drawn between the waterstoners and the oilstoners. The former use water as the lubricant; oilstoners use a petroleum-based cutting oil to aid in sharpening. Which kind of stone is preferable?

For a while, I thought the oilstoners had the upper hand, with their conviction that the Arkansas stone was the ultimate in sharpening stones. But in recent years the wetstoners have weighed in with the Japanese waterstones, which are excellent, too. For me, it comes down to this: In order to sharpen scissors, knives, chisels, or any other hand-cutting tool you need a sharpening stone. That's a given. And you need to do it right, with proper preparation, patience, and procedure. I'll leave the resolution of which stone is best to others: I suggest you buy a high-quality common sharpening stone and use it well, taking whichever side of the argument you wish. Experiment with both, if you like. But use and store the stone with the same care you lavish on your chisels.

Grinding the Bevel. Unless there are nicks in the tool or its edge has become flattened by many honings, there is usually no need to grind the edge on a wheel. If it is necessary, however, use a grinding jig to hold the blade at the precise angle of the bevel. Press the chisel gently against the wheel, moving it back and forth across the face of the stone, applying pressure evenly.

Preparing the Stone. Lubricate the stone according to the instructions that come with it. In the case of waterstones, that generally means immersing the stone in a bath of clean water for several minutes before use; with oilstones, it means wiping a sheen of fine cutting oil onto the stone. The water or oil allows the fine particles of steel ground off the edge that is being sharpened to float on the surface of the stone, preventing the stone from getting clogged. Make sure the stone is clean before beginning the honing.

Most sharpening stones have two faces, one coarse and one fine. You'll start with the coarse stone and then proceed to the fine surface.

The Whetting Process. Hold the chisel with the bevel flat to the stone. Use both hands to steady the chisel, and slide it backward and forward on the surface of the stone. Take pains to maintain the proper angle to the stone at all times (or, to put it another way, don't rock the chisel, but slide it precisely). Don't be in a hurry, either, but rub the bevel of the chisel along the stone in a smooth, even stroke.

Use the entire surface of the stone. Too many strokes in the same area of the stone will cause it to wear unevenly, perhaps leaving a hollow that will sharpen edges unevenly.

Repeat the whetting process on the fine surface of the stone.

Removing the Burr. The stone will have caused a small amount of the blade to extend beyond the back of the chisel, forming a slight burr. To remove it, turn the chisel onto its back (bevel side up) and hold it flush to the fine stone surface. Slide it back and forth a few times, taking care to keep the back flat on the stone surface.

Some people favor a thorough stropping at this stage, drawing the blade of the chisel across a leather surface that has had a polishing compound applied. A few stropping strokes certainly won't harm the blade, but aren't essential.

After you have completed the sharpening process, wipe off any residue from the stone with a clean cloth.

The Micro-Bevel. Another optional step favored by some is the addition of a second, steeper bevel at the tip of the blade. Only a few strokes on the finest stone are necessary, with the tip held at a pitch that is perhaps five degrees steeper than the previous whetting. Again, this is optional and, for the novice sharpener, an unnecessary complication.

Sharpening Plane Irons. The chisel-like blades in planes, called plane irons, are sharpened in much the same way as chisels. Follow the same procedure, except that the angle at which the plane iron is presented to the stone should be higher in jack or jointer planes (perhaps forty-five degrees) or lower for block plane irons (around twenty degrees). Match the original angle as closely as you can.

In sharpening a chisel, first you slide the bevel of the chisel, keeping it carefully flush to the surface of the stone, back and forth and around and around (above). Then you complete the process by removing the burr on the back of the chisel.

113

Storing Your Chisels. *Any cutting edge, whether it's a sawtooth, knife blade, or chisel tip, dulls rapidly when it comes in contact with other metal. The chisel is even more delicate than the others because its cutting edge is extremely fine.*

In order that your chisels remain sharp, you must store them away from the accidental dings and dents that are likely to occur if they were to mill about in the toolbox with the hammers, drivers, pliers, and the rest. Many new chisels come equipped with plastic tips; I strongly suggest you use these as one means of shielding the chisel's edge. But I'd suggest additional protection, too, like a sturdy leather or cloth pouch with separate pockets for each chisel. Individual leather sheaths also work well. Still another option is a chisel block, a honeycomb of wood like those used to store kitchen knives. Find a storage approach that suits your toolbox or storage closet.

Don't try to do all the cutting with single blows, but swing the hammer in a controlled rhythm. Watch the cutting edge of the chisel, not the handle.

Brick Chisel. Also called a bolster or brick set, the brick chisel is used to make smooth cuts on bricks. Rough cutting of brick is usually done with a brick hammer (which has a chisel-like blade opposite the face of the hammer).

Cutting a brick with a brick set isn't complicated. Position the chisel perpendicular to the brick, with the straight side of the cutting edge facing the end of the brick to be used. Strike the handle of the chisel with a small sledge or club hammer, hard enough to score the brick but not to shatter it. Score the brick on all sides, then strike it once more to break the brick in two.

Brick chisels should not be used for cutting stone, as they will quickly lose their edge.

Masonry Chisels. Some masonry chisels are designed for cutting soft stone, while others will stand up to harder use.

Like brick chisels, masonry chisels are generally used only to score the stone; as with glass cutting, the task involves scoring first, then breaking along the score line. Gentle taps on the chisel create the score line, allowing the stone to be snapped off when the line has been completed.

Floor chisels are another variety of chisel that can be used to scrape floors, clear off blobs of concrete, and other rough chisel work.

SCRAPERS

I've lumped together under a single heading a family of tools that are used to perform many tasks. They resemble one another in that they have flat blades mounted on handles, but differ in that some are light and flexible, others stiffer and heavier. The edges of blades vary, too, in the degree to which they are sharpened.

In a sense, the patriarch of this particular family is the hand scraper, which is a sort of simplified plane. Both the hand scraper and the plane are used to smooth surfaces, removing thin shavings. In cabinet and other fine finish work, the hand scraper – a flat piece of sheet metal also called a cabinet scraper – is an essential tool, but it is used almost exclusively in the workshop. For the purposes of this book, we'll consider its more rough-and-ready relation, the tool generically known as the paint scraper. As its name suggests, it's a scraper, too, used to remove old paint.

Paint Scraper. The tool has a flat steel blade and a handle of wood, plastic, or metal. Its uses are many, among them removing wallpaper or paint after they've been softened with heat, and it can be wielded

Flanking the safety glasses are a paint scraper (left) and a filling knife. Above are a razor knife, surrounded by a putty knife, four shave hooks with blades of different profiles, a narrow and a wide hook scraper, and a traditional cabinet scraper. You can see from the partially scraped mantel what a job it was . . . and how well it can be done.

in a grip similar to that you use to hold a screwdriver. The blade is used at a shallow angle to the surface being stripped, and the paper, paint, or other material peels up as the blade is advanced.

Another way to use the paint scraper that is particularly useful when scraping a wood surface is by gripping the blade with both hands, pinching it between the middle and forefingers and thumb of each hand. Bow the blade a little with the pressure of your thumbs to prevent the corners from digging into the wood. Angle it slightly away from you, and push the scraper across the surface. Scrape with the grain.

This is a tool that becomes easier to use with practice, so you may want to experiment and master the technique before trying to strip a piece that will end up at front and center in your home.

Putty and Filling Knives. At first glance, it's easy to confuse the putty knife with a narrow paint scraper. The difference is only a matter of weight: The lighter putty knife flexes more easily than the paint scraper. It's better suited to apply such thick or pasty materials as glazing compound, spackle, or other fillers.

Wider versions of this knife are often sold as a filling knife, and these tools can be purchased in a number of different widths, from one to four inches. These knives are a near relation to the wallboard knives used in applying the plasterlike joint compound (see page 198).

Hook Scraper. This tool looks like the runt of the litter, but it belongs here, too. Its handle is long, intended to be grasped with two hands, allowing for considerable weight and leverage to be put upon the blade. The blade is mounted at the end of the handle at almost a ninety-degree angle. The blade is also reversible. The hook scraper can be purchased with longer or shorter handles, and blades between one and a half and two and a half inches.

The hook scraper is designed for the most challenging scraping jobs, like removing stubborn paint from old floors.

Grasp the scraper between the thumbs and first two fingers of each hand, bending it slightly to keep the corners from cutting into the wood. Tipping the tool away from you, scrape in a pushing motion.

Razor-Blade Scraper. This small, inexpensive tool is really handy for scraping paint off windows, cleaning tile, and scraping other hard surfaces. It consists of a flat housing designed to hold a single-edged razor blade; most models are designed so that the blade can be safely retracted into the body of the tool for safe storage. Changing blades when they get dull is an easy matter of sliding the old one out and slipping a new one in.

I'd suggest two cautions regarding this tool. For one, don't ask it to do heavy-duty jobs for which it was not intended. Razor blades are thin and brittle and the handle is not designed to hold them so that a great deal of force can be used.

The second warning applies to all the scrapers: Remember, they are sharp, bladed tools which, to varying degrees, are capable of cutting and scraping flesh as well as paper, paint, and other materials. Use them with care and store them properly to prevent accidents.

SHAVE HOOKS

Also called molding scrapers, these sharp tools are used to remove old paint from cornice, baseboard, casing, and other moldings. The blades and shafts are made of steel, the handles of hardwood, usually beech.

As with any scraper, the blade should be at an acute angle of almost ninety degrees to the workpiece, with the blade tipped slightly in the direction you are scraping. This causes the edge to scrape along the surface, rather than to dig into it if it were presented to the surface. Shave hooks, like other scrapers, are often used together with a source of heat like a heat gun that softens the paint.

Molding scrapers can be purchased in different profiles, including triangular, pear-shaped, rectangular, square, arrow-headed, and a variety of other shapes. Purpose-made blades can be ground to order, too. Molding scrapers can be purchased with interchangeable blades, or as a set of handles and shafts with fixed blades.

The hook scraper and the shave hook are scrapers of related design and use. Both are used in a pulling motion, using one hand or two, depending upon the pressure required. The hook scraper has a straight blade for flat areas, the shave hooks have curves and points for scraping moldings and odd shapes.

117

Chapter 8.
Planes and Sanders

Planes and sanders are finishing tools, used to smooth rough surfaces, readying them for the application of paint or other finishes. Both come in an assortment of shapes, and in a range of sizes from hand-held models to stationary designs that are rarely used outside the confines of a workshop.

The pairing of planes and sanders in the same chapter is a natural one. Planes and sanders not only finish exterior surfaces, but allow their users to make ever so slight adjustments on a workpiece to achieve square, tight joints. The competent woodworker requires both, yet the degree to which an individual relies on one or the other of these tools speaks volumes about the woodworker's skill.

Consider it this way: Sanding is a technique a child can master, requiring only that paper with the proper grit (abrasive value) be used and that it be worked with the grain. But the plane demands much more: Using and maintaining a plane requires sophisticated tool sense, an alternately soft and forceful touch, a knowledge of the material being shaped, and sharpening skill.

Both planes and sanding devices are essential for countless tasks. But the woodworker who wields a plane with grace and ease has a degree of control no power tool can offer.

THE BLOCK PLANE

Quality planed stock can be bought from most lumberyards today, but wood that has been dressed on all four sides wasn't always the norm. Woodworkers only a few generations ago had to plane finished surfaces for themselves every time; as a result, planes both then and now were made in all shapes and sizes.

Even today a fully equipped workshop may well have large jointer or jack planes and smaller molding, rabbet, compass, and bullnose planes. There are important uses, too, for hand-held power planers and free-standing thickness planers. But it is the block plane that has survived as the most essential plane, a tool that belongs in every traveling toolbox. It's one of the finish carpenter's most valuable aids for fitting doors, moldings, and general trimming work.

The block plane is distinguished, in part, by its flat sole. Other common planes, like smoothing, jack, and jointer planes, all have slight curves across their widths. The low angle of its blade (twelve to

At the top are a block plane (left) and a bench plane. There's a palm-grip sander, too (left, center), and a range of sanding materials. At center is an antique sun plane, a tool used by a cooper to level the stave tops in barrel-making. Handsome as it is, that probably isn't a tool you'll need in your toolbox.

Store your block plane with care, always clear of any metal object or surfaces. A wooden or cardboard box or a cloth bag is a sensible housing precaution. Laying the plane on its side on a shelf, perhaps with a piece of scrap wood held by an elastic to its sole, will also help protect the plane iron. If you have no plans to use the plane for a period of time, withdraw the plane's cutting iron into the body, clear of the mouth.

Planes are like chisels: Sharp ones are a pleasure to use, friends and allies in the dressing and shaping of wood. But a dull plane will do little more than dampen your enthusiasm for the task at hand. Keep your planes sharp and ready.

twenty degrees, depending upon the model) is another peculiarity of the block plane, one that allows it to cut end grain (that is, it can be used to trim off shavings across the grain, unlike planes that are to be used only with the grain). This means that boards that need to be a shade shorter can be trimmed with a few strokes of the block plane, saving trips down the ladder or across the room to the saw. The blade of the block plane, called the plane iron, is mounted with its bevel up.

The block plane is also useful for trimming small stock with the grain, so it can be used for a great deal of any final trim and fitting work. The finish carpenter applying moldings will find the block plane fits nicely in a pocket and comes to hand in a moment for matching one length of molding to the next.

The block plane is small, typically five to seven inches long, though both longer and shorter models are available. The frame is made of iron or brass and the blade of steel. The plane is designed to be used one-handed. The tool fits into the palm, with the fingers fitting around the bulbous frame, and the fingertips holding the knob at the front (toe) of the plane. The blades in various models range from about one and a quarter inches in width to one and five-eighths inches.

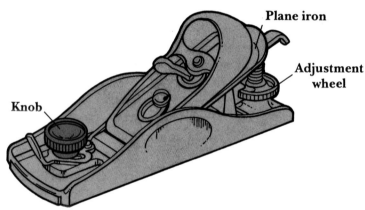

Plane iron

Adjustment wheel

Knob

Block planes are sold in a number of different configurations. Some have their blades set at a very shallow pitch, as low as twelve degrees, in comparison to a more usual twenty or so degrees. The models with the lowest angles work best for trimming plywood, end grain, or other difficult stock.

The simplest models allow only for the blade to be adjusted; it is tightened in the proper position, then put to use. Others have a lever for adjusting the blade laterally and a screw or wheel for raising or lowering it. On some models, the mouth of the plane can also be adjusted for fine or coarse work. Any block plane that has a sharp blade can be used effectively; the more expensive models simply allow for easier adjustment. Selecting one rather than another is a matter of

PLANING TECHNIQUES

Get comfortable with the block plane in your hand. It is designed for one-handed work, so hold it, blade up, in your palm. I find it always feels heavy for its size but offers me a sense that it's ready to go to work.

Assume the Position. One great virtue of the block plane is that it is used one-handed, so you can plane a piece almost anywhere. But before you try planing on a ladder or in a cramped space, get familiar with the tool on a workbench, fixing the piece firmly in place.

Whenever you use the block plane, assume a balanced stance, with the workpiece held firmly with one hand, the plane in the other (the workpiece-hand should be out of the intended path of the plane – or the trajectory it will take should your hand slip). You'll also find that planing horizontally or even downhill is a great deal easier than trying to plane upward.

Adjust the Plane Iron. On a piece of scrap that resembles the workpiece you'll be planing, take the plane on a trial run. If the blade extends too far through the mouth, it will jam, choking on great chunks of stock. If it's withdrawn into the frame, you'll remove no shaving at all. Adjust the plane so that thin shavings are removed.

Let the Planing Begin. Hold the plane flat to the surface. Let your fingertips guide the plane. Be firm, but don't force the tool.

Try Working Diagonally. The block plane is often most effective when held at an angle to the workpiece, especially when trimming end grain.

When planing end grain, plain from each edge to the middle – a full stroke across the end grain is likely to split the wood at the edge.

Like the kangaroo that carries her young around in a pouch, many a finish carpenter carries his best friend, the block plane, around in his back pocket. Before you know it, the block plane may be a valued collaborator of yours as well. Remember, there are those who say that what separates the skilled from the semi-skilled carpenter is the ability to use a plane well.

The block plane generally works best when it is presented to the work at an angle to the grain. That's true whether you're cutting off circular sawmarks with the grain (below), or trimming end grain.

balancing the desire for a plane that is slightly easier to use with its added cost.

The block plane is intended for fine work. If you need to level a workpiece, smooth a long, wide surface, or plane a drawer slide, the block plane is probably not the answer. Its body is too short to flatten a surface, and with the rise and fall of the waves in the stock, it may even exaggerate the contours.

THE PALM-GRIP SANDER

Belt sanders, disk sanders, orbital sanders, finish sanders, random sanders, drum sanders, combination sanders . . . like planes, there is a dizzying array of sanders. But at the work-site, there is one hand-held model that can perform a wide variety of tasks with ease and efficiency.

The palm-grip sander, as its name suggests, is designed to fit comfortably into the palm of the hand. Powered by an electric motor, this sander works with the sandpaper mounted in twin jaws that hold the paper tight to a rubber pad at the base of the unit.

The palm-grip sander fits naturally into the hand and makes quick work of finish sanding, even on curves and corners. For most jobs, though, a dust mask is a good idea.

The palm-grip sander's motor generates an orbital (spinning) motion that produces a rapid series of cuts, up to ten thousand a minute. The paper used, however, is the biggest single factor in how much material the tool sands from a surface.

Palm sanders can be purchased in different sizes that are distinguished by the size of the sheet of sandpaper required. Common variations require a quarter sheet and a sixth of a sheet of sandpaper.

Some models come with a dust-bag attachment. This reduces the frequency with which the dust clogs the paper on the machine, and results in a cleaner work area. However, sanding remains a dusty business, no matter what.

To use the sander, switch it on and let it come to full speed. Then set it on the surface to be sanded. Move it in the direction of the grain, exerting gentle pressure on the tool. Remember, the palm sander is a finish sander. It is used to put a finish surface on a workpiece, not to give it a basic shape, so don't put too much pressure on it. Keep the base of the palm sander flush to the surface being sanded at all times, to avoid creating undulations in the surface.

THE SANDING BLOCK

The sanding block can be, as its name suggests, a block-shaped tool for sanding flat surfaces. But that doesn't mean that all sanding blocks are the same.

At its simplest, a sanding block is simply a piece of scrap wood with a piece of sandpaper fitted around it which is held in place by the grip of the sander. To prevent cramping, some commercially available blocks of wood or rubber are formed to fit the shape of the hand. The block produces a more even pressure on paper during sanding, preventing the paper from following the waves of the stock and helping to flatten the surface. Sanding blocks also make getting into corners easier, and allow you to sand with added force over a larger area than you could using your hand alone.

When using a sanding block, hold the surface of the block flat and tight to the surface being sanded. That's especially important when sanding at an edge, because if you allow the block to angle over the edge it will tend to round out the edge.

Other Options. Abrasives are sold in numerous configurations these days, including foam blocks that are manufactured with abrasives integral to the foam itself. There are plastic sticks to which a sheet of sandpaper is attached. A teardrop shape is also available which can reach into narrow grooves and molding profiles.

A basic sanding block: Take one end-cut of one-by-four stock, add a sheet of sandpaper, and let the sanding begin.

Surrounding the palm-grip sander are a variety of hand sanding tools. At bottom left is a simple sanding block, made from a piece of scrap stock with sandpaper wrapped around it. To the right are a sanding stick and a form hand sander, a prefabricated sanding block that can be washed and reused. The blue disk is for a sander attachment for a drill. That's a teardrop sander to the left of the palm sander, with steel wool and a miscellany of sandpapers above.

SANDPAPER AND STEEL WOOL

These days sandpaper isn't made out of sand at all. Instead, a range of abrasive materials are used, backed by either paper or cloth. The backing material is impregnated with stearate (a waxy fatty acid), aluminum oxide, or silicon carbide. The aluminum oxide papers are perhaps the best buy, but the aluminum oxide cloth is more durable. Garnet papers are well suited to finishing wood, as the paper holds up well and is available in fine grades. For wet sanding, the silicon carbide paper is best.

Sandpaper (or abrasive paper, as some people prefer to call it) is sold in grades, depending upon how coarse, medium, or fine is its abrasive surface. There are also numerous subdivisions beneath the three main headings and these are identified by the size of the abrasive particles or "grit" to be found on their surfaces. Coarse papers have a grit of 40 or 50; medium paper, 60 to 100 grit; fine, 120 to 220; and extra-fine, 240 to 600 grit. Wet/dry papers are sold in superfine, up to 1,200 grit.

Sandpaper can also be purchased with pressure-sensitive (peel-and-stick) backing or even with Velcro to adhere to sanding machinery or blocks.

When fitting sandpaper to a machine or block, fold the paper and tear it along the fold. Don't cut it with a knife or scissors, as it tears easily and will rapidly dull an edge.

Steel Wool. Made of steel thread, steel wool is loosely woven into hand-held pads that are used to smooth surfaces prior to painting or finishing. Like sandpaper, it comes in grades identified by the fineness of its surface, ranging from coarse (number three), up through medium coarse (number two), medium (number one), and medium fine (zero), very fine (zero, zero), extra-fine (triple zero), and superfine (four zeros). Metal wool can also be purchased that is made of brass.

SANDING TECHNIQUES

Whether you are using a palm sander, a block, or are sanding with paper in hand, the process is basically the same.

Prepare the Surface First. Remove all tape or staples from the surface to be sanded. If necessary, scrape off blobs of plaster, paper, or flooring residue, glue, or any other material. Set all nails beneath the surface; one nail or staple can tear and ruin a fresh piece of sandpaper instantly.

Sand in Sequence. In smoothing a rough surface, you will need to use a sequence of two or three sandpapers, moving from coarse to fine. A medium-coarse paper of 80 to 100 grit might be an appropriate first step, followed by a finer paper in the 120 to180 range to smooth the surface.

Protect Yourself. If you're sanding old paint or plaster or sanding a great deal of anything, wear a mask or respirator (see page 67). Some sanding dust is toxic; even when it isn't, inhaling the dust is a choking, unpleasant sensation. Wet/dry sandpaper is an option, too, for limiting the amount of dust generated.

Clean the paper periodically: It will clog with dust, reducing its efficiency. Simply tapping the paper will cause most of the dust to fall free of the paper's surface.

CONTENTS

FASTENING
TOOLS

In Part I I talked of measuring and marking tools. In Part II the subject was cutting tools, and in the previous section we examined shaping tools. So now we come to the tasks of fastening together the pieces we measured, cut, and shaped.

The fasteners most often used in home construction are nails and screws, but occasionally bolts are put to good use as well. The hammers, drivers, pliers, and related tools discussed in the pages to follow offer a range of options for employing these traditional fasteners. I haven't attempted to include all the driving tools that a professional auto mechanic would require – those alone would fill more than a book or two – but a basic array of sockets and wrenches are covered here.

Extraordinarily strong glues are playing an increasingly important role in house construction. Sheet flooring and walling surfaces are often held in place, at least in part, by construction-grade adhesives. Caulk and glue guns are routinely used in maintenance and projects around the home; they're easy to use, the supplies are commonplace and reasonably priced, and some of the adhesives themselves have proved very durable. You'll find the glues and guns in this chapter, too.

Finally, we'll talk in brief about the flip side of fastening things: That is, about the wrecking and pry bars that are needed to dismantle something. After all, most renovations begin with demolition, or at least a little surgery to get through the flesh to identify what ails the bones of the structure beneath.

The handscrew clamp is one the woodworker's best friends, especially when used in conjunction with its numerous cousins, bar clamps, pipe clamps, C-clamps, and all the rest.

Chapter 9.

Hammers

Hammers are among our most basic, and our oldest, tools. No doubt the tool was first improvised in an instant by some clever caveman who picked up a stone many thousands of years ago to crush a nut or pound in a stake. We know that stones were used as hammers in classical antiquity because some of the large, handled jars called amphorae that survive from that period carry illustrations of Greek bronzesmiths plying their trade with stones in hand.

The hammer has had many improvements in the years since (that's linguistically true, too, as some pedants insist upon calling this family of tools the percussives). A bent wood handle was fabricated, and it eventually evolved into the design we know today, the straight handle that fits into the "eye" in the hammerhead. Stone heads were replaced in turn by bronze, iron, and eventually steel. The claw is thought to have been devised after the birth of Christ, as there is pictorial evidence of clawheads' use in Roman times.

Today, there are hammers of a dozen or more different designs manufactured for many kinds of tasks. In the pages that follow, I'll talk about several of them, in particular the claw hammer, ball peen, club hammer, wooden mallets, and soft mallets. But there are others available, too, for specialty needs, including upholsterer's and drywaller's hammers, veneering hammers, brick hammers, and sledgehammers. Still others are more often found in museums and antique shops, like cooper's, clench, double-clawed, saddler's, and wheelwright's hammers.

In general, hammers of the same kind are identified by their differing sizes, as a twenty-four-ounce hammer, for example, is larger (and heavier) than a sixteen-ounce hammer. The weight referred to is that of the hammer's head rather than the tool's overall weight.

Another variable in buying a hammer is the face of the hammer (the face is the surface used for striking; the opposite side of the head, whether it has a claw or another shape, is known as the peen). Some faces are smooth, others have serrations often machined in a waffle pattern. Some are flat (plain-faced), others convex in shape (the latter are called bell-faced).

The bottom line is that every household needs at least one hammer. Whether it's for tacking a picture onto the wall or renailing a floorboard or piece of molding, the hammer should come quickly and easily to hand.

Here are hammers, mallets, and nails galore. The greater the variety of jobs you take on, the broader the range of striking tools you'll need (although you probably won't need quite this many).

An early, hand-forged iron hammer.

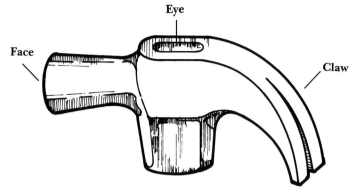

Eye

Face

Claw

Though this drawing features a claw for pulling nails, the rear of the hammerhead, whether it has a claw, a flat surface like a thick chisel, or a ball-shaped tip, is called a peen, pein, or, in England, a pane.

Hickory hammer handles, though less durable than those made of steel or fiberglass, have a flexible "feel" that has long been favored by craftsmen. I don't find this makes a great deal of difference when bashing large nails, but in finish work, especially when using square-shafted cut nails, more of a sense of the nail's progress is transmitted along the wooden shaft.

CLAW HAMMERS

For most of us, this is the design we reach for when we need a hammer. Its head has a face that is used to drive nails; the peen opposite the face is a two-pronged claw that is used to pull nails out of wood. The claw hammer is one of the carpenter's basic tools.

The head on a claw hammer is made of steel, the handle of fiberglass, wood (commonly hickory, a tough, springy wood), or steel. Fiberglass and steel hammers typically have rubber, plastic, or vinyl handles for comfort and shock absorption.

Claw hammers can be purchased in many sizes, ranging from small tack hammers weighing only a few ounces to large framing hammers (designed for driving large nails) that have heads weighing up to twenty-eight ounces and handles reaching eighteen inches in

length. The shape of the claw varies from one hammer to another. Larger hammers often have a flattened claw, and sometimes are referred to as wrecking or rip hammers because the claw can be used to pry apart wooden elements in demolition work. Smaller hammers usually have claws with sharper curves.

A moderate-sized hammer with a head of sixteen ounces and handle of sixteen inches will perform a wide variety of tasks, though for framing work a heavier hammer, perhaps of twenty ounces, will offer added power. (I'd suggest you leave the really big ones to those who frame buildings for a living; in the hands of the occasional user, they are unwieldy and a liability for most jobs around the house.)

When selecting a hammer, consider the face, too. A patterned face (also called a mill face) will help prevent glancing blows, because the serrations grip the head of the nail. This is especially handy when doing work that involves forceful hammering, like framing and toe-nailing. A smooth, slightly convex (belled) face is preferable for finish work. In claw hammers, flat faces are usually an indication of second-rate goods.

Pulling a nail puts tremendous wrenching stresses on a hammer. If you favor a wood-handled hammer (and many of us do), use it sparingly for pulling nails. Keep a pair of nail pullers or a wrecking bar handy in your tool bag for pulling all nails larger than eightpennies (two-and-a-half-inch-long nails).

When you wish to remove a nail from what will be (or is) a finished surface, you need to protect the wood from the head of the hammer. To do so, use a piece of scrap to rest the hammerhead on as you lever the nail out.

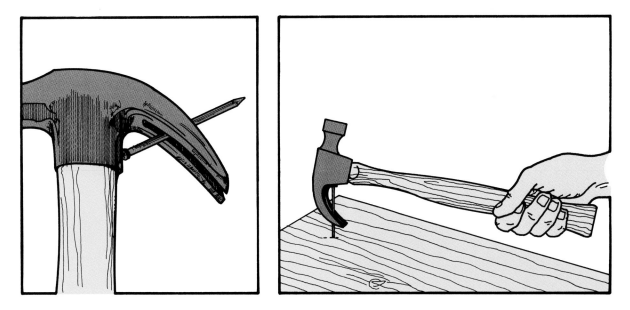

To start a nail one-handed, cradle the nail between the claws of the hammer, with its head flush to the base of the hammerhead. With a short swing, plant the tip of the nail in the workpiece. Then gently detach the claw and hammer the nail in as you would any other nail.

BASIC HAMMERING 101

At first, I felt a bit foolish explaining how to use a hammer. Most of us have seen children banging away with toy mallets before the age of two, and even at that tender age hammering seems natural. After all, the act was probably encoded in the human genetic program well before the word was adopted.

Yet proper hammering technique, like so many skills that we take for granted, isn't as self-evident as people think. I have seen a fair number of professionals swinging hammers with great confidence – and minimal technique. If you know it all already, let the following serve as a refresher. Who knows, you might just learn something, too.

Gripping the Hammer.
Whether you're nailing a twenty-penny spike or a finishing nail, the grip is the same. Make a fist, either wrapping your thumb across the index and middle fingers or gripping the handle just above the first finger.

Make sure you hold the hammer near the end of the handle. By holding it there, you'll get maximum leverage and the tool will be better balanced. It may not feel that way at first, especially if you are a self-taught carpenter who has always choked up on the handle. But you will do well to retrain yourself and learn to use the whole hand. You'll find that you bend fewer nails, too, because the angle of approach will be more in line with the shank of the nail, while a choked-up grip tends to bring in the blows at a lower angle.

Swinging the Hammer. Holding the nail upright with the fingers of your other hand, rest the hammer's face on the head of the nail. It's like golf: You line up the shot first, then you swing.

Raise the hammer slightly, and drop it back onto the nailhead a few times, tapping the nail into the wood until the grain grips the tip. Now, holding the hammer gently but firmly, aim the head at the nail, and swing in a motion that might be best described as a half chop, half throw.

Let the weight of the hammer do the work for you. Most of your work is actually done at the beginning of the stroke. Don't muscle the hammer all the way to the nail, merely guide it to the nailhead, letting momentum and gravity help you. Control the hammer, but not in a rigid grip.

Even the return stroke is easier when the hammer is gripped gently. Thanks to Newton's third law of motion (the one about an action resulting in a reaction), the hammerhead will bounce back. Use that bounce to advantage, letting it guide your backswing, returning the hammer along the same line it took on the striking stroke.

If you feel a jar in your shoulder or elbow when the hammer strikes, you're too tight.

One last thing: Wear your safety glasses when you hammer. Even the most skilled of carpenters mis-hits now and again, and in an instant a nail can become a missile. Airborne nails – or pieces of nails – are dangerous indeed.

Remember, the slight swelling at the heel of the hammer's handle should fit into the pad at the heel of your hand. And the line of the handle should be perpendicular to the shaft of the nail.

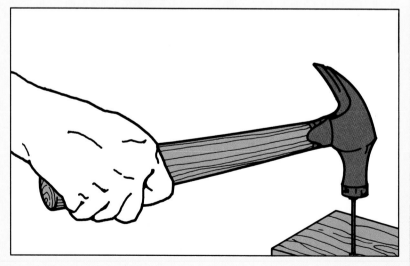

THE BALL PEEN HAMMER

The claw hammer is designed for working with wood, the ball peen hammer for metalwork. Sometimes called an engineer's hammer, this tool is used to drive punches and cold chisels, set rivets, and shape metal. Its head is hardened and is less likely than a claw hammer's to chip when used to pound cold chisels. Rather than having a claw, the ball peen hammer has a flat striking surface on one face and a rounded one on the other.

Ball peens, like claw hammers, are sold in many sizes. Common head weights are four, eight, twelve, and up to thirty-two ounces. The heads are steel, the handles usually made of hickory.

When driving a cold chisel or punch, a ball peen hammer with enough weight to drive the tool is required. On the other hand, though this may seem contradictory at first, when shaping metal it is important to use a hammer that doesn't weigh too much. A hammer that is too large will scar or distort the material (especially brass), while a smaller one will tend to shape it more efficiently.

The ball peen hammer is not essential for the woodworker's toolbox. But when it comes to driving cold chisels, the claw hammer isn't the right tool, so having a club hammer (see below) or a ball peen at hand is a good idea. The ball peen can also be used for driving heavy nails and other tasks where its weight and hardness are an asset.

THE CLUB HAMMER

The club hammer is essentially a small sledgehammer. It is short handled (ten inches long is typical), and light enough that it can be managed comfortably with one hand. A club hammer with a two-and-a-half-pound head is a useful size, though three- and five-pound models are also common. As with most other hammers, wooden handles are typically made of hickory, though fiberglass-handled club hammers are available.

Most club hammers have two identical faces. Both faces can be used, though the primary reason for the second face is that the hammer would be awkward to use if the head were not evenly balanced.

The club hammer and its bigger brethren, the sledgehammers, are used to drive stakes or cold chisels and to demolish masonry. They are sometimes called hand-drilling hammers because they are often used to drive masonry drills.

In using this tool, let the weight of the club hammer's head do as much of the work as possible. For light blows, the weight alone will provide sufficient force; merely allow the head to drop on the object being hammered.

For more force, swing the tool as you would other hammers, again with a firm but not rigid grip. This is especially important when

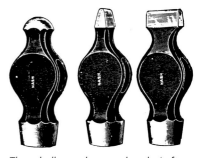

Three ball-peen hammerheads: Left to right are a ball, cross-peen, and straight peen, all of which are occasionally found in woodworkers' toolboxes.

The sharper the nail, the more effortlessly it will slide through the fibers of the wood. That goes without saying, right?

Wrong. To prevent splits when nailing, especially near the end grain, dull the tip of the nail, blunting it with a couple of blows of your hammer. The blunted nail will crush its way through the workpiece, rather than forcing the fibers apart as a sharp nail does. This is a great trick to know when you're nailing thin stock (like siding) or toe-nailing and the lumber keeps splitting.

using the club hammer for demolition, as the shock of striking a masonry wall, for example, will carry through to your arm if you hold the hammer too tightly, putting you at risk of wrist, elbow, or even shoulder soreness.

Always wear safety goggles when putting the club hammer to use: Stone, masonry, or other bits of debris can easily become airborne and present a grave danger to your eyes.

NAILING TECHNIQUES

Nailing a nail isn't just a matter of ready, aim, and swing. Other elements enter in, like the size of the nail, the angle at which it is driven, and the nature of the pieces being joined. When it comes to understanding the advantages of face-nailing versus toe-nailing, for example, a lot of people have a lot to learn. Here are some issues and options to consider.

Nail Size. A general rule of thumb is that to attach one piece of wood to another, you should use a nail that is three times the thickness of the piece being nailed. While that's a good starting point, it isn't the whole story.

If the nail will pass through the second piece, then a times-three-length nail is too long (except when clinch nailing, see facing page). Another consideration, especially when doing finish work, is the potential for splits. These are most likely to occur when nailing through the end grain, and oversized nails may be the cause.

A little practice, experience, and, if you're unsure, some experimentation on scrap pieces will tell you what you need to know in individual cases. (See also *Nails for All Occasions,* page 219.)

Hammer Size. Choose your hammer properly, too, matching the weight and shape of the hammerhead to the job you are doing. Small nails are a great deal easier to nail with lighter hammers, and large nails difficult to drive with small hammers. Again, a well-balanced, twenty-ounce, bell-faced hammer will perform the widest range of tasks.

Face-Nailing. This is the rudimentary nailing we learned first. It can be used in the widest variety of situations, when the nail is driven straight into the face of the workpiece, through to the second piece. Face-nailed joints aren't particularly strong (especially when the workpieces being fastened are perpendicular to one another), but the technique is fast and easy.

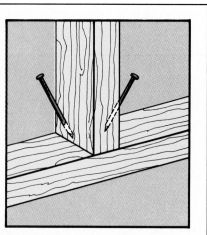

Toe-Nailing. In contrast, toe-nailing produces a strong joint. The technique requires a pair of nails, driven at opposing forty-five-degree angles. It isn't suitable for all joints, as the grain of one workpiece needs to be at an angle to the other.

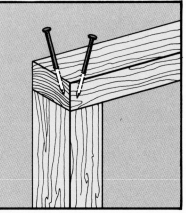

Dovetail Nailing. This technique is akin to toe-nailing, as it involves driving nails on a bias. Nailing pairs or sets of nails at alternate angles strengthens the nailed joint. In this case, however, it is the

face of the board that is nailed (rather than the opposite sides of the board).

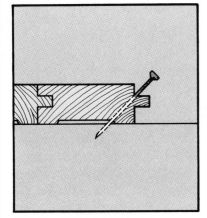

Blind Nailing. Tongue-and-groove boards are blind nailed. The nail is driven at about a forty-five-degree angle into the tongue of the board. Then the groove of the next piece is slid over the tongue, obscuring the nail.

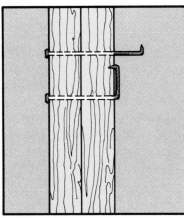

Clinch Nailing. A commonplace technique in the past, this is less often employed today. A clinched (or clenched) nail is driven through the pieces being joined, and the protruding tip is bent and nailed flush for extra holding power. Batten doors were traditionally made using this technique, leading to the cliché "dead as a doornail."

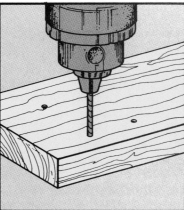

Pilot Holes. If you are working with hardwood or nailing any thin stock near its end grain, you will need to drill a pilot hole first in order to avoid splitting the wood.

I'll talk about another nailing technique, setting finishing nails, when we come to nail sets (see page 138).

To develop a proper hammer grip, try this little exercise.

Let the tool dangle, head down, with your arm extended along the side of your body. Cradle the handle in your hand, holding it just tightly enough that when you shake your wrist you don't drop the hammer. That's the proper grip.

If you hold the hammer more tightly, the shock from striking the nail will carry through the tool into your hand, wrist, and arm. A wrist injury called carpal tunnel syndrome (in which a buildup of calcium deposits puts pressure on a nerve, causing pain and numbness in the wrist and hand) is one result of too much – and especially of improper – hammering.

If you are driving a series of nails along the length of a piece, don't align them. Stagger the nails instead to avoid splitting the wood.

WOODEN MALLETS

Mallets are hammers that are used to drive chisels, gouges, or to shape soft metals. Firmer chisels are often driven by mallets, as are other wooden objects that might split or break if struck with a hammer, like dowels, pegs, and spindles. Mallets are not to be used to drive nails, screws, or other metal objects with sharp heads that could mar the face of the tool.

Typically made of beech, wooden mallets are found in a number of different shapes (mallets of other materials, including rawhide and rubber, are discussed on the facing page). The carpenter's mallet is flat-sided, though the two faces are usually not parallel, as if the head were cut from a segment of a wheel. The carver's mallet is rounded, more or less cylindrical in shape, enabling the carver to strike his chisels at various angles without shifting the mallet or arm position each time. Some mallets have iron bands around their heads for reinforcement.

These hammers are used more often for driving than for striking. The three with wooden heads (left to right, across the back) are for chiseling, framing, and carving; the metal-headed club hammer (left) is used with cold chisels or for demolition duty. The rubber and rawhide mallets (foreground) can be used as persuaders on a great many materials with little risk of marring or breakage.

A carpenter's mallet and carver's mallet; one for power, the other for finesse.

Though a range of sizes is to be found, most mallets are intended to be used one-handed. Their heavy heads are swung in short, controlled strokes, rather than in full swings.

The beetle, a large, two-handed mallet, is used when working with timber. These giant mallets have cylindrical heads, typically a foot long and six inches in diameter, and handles that are three feet or so in length. Ask any timber framer: These tools are very good indeed at convincing recalcitrant joints to cooperate.

SOFT MALLETS

Soft-faced mallets have a long history. Boxwood and leather varieties were used by silversmiths in the distant past. Today's soft mallets, which may have heads of rubber, coiled rawhide, or plastic usually mounted on handles of hickory, have much wider applications.

A soft mallet is useful in a great many situations, but for the woodworker its principal application is as a persuader for workpieces that seem reluctant to go where you want them to go. The rubber or rawhide head is soft enough that it will do no damage to hardwoods and will dent softwoods only after repeated, heavy hammerings. Soft-faced mallets are also used in automobile repair to reshape sheet metal.

Deadblow Hammer. A related tool, the deadblow hammer, has metal pellets in its head. The presence of such metal ballast means that when the deadblow hammer strikes something, much of the shock is absorbed by the pellets, minimizing the rebound. Many deadblows these days have plastic or urethane faces, but are not truly woodworkers' tools.

NAIL SETS

The nail set belongs to a family of tools known as punches. They are designed for penetrating or creating indentations in wood, plastic, sheet metal, or other materials. Prick punches and center punches have sharpened points, while the tips of nail sets are ground square.

When hammering finish nails, the last blow or two required to drive the nail flush to the wood's surface often leaves an indentation in the wood (referred to derisively in some quarters as an elephant's foot or novice's knock). Nail sets are used to avoid such unsightly mars, as they enable the carpenter to keep the head of the hammer a discreet distance from the finished surface. Rather than striking the nail directly, the last few strokes are delivered indirectly, using the nail set to relay the blows. The nail is set flush to or slightly beneath the finished surface of the wood; the head hole can then be filled with carpenter's wood filler.

Punches and nail sets are made of steel and shaped like thick pencils. A nail set tapers at one end to a blunted tip, while the other end (in the position equivalent to that of the pencil's eraser) is squared off to form a small striking surface, or anvil. The shaft in between is knurled, the better to grasp it. The points on some nail sets are concave (cupped) to prevent them slipping from the nail that is being set.

An unusual hammer much favored by cabinetmakers is called a Warrington hammer. It's thought to have been used originally by modelmakers working with wood in a foundry. Rather than having a claw, this more nearly resembles a ball peen hammer, though it is certainly a wood hammer. The flattened, wedge-shaped design of the peen is actually a second face, and is handy for starting small nails or brads.

The diameter of the nail-set tip should match the head of the nail being set. If it's too big, the set will leave a larger hole to fill; if it's too small, more force will be required to drive the nail. Nail sets are often sold in a cluster of four or more. Varying sizes are identified by the diameter of the set's tip. Common and useful sizes are $\frac{1}{32}$, $\frac{1}{16}$, $\frac{3}{32}$, and $\frac{1}{8}$ inches.

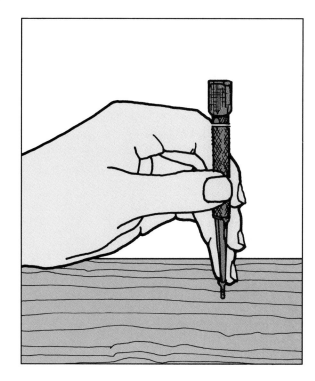

To set a nail, drive a finishing nail within an eighth of an inch or less of the wood's surface. Hold the nail set between the fingers and thumb of one hand, your hammer in the other. The set should be aligned with the shaft of the nail and, preferably, perpendicular to the surface of the wood. Strike the top of the set with sharp, short blows until the nail is completely set into the wood, perhaps a sixteenth of an inch below the surface. Fill the hole with carpenter's putty.

Don't store your rawhide or wooden mallets in the sun, as they can dry out and crack. Apply an occasional film of oil to the face of the mallet to maintain some moisture in the head.

Chapter 10.
Drivers and Other Fasteners

Unlike some fastening tools (like the hammer, for example), the screwdriver is a relatively new implement. The term "screw driver" wasn't even coined until the turn of the nineteenth century (in earlier days, the tool was known as a turnscrew). It wasn't until the advent of the Industrial Revolution that mass production of metal fasteners like screws and bolts became easy and inexpensive.

Before that era, screws were often made out of wood, and even those made from metal had to be shaped and threaded by hand. To this day, evidence of the handwork required to shape a screw can be seen in the heads of the old screws that hold together antique furniture or that fasten old hinges. The slots were cut by hand, and as a result are more often off-center than precisely placed.

Today, screwdrivers are omnipresent; everybody uses them, from auto mechanics to housewives. In the case of woodworkers, another set of fastening tools are equally as common – the clamps that are used in conjunction with glues and adhesives. We'll talk about those, too, in this chapter.

SCREWDRIVERS

To the uninitiated, a screwdriver is a screwdriver is a screwdriver. The truth is, however, that simply isn't so.

Most screwdrivers do share an overall design. Each consists of a metal shaft called a shank, usually made of steel (though sometimes it's an alloy of vanadium or chrome). There's a handle at one end and a tip at the other called the blade. But the commonalities end there, because there are many variations in blades and handles; not to mention those oddball screwdrivers that have no shafts at all, but instead use ratchets offset at a ninety-degree angle to the tip and are used for driving screws in confined spaces.

I've found that the handle offers as good an indication as the tip of the purpose for which a given driver is used. Most are shaped like a bulb, large enough to be gripped comfortably in the palm of the hand. Electrician's screwdrivers usually have plastic handles – because plastic insulates the user's hands from the risk of electric shock – as well as plastic tubing that runs much of the length of the shaft. Not surprisingly, wooden-handled drivers are more often found in

Here are some fasteners, including clamps and drivers (electric and muscle-powered). And caulk guns and more clamps, and glue guns and more drivers. Clamps, in particular, are tools of which you can never really have too many different types and sizes.

When tightening or removing a screw, take special care to select a screwdriver whose tip fits snugly into the head of the screw. With slotted drivers, the head should be approximately the width of the screwhead. If it's wider, it may mar the surrounding material; one that is too small or worn may mangle the screwhead. An improperly sized driver will also increase the amount of force needed to hold the driver in place in the screwhead.

(And don't use slotted-head drivers on Phillips-head screws; you could irreparably damage both the driver and the screwhead.)

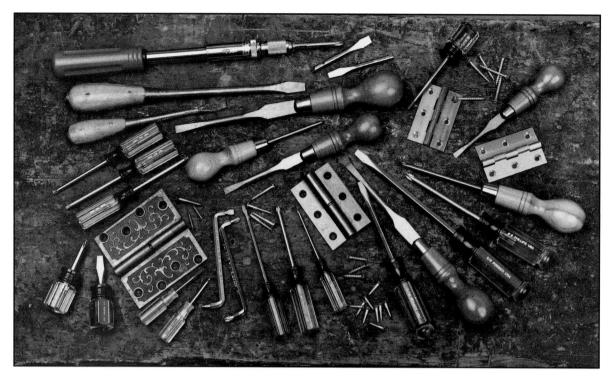

*That's a Yankee ratchet driver at top, left, and two different types of wooden-handled drivers designed specifically to drive wood screws. Amidst the rest of the familiar insulated-handle screwdrivers are two **S**-shaped offset drivers that make tightening (or loosening) screws in confined spaces easier.*

These rather dated-looking drivers have a flat blade (so that they won't roll off the bench). Though rare today, these drivers offered their users surprising torque for loosening seemingly immovable screws.

woodshops (the handles are usually beech, but are sometimes made from boxwood or other hardwoods). Some have oval handles, others iron shafts that run the length of the tool with wood riveted to two sides to form a handle. Auto mechanics often favor screwdrivers that have rubber sleeves on the handles for a firmer grip.

Screwdrivers also can be purchased with built-in ratchets and other mechanisms that save on twisting and turning. Sometimes called Yankee drivers or pump drivers, most have spiral grooves in the shaft that turn when the handle is pushed toward the workpiece, only to spring back when released without turning. By shifting a lever, the process is reversed for screw removal. These drivers resemble the push drill (see page 101).

The variations are truly endless: I've even seen one clever ratcheted drive that features a short handle in the shape of a fore-shortened crutch that fits comfortably into a fist for close work. Power drivers are still another option (see facing page).

Screwdrivers can be purchased with long shafts or short, and are generally identified by the combined length of the shaft and handle. Common sizes range between stubby drivers that are two and a half inches in length and longer drivers about a foot long. But there are also many other drivers, both shorter and longer, ranging up to twenty-four inches long. The tips can be wide or narrow – instrument screwdrivers have slotted tips in the range of $\frac{1}{32}$ inch wide. Screwdriverlike tools can also be bought to drive nuts and bolts, but those tools are really members of the socket family.

At a minimum, a pair of large and small slotted screwdrivers and another pair of Phillips-head screwdrivers should inhabit your tool-

box. Often, the most economical way to purchase screwdrivers is in a set, some of which contain as many as twenty screwdrivers. You just might be surprised how, over time, each and every one of those drivers comes to have at least an occasional job to do.

POWER DRIVERS

Power drivers are, for practical purposes, redesigned and re-engineered electric drills. Drills and drivers look much like one another, but instead of an adjustable chuck that can grip a wide range of drills, the power driver accepts only standardized screwdriver bits, usually Phillips-head, but slotted and other head types can also be used.

SCREWHEADS

Screwheads, and the tools used to drive them, come in a variety of configurations. The most common are slotted and Phillips-head varieties. Other designs, once largely the province of industry, are increasingly coming into more general use.

Slotted Head. The most common screwdrivers have blades that are shaped and hardened to drive screws with a straight slot in the head. The slot is flat-bottomed, and the driver is usually ground flat and flared.

Phillips Head. A symmetrical cross is cut into the top of Phillips-head screws. The shaft of a Phillips-head screwdriver is usually round, with a pointed tip that strengthens the grip between the driver and the screw.

Torx Head and Square Drive. There are some innovative screwheads on the market that are designed for added driver torque. Some of these specialized screws are often found on electronic and communications equipment. At least initially, the new designs reduced the likelihood of tampering, because the drivers were relatively uncommon. As the screws have become more widely used, this advantage has gradually diminished.

Both of these designs offer a more positive drive than traditional Phillips-head screws. Given their relative rarity, they offer some tampering protection, too. If you don't have a square-head driver on hand, you can make one with an old driver and a grinder.

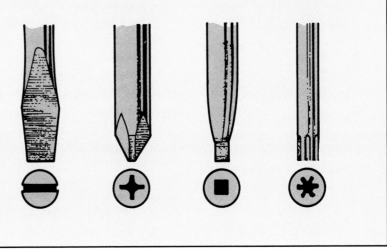

The power drivers for drywalling (left) and for lighter duty.

Whether your driver is powered by electricity or the muscles in your hand and arm, be sure the tip of the driver is firmly set into the head of the screw before trying to torque the screw. Failure to do so can damage a screwhead in an instant, sometimes rendering it impossible to remove.

Not everyone needs a power driver. Originally, they were designed for use by installers of drywall (hence, another name by which they are known, drywall screwdrivers). In the hands of an experienced user, they drive drywall screws at a remarkable rate, saving time and, for a contractor, money.

Like electric drills, a power driver should be reversible and have a variable speed control. Drywall drivers are approximately the size of three-eighths-inch drills, and share their pistol-shaped design equipped with trigger control. Drivers also have a locking button that, when engaged, keeps the drill running continuously.

Power drills look slightly different because they have an adjustable cone that surrounds the tip of the bit. This nosepiece acts as a stop, causing the bit to cease driving the screw at a preset depth. To facilitate feeding screws onto the bit when the driver is running continuously, a positive clutch mechanism at the base of the bit holder acts to engage or disengage the spinning motor. Only when the bit is pushed onto the workpiece does the clutch cause the bit to turn.

A standard electric drill will accept screwdriver bits and, for occasional use, will perform the same jobs quite adequately although it lacks the power driver's stop and clutch mechanisms. However, if you are planning on hanging a quantity of drywall, a drywall screwdriver is by no means an unnecessary extravagance. Off-the-shelf electric drills are not designed for the demands of driving screws and if they are used as drivers for extended periods, their life expectancies may be shortened significantly.

There is another class of driving tools on the market that can perform a range of light-duty driving chores. Known as in-line screwdrivers, these rechargeable cordless drivers are light (most models weigh less than two pounds) and handy for removing and driving screws around the house. They do not have the torque for heavy-duty tasks, but are easy to store and use.

WOOD CLAMPS

Wood is a remarkable material. It's widely available, handsome, and immensely diverse. Many of its varieties can easily be cut, sculpted, bored, and otherwise shaped in a hundred different ways. Wood can be fastened to metal, plastic, or other pieces of wood, using nails or screws. But the most miraculous of its tricks, at least for me, is wood's willingness to be clamped and glued.

A properly prepared glue joint (and this is the amazing part) is as strong as the sinews of the wood itself. I've seen many broken pieces of furniture that snapped and cracked not at a glue joint but as a result of flaws in the wood itself. Not every glue joint is perfect, of course, but those that are can endure for centuries.

No, it's not a Christmas present wrapped in ribbon. . . it's an Empire side chair that spends a lot of its time requiring repair. In this case, pipe, spring, hand-screw, bar, and C-clamps are tightening its joints and affixing its veneers. As for the ribbon . . . well, that's actually a strap clamp.

The first key to a good joint is proper clamping. The clamp – most are devices with pairs of jaws that are drawn together with screw mechanisms – is responsible for pulling together the pieces to be glued, and for holding them tight and flush until the glue sets. The other key is the glue, and using the right kind in the right way. But first let's talk about the array of clamps that are available.

Clamps (or, as they like to call them in England, cramps) are invaluable tools in the workshop, and in the companion volume to this book we'll talk at length about the services they can perform there. But unlike the vice, another tool that can be used to hold workpieces together, clamps are easily portable, which makes them most convenient problem solvers at the work-site. Here are a few clamps for which you may well find many applications.

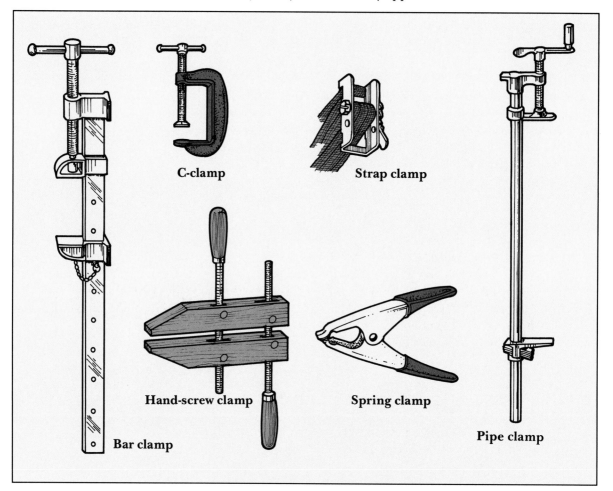

C-clamp

Strap clamp

Hand-screw clamp

Spring clamp

Bar clamp

Pipe clamp

C-Clamps. These multipurpose clamps get their name from their shape. Especially practical for gluing in tight spaces, these clamps have jaws in the shape of the letter **C**, and rely upon screwdrives with metal shoes at their ends to hold workpieces tightly. The screwdrive is driven by a T bar that forms a handle on the screw; in general, finger-tightening will provide adequate force. The shoe is mounted on a ball joint, allowing it to sit flush even to slightly angled stock.

C-clamps are made of aluminum, iron, or steel, and are designed to clamp metalwork. When used with plastic or wood, pads are generally used to protect the material from telltale indentations that are left by the metal jaws and the shoe of the clamp when tightened. Clamps come in a range of sizes, with jaws as small as one inch and as large as twelve inches. Some have deeper throats than others, to accommodate clamping some distance from the edge of the workpiece.

Bar Clamps. The bar is the backbone of this clamp, a rectangular length of steel or aluminum. There is a jaw at one end of the bar, and a tail slide that moves up or down its length. The tail slide can be fixed in the desired position at one end of the workpiece that is to be clamped. Depending upon the design of the clamp, this is done using a peg that passes through the bar or by locating the slide at one of the notches in the bar. The adjustable jaw device, which uses a screwdrive, can then be tightened over the workpiece at the other end.

Bar clamps, which are also known as joiner's clamps, are sold in two- to six-foot models. The steel clamps, in particular, can exert considerable force in clamping. Pipe clamps (see below) and bar clamps have strong jaws, and can be used in rough framing to pull a reluctant joist or header into place. More often, they're used in cabinetwork or to repair doors or windows.

Pipe Clamps. At first glance, the pipe clamp resembles the bar clamp, save that the spine is in the form of a length of pipe. As with the bar clamp, the pipe clamp has a jaw that in most models is fixed to one end of the pipe. A second sliding jaw can be positioned anywhere on the length of the pipe, with a cam operated by a lever mechanism or a clutch that is engaged when an object is clamped in place.

The fittings for pipe clamps can be used on any length of pipe. Two sizes of fittings are common, designed for half-inch and three-quarter-inch iron pipe.

Hand-Screw Clamps. All-wood hand-screw clamps were the rule for generations. One great advantage of wooden hand-screw clamps is that, when used properly, they apply pressure evenly over a larger area than most clamps, meaning they are less likely to mar a workpiece than other clamps.

The wooden screws in the older models travel freely through one jaw and thread into the other; the front and rear screws are the reverse of one another. The newer, steel-screw models have threads at each of the points of connection with the jaws, but the thread on each rod reverses at its midpoint, for ease of adjustment. Both wooden and wood-and-steel designs can be loosened or tightened by gripping them with both hands, a handle in each hand, and rotating the clamp. A clockwise rotation tightens the clamp.

When using more than one clamp in gluing workpieces together, tighten the clamps gradually, working back and forth from one clamp to the other. Too much force on one clamp may produce an uneven joint.

The all-wood hand-screw clamp has hardwood jaws (often made of beech or maple) and screws (commonly of hornbeam). Many antique wooden hand screws survive and are cherished by their users. But they've been joined by wood and steel models, which retain the wooden jaws while substituting steel screws and spindles.

WOOD GLUES

Glues really used to be made from old horses (the hoofs, skins, bones, and other parts, when boiled, produce a protein gelatin that forms the glue base). Such organic hide glues are still in use today, though fine furniture restorers are most likely to use them when repairing pieces of cherished antique furniture in homes and museums.

A once clear line of usage has now been blurred between the word *glue* (traditionally used to refer to such organically based materials) and the word *adhesives* (for manmade materials). Today, most wood is glued together using glue consisting of manmade polyvinyl or aliphatic resins.

Polyvinyl Acetate Resin Emulsion Glue. Also called white glue, polyvinyl resin glue is a near relation of that white stuff we used in grade school that was sold under the brand name Elmer's (and, today, under that and about a hundred other names). It'll glue china, paper, and wood.

White glue sets fairly quickly, hardening as the moisture in it evaporates and the glue line becomes transparent. It cures hard in a few hours, though when you are clamping glued pieces together, letting them set overnight is always a sensible precaution. When buying white glue, be sure that you are buying a full-strength glue, since some are watered down for children's use.

Polyvinyl resin is not waterproof, so is not suitable for damp or exterior application. In situations where the glued pieces will be near a source of heat like a furnace, fireplace, or heater, other glues are also preferable. But white glue is inexpensive, easy to use, non-toxic, and non-flammable. It has a long shelf life (when the container is kept properly sealed), and won't stain your tools or most workpieces, though metals and oak are exceptions to that rule. White glue works best at room temperatures.

Aliphatic Resin Glue. The generic name *carpenter's glue* describes the aliphatic resins. Like the white glues, these are sold in squeeze bottles, but aliphatic resin glues are actually a good deal stronger than the polyvinyl resins.

This creamy yellow glue dries very quickly (you can leave the pieces clamped a minimum of an hour, but two hours is preferable, and there's no harm in waiting still longer). Carpenter's glue is easy to use, dries a translucent amber color, and is more easily sanded than white glue, which tends to soften due to the heat of the sanding process. Like white glue, however, carpenter's glue is not for use in damp or exterior applications. It sets more quickly at warm temperatures, but can be used effectively at temperatures as low as forty-five degrees.

Resorcinol Formaldehyde Glue. Though there are other moisture-resistant glues available (including urea formaldehyde resins), resorcinol glue is completely waterproof and can be used on aquatic equipment (like boats and water skis) as well as exterior finish on doors, windows, and moldings. It dries a deep maroon color.

Resorcinol glue is expensive, and must be mixed at the time of use, blending the resin and a catalyst. It also requires eight to ten hours to set and can only be used at warm temperatures. Resorcinol is less convenient to use than carpenter's glue, but it is the only option for joints that are to reside in damp locations.

Other Adhesives. Contact cement is bought premixed, often in small bottles, and is invaluable for attaching (or reattaching) veneers. Epoxy bonds metals and glass to wood but, like resorcinol, requires mixing. Milk-based casein glues are useful for gluing teak, ebony, and other oily woods. Neoprene cement works well with tile.

For most uses, the clamp should be tightened to fit the workpiece with the jaws roughly parallel. When the mouth of the clamp is snug over the workpiece, turn the rear handle to fully tighten the clamp. When gluing, take care to avoid gluing the wooden jaws to the workpiece.

Over the years, these clamps have been manufactured in a great range of sizes, and today clamps can be purchased with jaws that open up to a maximum of twelve inches or more. Typically, the hardwood jaws are between eight and eighteen inches long, and between one and a half and two inches square.

Spring Clamps. These clamps mimic the shape and function of the human hand when you are grasping something between your thumb and forefingers. Only this clamp is quite happy to remain in place indefinitely, exerting uniform pressure, enabling you to go off and do something more interesting.

The clamp's jaws are usually made of steel, sometimes with a layer of plastic applied to reduce scarring on soft materials to be clamped. A spring holds the jaws tightly closed, until the action of squeezing the handles together opens them. Spring clamps are sold in various sizes that open one, two, three, or more inches.

Strap Clamp. Also called web or band clamps, these clever devices rely upon a beltlike length of webbing to tighten joints in a structure. A mechanical device functions as a kind of elaborate buckle, with a ratchet that allows the one-and-a-half-inch-wide belt to be tightened.

Belt clamps are especially useful in furniture work, tightening frames and cases (even round ones), and those seemingly impossible clamping tasks that most clamps just don't seem to suit.

As with any clamp, make sure you remove any extra glue from the clamp. Not only can excess glue cause the strap to adhere to the clamp, but it may leave an abrasive residue on the strap for the next job. Either way, you can mar your work.

Make sure that the wooden jaws of hand-screw clamps are parallel to the clamping surface. These tools are more likely to scar the workpiece – and will be unable to exert maximum clamping pressure – if the clamps grip the workpiece with only the front or back of their jaws.

CAULKING AND GLUE GUNS

Modern chemistry is bringing us new formulations of glues, caulks, sealants, and cements. Using these adhesives and other materials has been made simpler with the innovation of inexpensive and easy-to-use applicators like caulking and glue guns. These devices are shaped like guns, more or less, with trigger controls in the handles and reservoirs of glue, caulk, or other material in the barrel portions of the guns.

Glue guns use sticks of dried hot-melt glue. A molded plastic handle contains an electrically powered heating element within the gun which heats up the glue in a matter of a few minutes. The trigger

The fastening guns: A glue gun (center) surrounded by small and large caulk guns (bottom and top, along with two staple guns), one electric and the other spring-powered.

then feeds the glue through a nozzle, producing a thin steam of liquefied glue.

Most glues set in about a minute, but the glue sticks can be bought in a variety of shapes and kinds so the actual working time does vary. Among the varieties are general-purpose adhesives that dry clear, and wood glues, designed to bond with wood, which dry a cream shade. There is a fast-drying adhesive that dries quickly, usually in less than half a minute. And there are specialty glues for ceramics, glass, and crafts works, as well as caulks that are used to weatherproof doors and windows and other exterior joints.

Nozzles can also be fitted to glue guns. A needle-shaped nozzle will help you deliver small quantities of glue into tight spots, while a spreader nozzle, with a wide opening at its mouth, is a help when applying caulk or glue to large areas.

Caulk guns use sealed cartridges of adhesive or caulk. No heat is required to operate a caulk gun, though under very cold conditions

CLAMPING A GLUE JOINT

Use blocks of pine or other softwood when clamping with metal-jawed devices. The blocks will protect the workpiece, preventing it from being marred by the unforgiving metal.

A properly glued wood joint is very strong, but one that is glued improperly is likely to fracture given a minimum of hard use. So do it right in order to avoid having to do it twice.

Plan the Process First. Decide which clamps will provide the right amount of pressure – enough but not too much. You want the pressure to sandwich the glue in the joint, squeezing out any excess.

Select the right glue. Carpenter's glue is appropriate for most wood-to-wood joints, but in wet applications (or when gluing materials other than wood), look to other options. Read and follow the instructions on the glue container.

Assemble the elements you need before proceeding: Workpieces, clamps, glue, clamping pads, and paper towels or a rag to clean up any excess glue.

Prepare the Pieces. This may be the most important step. You must scrape off the old glue residue, if any. Fit the pieces together *before* applying the glue. Is the joint tight? If

there are evident gaps, you will need to fill them first, either with a wood filler or, in the case of large gaps, with carefully cut and fitted pieces of wood. Wood glue will fill small voids, and adding a small quantity of matching sawdust will help. But you cannot count on the glue to fill the larger gaps.

Do a Dry Clamp. Before you even open the glue container, fit the pieces together and clamp them tight. If the clamps you've chosen slip or otherwise prove inadequate, try another kind of clamp. When working with softwood or using clamps with metal jaws, use wooden or leather pads to protect the parts.

Apply the Glue. Once you have found a clamping arrangement that works, spread the glue as directed on the package. Some glues are best applied to both surfaces to be clamped, others not. Certain glues need to set to tacky first, though most should be clamped immediately.

Wipe Off Excess Glue. Too much glue is indeed too much of a good thing. Using a scraper, wipe off any excess from the surface of the workpiece as you tighten the clamps. Be sure that you aren't gluing your clamps to the piece being clamped. A damp cloth will help, too, with white or carpenter's glue.

Take Your Time. Check the joint for square. Don't make it too tight: you may crush some the fibers of the wood or even cause another break if you tighten the screws too much.

the material in the cartridges may be stiff and more difficult to work. The gun itself is metal, with an **L**-shaped notched rod that extends from the back of the gun where the hammer would be on a pistol. Most caulk guns are strictly mechanical, powered by the human hand.

Like glue guns, they are remarkably easy to use. You simply cut the tip of the tube at about a forty-five-degree angle (which produces a simple nozzle that will help direct the flow of the caulk) and insert the cartridge into the gun. The trigger is then pumped to advance the rod and plunger in its handle into the body of the cartridge. There it exerts pressure on the contents, causing it to eject a bead of caulk out of the cartridge.

Remove the cartridge from the gun when you've completed the task at hand. Clean any residue of caulk or adhesive from the plunger or other parts of the gun. A cap may have been provided to seal the tube, but a large common nail inserted into the nozzle will also prevent the remaining material from drying out.

Caulking guns are used to apply waterproof caulking (latex, silicon, or other materials) in order to seal gaps or cracks and to limit the infiltration of air or water. They are also useful in applying construction adhesive for flooring or paneling.

THE STAPLE GUN

You don't have to be a big-time contractor to appreciate this tool: The staple gun, in any of its numerous shapes and sizes, can be used to fasten all kinds of materials in the work of home construction and maintenance. Roofing contractors, insulation installers, carpenters, and lots of other tradesmen rely upon staplers every day, even every hour, to do their jobs.

The staple gun is a larger, tougher sibling of the desk stapler that's a fixture in every office. Its ammunition is bigger, too, as most guns take staples that are from a quarter to nine-sixteenths of an inch long. The staples required for a given job depend upon the nature of the material being used. The width of the staple varies with the manufacturer of the gun.

Staple guns come in hand-powered and electric models. The most common configuration is powered by a spring; a large lever built into the handle at the top of the stapler acts as a trigger, and the spring squeezes out a staple when the gun is pressed onto the workpiece. The electric models are a bit faster to use, bury larger staples more efficiently, and don't tire out the hand and wrist as hand staplers do. Another variety fits somewhere in between: It is hand-powered but delivers staples not when a trigger is depressed, but when the tool is swung like a hammer. When its head makes contact, the staple is released. All models have a magazine that accepts a strip of staples.

Staples are used to fasten plastic sheeting, upholstery and other fabric, ceiling tiles, carpeting, wire netting, and other materials. The alternative to the staple gun is tacks, and hammering in lots of small nails takes two hands, more time, and generally produces sore fingers. I think you'll agree, the staple gun is a lot easier to use.

When using carpenter's glue to make a particular tricky repair, try mixing a little water with the glue. This will allow the glue to penetrate more deeply into the grain of the wood, adding strength to the bond. Allow additional clamping time for the extra moisture to evaporate.

Though more expensive than traditional staple guns, the hammer stapler is a real time-saver for attaching large sheets of materials like building paper or poly for vapor barriers .

Chapter 11.
Unfastening Tools

Pry bars, crowbars, pinch bars, flat bars, and cat's-paws – those are the names of some of the sturdy steel tools that pull nails, pry boards, and perform other demolition tasks. One manufacturer goes so far as to call its crowbar a "Renovator's Bar."

Several of these tools belong in the fully equipped toolbox. They save wear and tear on the claw hammer when pulling large nails, as well as on the muscles of the arm and back. The leverage a wrecking bar provides makes a number of demolition jobs seem possible – or even easy. When used with care, some of them (in particular, the flat bar) can remove quite delicate wood pieces intact, allowing for restoration and reconstruction.

These are the tools needed for removing such architectural salvage as this corner bracket. From left to right, the three large tools are a wrecking bar, a shingle remover, and a flat bar. At center is a pair of nail-pullers; two cat's-paws are at far left and far right.

THE FLAT BAR

The pry bar or wonder bar, as this tool is also known, is made of flat steel. Typically two inches wide and fifteen inches long, the flat bar is an invaluable tool for separating wooden elements that have been nailed to one another.

Unlike the pinch bar (which, given its bulk and shape, is a brute and difficult to wield gently), the flat bar can, when used with care and patience, help dismantle delicate woodwork while causing a minimum of damage. Its ends are beveled and notched, and can be driven between clapboards, for example, and then be used to pry them apart. Nails can be removed using either of the notches or the teardrop-shaped hole cast in the middle of the bar.

THE WRECKING BAR

Made of steel that is octagonal in section, the wrecking bar has a flattened blade at one end and a hook-and-claw shape at the other. Though sold in several sizes from one to four feet in length, in none of its incarnations is this a gentle or fragile tool.

The pinch bar, as it is also commonly known, is for wrecking. It's designed so the hooked end can be hammered, driving the blade at the other between wooden elements. The length of the bar then provides leverage to pry the wood apart. The claw at the curved end can also be used to remove nails; again, the length of the tool offers sufficient leverage to make removing even large nails a relatively easy matter.

The wrecking bar belongs in the toolboxes of almost all carpenters, even if the plan is only to attempt new construction. As any experienced carpenter will tell you, mistakes get made even by veterans; and the wrecking bar comes in very handy for undoing rough framing, or for small, medium, or large demolition jobs. Along with its cousin the flat bar, the wrecking bar is one of those tools that doesn't seem essential – until it's the only one that will do.

Like a crowbar (a larger-scale wrecking tool with no hook on its end), the wrecking bar can also be used as a lever to lift heavy objects like stones or machinery. For most purposes, a twenty-four-inch wrecking bar will prove adequate.

THE NAIL-PULLER

In our time, these practical tools are known as nail-pullers, but your grandfather's grandfather would have known them as carpenter's pincers. Made of steel (or, in the case of antique nail-pullers, of iron), the flat head of the tool is positioned flush to a wood surface in order to remove nails, tacks, or even screws clamped in its straight jaws.

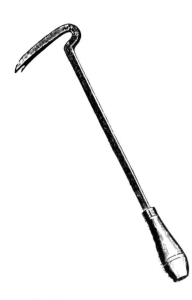

A nail-puller, yes, but in its own day it was termed a "Pelican nail-puller."

To use nail-pullers, hold the tool vertical to the surface, gripping the nail to be removed in the jaws as close to the workpiece as possible. If the surface of the workpiece will be visible in the finished product, protect it by using a shim or scrap of wood to prevent the nail-puller from marring the wood.

Nail-pullers are especially handy in tight spaces or angles where a claw hammer hasn't room to work. The nail-puller is a multipurpose tool, as it can also be used to drive nails, using the flattened exterior of its head. Nail-pullers are found in several sizes, typically from about six to ten inches in length.

A related tool, called end-cutting pliers, closely resembles nail-pullers except that the jaws are sharpened for cutting nails, wire, or other metal items.

THE CAT'S-PAW

If the pry bar is the bulldog of the demolition tools, then this is one tough tomcat. It's a smaller pry bar, and designed for pulling nails (hence, one of its nicknames, the nail-puller).

Some varieties have a handle on one end, others have a thin, flat prying surface, a more delicate version of the hook on a flat bar. Still others have claws at both ends, one aligned with the shaft of the tool, the other at a ninety-degree angle to it. The claws on a cat's-paw are usually spoon-shaped.

This one is handy for a variety of dismantling tasks. One of its specialties is removing nails buried in wood. The tool is driven below the nailhead, so when leverage is applied it scoops out the nail.

The shingle remover – also called a slater's ripper – can be an invaluable tool, and not only when re-roofing. For dismantling tasks (like removing clapboards), the thin blade can be slid beneath the boards (without damaging the wood as a larger tool might) to pry them loose.

An utterly useless hulk, of value to no one but a fire department looking for practice. Right? Not necessarily, as even the most tumbledown structure can yield surprising finds to the intrepid salvager armed with the right demolition tools. This house, for example, had some good old glass, hardware, and even six-panel doors. But be sure the building is still sound enough to carry your weight before you venture in.

Chapter 12.
Pliers, Wrenches, and Sockets

Like the driving tools in the previous chapter, these implements have a briefer history than the hammer, saw, and chisel, to name a few of the tools that have been in use for most of recorded history. While blacksmiths, tinsmiths, and other metalworkers have always used tongs in performing their operations, pliers as we know them are not ancient tools but comparatively modern ones.

Most of the early pliers are fragile looking by today's standards, resembling needle-nose pliers, and were used for shaping sheet tin, brass, wire, or springs. But the array of tools that fill any mechanic's toolbox today are sturdy indeed, products of the Industrial Revolution and its reliance upon nuts, bolts, screws, and a variety of other metal fasteners.

Pliers are used to grip, position, tighten, loosen, and cut certain metal elements. Wrenches are used to turn nuts or bolts, but some are designed for gripping pipes. There are two kinds of wrenches, fixed and adjustable. Fixed (box- or open-end) wrenches have jaws of designated dimensions, while adjustable wrenches can be used to fit a range of different nuts or bolts.

Here is an array of turning tools, implements that are used to exert a twisting force on nuts, bolts, and pipes.

SLIP-JOINT PLIERS

The slip-joint pliers were the tool that I first learned to call pliers. Only later did I discover that there were more kinds of pliers than there were kids in my neighborhood.

A pair of slip-joint pliers isn't exactly a high precision tool, but even as a boy I discovered that pliers could help perform a great many everyday tasks around the house, whether it was fixing my bicycle, the kitchen stool, or a bit of wiring. They are handy for holding or bending flat or round stock, can crimp sheet metal, loop a wire, cut soft wire nails, remove cotter pins, and, if necessary, loosen or tighten a nut.

The key to the versatility of this tool is the slip-joint that gives the pliers their name. Like most pliers, they are operated by opening and closing the handles, which produces an opening and closing action of the jaws. But slip-joint pliers have the added advantage of an adjustable pivot point, which allows the two parts of the jaws to be

Surrounding the giant open-end machine wrench are sockets, two pairs of locking pliers, four nut drivers (they look like screwdrivers), a miscellany of pliers, a set of allen wrenches, a handful of combination wrenches, and a trio of adjustable wrenches. In short, quite enough tools to assemble (or disassemble) quite a lot of things.

Most pliers are meant to be used one-handed. In order to open and close the jaws, hold the tool with your little finger (and your ring finger, if that's more comfortable) inside the lower handle. That'll enable you to open and close a straight-handled tool as if they had scissorlike handles.

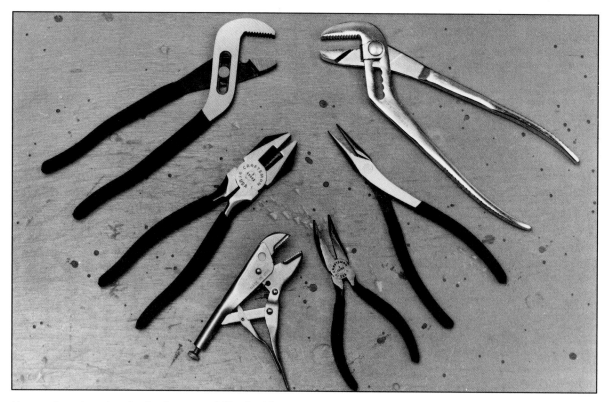

Now, to introduce the plier family: Moving clockwise from top right, there are a pair of slip-joint water-pump pliers, two sets of needle-nose pliers (one with a bent nose), a diminutive pair of locking pliers, a pair of linesman's pliers, and another pair of water-pump pliers with insulated handles.

shifted with respect to one another. So a pair of slip-joint pliers can be used to grip securely objects ranging in thickness from a single sheet of paper to a half inch or more, depending upon the size of the pliers. Most slip-joint pliers have two or three options for positioning the pivot point.

At its mouth, the pliers' jaws are flat and serrated, but they curve at the back of the jaw near the pivot. This curved area, once known as the burner grip because it was originally used for removing the jets from gas lamps, will grip rounded objects like pipes or rods. Many slip-joint pliers also have a wire cutter built into the neck of the pliers, just behind the curved serrations.

Slip-joint pliers can be purchased in various sizes, ranging from almost toylike models only a few inches long up to ten inches. A pair of seven-inch slip-joint pliers probably belongs in your kitchen-drawer toolbox (or its equivalent, wherever it is) that contains a handful of small-scale tools that come to hand quickly and easily for minor repair or adjustment tasks in your household.

Slip-joint pliers are also manufactured in bent-nose and narrow-nose configurations, but a standard pair is the most useful for most purposes. Buy a pair with insulated handles for added comfort.

WATER-PUMP PLIERS

This grouping of pliers features several variations on the same theme. Sold in designs known as arc-joint pliers, Channel-Lock

Pliers (a proprietary name), and known in conversation simply as pumps (as in, "Hand me those blue-handled pumps, will you, Michael?"), these tools are designed for gripping pipes. The jaws are angled to the length of the handles so that reaching between joists and into awkward spaces is easier.

Water-pump pliers are not the sole province of plumbers, as they have a variety of other applications.

The jaws of water-pump pliers are serrated, with a curved shape. Like slip-joint pliers, they can be adjusted to grasp various sized objects. The pivot point on arc-joint models shifts like that on slip-joint pliers, while on others there are a series of grooves that allow the jaws to be positioned at different openings but that keep the jaws parallel to one another. The varieties with the channel design offer a more positive grasp of the pipe or other object. The jaws may be set in seven different positions on many varieties of plumber's pumps.

Water-pump pliers come in various sizes, ranging from four to sixteen inches in length, and the models in the middle of that range are the most generally useful. On all models, the handles are long in proportion to length of the tool, providing for maximum leverage. Water-pump pliers are made of steel, and the kind with handles sheathed in plastic are the most comfortable to use.

LINESMAN'S PLIERS

Sometimes called electrician's pliers or engineer's pliers (the latter variety is often sold without insulated handles), these are very versatile steel tools. Linesman's pliers are descendants of nineteenth-century tools called bell pliers, because they were used by bellhangers for cutting and twisting the wires used to connect unelectrified household bells.

Like other pliers, they hinge at a pivot point, so working the handles together or apart causes the jaws to close or open. The jaws have shallow serrations for firm gripping, especially of flat objects like sheet metal, which explains their popularity among sheet-metal workers. An electrician relies upon the jaws for twisting together wires into a cone-shaped knot that is then protected by a plastic insulator called a wire nut. Immediately behind the jaws are a pair of side cutters, designed for cutting wire. Using them to cut nails will dull them quickly.

Though the pliers are sold in various sizes, with lengths from five to ten inches, the eight-inch size serves most needs. Buy a pair with plastic grips, but keep in mind that the plastic alone is not sufficient to protect you from electric shock. Do not use these – or any other tools – on live wires. Always remove the fuse, turn off the breaker, or unplug the cord before performing any electrical work.

"Bellhanger's pliers" as illustrated in a 1909 catalog.

THE RIGHT WRENCH FOR THE JOB

When using pliers or adjustable wrenches – rather than precision-fixed sockets or wrenches – you risk grinding off portions of the nut or bolt head. This is a particular concern when using a tool with a serrated jaw, like water-pump pliers, slip-joint pliers, or a pipe wrench.

Use the Right Tool. The first lesson is: Use the right wrench for the job. If you don't do this then, for example, a pliers' grip on a nut or bolt head being loosened (or tightened) will not be firm, and the tool will move while the nut or head does not. As a result, the tool will abrade the piece. If repeated over time, this grinding action can result in a complete inability to move the piece.

Try to use only square-jawed wrenches to loosen and tighten nuts and bolts. Use pipe wrenches on pipes, not on nuts (except in rare instances where nothing else will work and you can easily replace the nut, after it's been removed, with a new one).

Size Up the Situation. There's no one wrench that's right for all jobs because, as obvious as it may sound, big wrenches suit big ones and little tools small tasks. Select a wrench or pair of pliers in proportion to the bolt or pipe to be worked.

Look for a Tight Fit. Be sure the fit of the wrench or pliers is snug and square. That means tightening the jaws on pliers or an adjustable wrench, or sliding the nut or bolt head deep into the throat of the wrench.

Determine Direction. Most bolts are threaded so that turning them clockwise tightens them and counterclockwise loosens them. Most, that is, but not all. The arbor bolt on some circular saws, for example, tightens counterclockwise. So before you put all your weight and strength into loosening a resistant nut or bolt, check out which way it goes.

Pull, Don't Push. Last, but not least, always *pull* on the wrench if the working space allows. Pushing on a wrench increases the risk of bloodying your knuckles if the nut should suddenly break loose and your hand goes crashing into whatever lies in its path. If you must push, do so with an open palm.

LOCKING PLIERS

These adjustable pliers are designed to be used as a hand-held vice or clamp that locks firmly onto a workpiece. Also called plier wrenches, lever-wrench pliers, and by the proprietary name Vicegrips, they have a double-lever action.

Their jaws are closed like those on other pliers by squeezing the handles together. However, the jaw opening is adjusted by turning a screw-drive in one handle and when the jaws contact the object to be gripped, the added pressures lock it in a vicelike grip. To release the tool's grip, a lever in the other handle is triggered. The compound lever action of the tool means that the jaws can apply tremendous force.

Locking pliers are manufactured in several different configurations and sizes. Most have serrated, straight jaws, and are found in lengths ranging from four to twelve inches. Models with curved jaws are also sold, as well as long-nose, flat-jaw, smooth-jaw, and C-clamp configurations. The multipurpose locking pliers can be used in place of pipe wrenches, adjustable wrenches, or even clamps.

As with other varieties of pliers, locking pliers should be used rarely, if at all, on nuts, bolt heads, pipes, or fittings that are to be reused. The serrated teeth on most locking pliers can permanently damage the parts onto which they are clamped.

NEEDLE-NOSE PLIERS

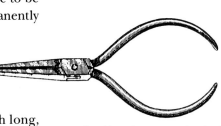

These are essentially small-scale electrician's pliers, with long, tapered jaws. Smaller in scale than linesman's pliers (see page 161), the needle-nose pliers are particularly well suited to working with wire in confined spaces like electrical boxes, though they are also useful for bending and holding metal fittings. Their jaws taper to a point, and at the nose have serrations on the gripping surface. At the throat of the tool near the pivot there is a side cutter.

Actually, this rather unusual pair of needle-nose pliers was referred to by its maker as pendulum pliers, *but such pliers functioned very much as the less elegant needle-noses do today.*

Sometimes called radio pliers, this tool is also handy for working with small nuts, washers, or other pieces that need to be precisely placed, perhaps out of the reach of your fingers. Needle-nose pliers can be purchased that have their tips bent at angles of forty-five or ninety degrees to the line of the handles.

In using needle-nose pliers, keep in mind that they are not for heavy-duty work. They are delicate tools, and their jaws can be sprung, bent, or broken, if abused. Use them for the kind of spot jobs for which they were intended, not for more demanding tasks.

BOX-END AND OPEN-END WRENCHES

The first nuts and bolts, which were put to use during the early years of the Renaissance, had square heads. The six-sided hexagonal design followed soon afterward and remains the dominant variety today, although square heads are still the rule on carriage and lag bolts.

Whatever the number of sides (called flats) on a nut or bolt head, there are several tools designed specifically to tighten or remove them. Each of the different types have significant attributes and disadvantages, but there are some dissimilarities between box-end, open-end, and combination wrenches.

Wrenches are made with openings that are slightly larger than the nuts or bolts they are designed to fit (typically, the clearance is a few thousandths of an inch). If the fit of the wrench is too loose, however, it will round off the points of the nut or bolt head.

All wrenches are available in many sizes, and can be purchased individually or in sets. A small set may have, say, six to ten wrenches, ranging in size from perhaps five-sixteenths to one inch. Standard wrenches are sold in sixteenth-inch increments up to one and a half inches (and in metric sizes, too, of course). The length of the tool varies in proportion to its size, ranging from about four inches to

Whether you're using an open-end, box-end, adjustable, or any other kind of wrench, always take the time to be sure the jaws of the wrench are snug and square on the nut or bolt head. Working with a loose-fitting or angled wrench will gnash the nut, rounding the corners of the flats. A badly damaged nut or screwhead can be impossible either to remove or to tighten.

So here's the wrench family, featuring a combination, socket, and adjustable wrench, along with an allen wrench (bottom, left) and a nut driver.

almost two feet. The logic is that the shorter (or longer) tool minimizes (or maximizes) the amount of force you can use to tighten a smaller (or larger) nut. This helps avoid shearing off bolts through the application of too much pressure.

Box-end and open-end wrenches are both sold with different-sized wrenches at either end of individual tools. This economical approach means that a five-piece set will actually contain twice that many sizes of wrench.

You'll also find that two wrenches of the same size and kind can have wildly different price tags. The explanation lies in the materials and manufacturing process. The best wrenches are made of alloys like chrome or vanadium, while less expensive tools are made from molybdenum steel or are simply stamped from sheet metal. The stamped wrenches are bulkier (more material is needed for strength), and are quite useful for occasional light duty. For frequent use, however, and for virtually any automobile applications, more expensive tools will prove the better investment.

Box-End Wrenches. These are closed-end wrenches, typically with six or twelve points around the inside diameter of the jaws. The six-pointed jaw is designed to fit hexagonal heads and nuts, while the twelve-point configuration will also accommodate a square nut. The ends of the wrench are offset slightly.

Box-end wrenches usually offer a firmer grip than do open-end wrenches. The thin wall of the jaw also makes access to nuts in tight spaces easier, but there are situations where these wrenches cannot be used, since they have to be slid on over the end of the bolt.

Open-End Wrenches. The flat jaws of these wrenches are slid around nuts or bolt heads and levered for loosening or tightening. The open ends allow the tool to be slid over the nut in tight quarters where there would be insufficient space for a box wrench or a socket, or where the length of a shaft or pipe interferes. Open-end wrenches are the quickest and easiest wrenches to use, but they will not always fit into tight quarters.

Combination Wrenches. Combination wrenches have an open-end jaw at one end of the tool and a box-end wrench of the same size at the other. As there are many situations where one or the other type simply won't work, combination wrenches can be handy indeed. However, if you require wrenches only infrequently, the added expense of combination wrenches may not be necessary.

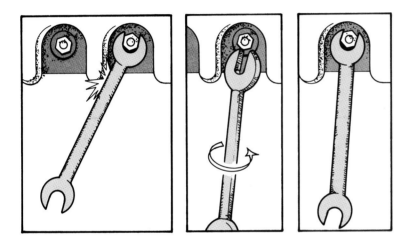

When using a wrench in a tight space that limits the turning arc, turn the nut as far you can . Then flip the wrench in your hand 180 degrees and fit it back over the nut. This will allow you to turn the nut.

THE ADJUSTABLE WRENCH

If space or budget considerations dictate buying only one wrench, an adjustable wrench is likely to be your best investment. The most widely used kind of adjustable is called a crescent wrench in honor of the shape of its jaws; another, called a monkey wrench, is less often used today.

An adjustable wrench is larger than a fixed open-end or box-end wrench, but one adjustable alone can do the work of a number of fixed wrenches. The crescent has one jaw that is fixed and one that is adjusted by turning a worm screw. Both are open-ended, but their adjustable nature also means that they can be used on inch, metric, Whitworth, and other dimensioned bolts.

As flexible a tool as the crescent wrench is, the limitations of its design prevent it from having the gripping strength of a fixed wrench. It is more likely to round the points on a nut or bolt head; especially when working with machinery, fixed wrenches are preferable. As you use the adjustable, check it periodically for tightness, as sometimes the wrench will loosen.

When using an adjustable wrench, set the jaws to fit precisely over the nut, rocking the wrench slightly as you tighten the jaws to help assure a firm fit. Make sure as well that for added strength the nut is positioned as deep as it will go into the throat of the adjustable wrench.

Adjustables can be bought in different sizes. A four-inch wrench, for example, has a maximum "bite" of half an inch, while a twelve-inch model opens to one and five-sixteenths inches. Both larger and smaller models, as well as a number of sizes in between, are available.

A sensible strategy is to buy two adjustable wrenches of complementary sizes, say, one that is six or eight inches long and another, larger wrench perhaps twelve or fifteen inches in length.

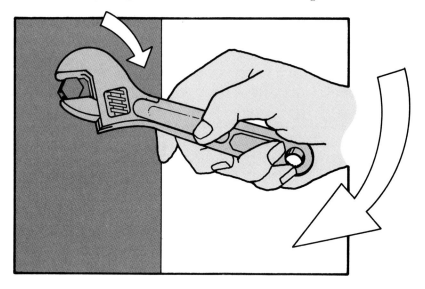

When using an adjustable wrench, keep in mind that the tool will "bite" better if pushed from the side of the tool with the fixed jaw.

ALLEN WRENCHES

Allen wrenches are steel bars, hexagonal in section, bent into L-shapes. The shorter length is called the head, the longer one the handle. Either end can be slid into matching openings in the tops of bolts or machine screws, most often set screws used in tools and machinery to hold one part firmly in position with respect to another. Pulleys on shafts, for example, are often fixed with set screws that are recessed into the body of the pulley.

Also known as allen keys, set-screw wrenches, and hex wrenches, these small tools seem utterly irrelevant – until the moment you need one. Then they are the only solution to the problem.

They are manufactured in a variety of sizes, from a sixteenth of an inch up to three-quarters of an inch, though allen wrenches larger than three-eighths of an inch are rare except in working with very large machinery.

Either end of an allen wrench can be used to drive the set screws, but the handle provides more leverage. In some cramped spaces, the shorter one must be used. If added torque is required, a pair of

Vicegrips or pliers may prove useful in grasping the handle of the wrench and turning it.

SOCKET SETS

Sockets are another option in the world of wrenches. They are highly convenient and, in experienced hands, allow for remarkably speedy tightening and loosening of nuts or bolts. While they are standard in automobile shops, they have a number of uses elsewhere, in particular when working with machines.

The sockets themselves are cylindrical receptacles. One end has points that resemble those in the jaw of a box wrench, while the other has a square hole into which the driver mechanism fits. Individual sockets are referred to by the square opening (the drive size) and the dimension of nut over which the opposite end will fit.

The handle that drives the sockets may resemble a screwdriver, though more common are ratchet handles. The ratchet eliminates the necessity of removing the socket from a nut only to refit it for another stroke when working in tight quarters where there is limited room to swing the handle. The tool will turn the bolt when swung in one direction, but will return without backing up the socket. A lever allows the process to be reversed, so that the tool can be used alternately for tightening or loosening.

There are also cranks, extensions, hinged handles, universal joints, and other devices that are used to drive the sockets.

The sockets, and the attendant mechanisms, come in many sizes. A truly complete socket set, in fact, might well consist of several hundred pieces at a cost of many hundreds of dollars. However, a good basic household socket set with about half a dozen sockets (ranging from a quarter inch to perhaps five-eighths of an inch) and a ratchet and extension will prove useful for driving lag bolts, occasional repairs, and other tasks.

As with box-end wrenches, sockets must be set squarely on the nut or bolt to be tightened. When considerable torque is required, having one hand on the handle of the ratchet and the other hand keeping the socket aligned with the length of the bolt will help insure that the flats of the head do not get rounded.

CONTENTS

SPECIALTY
TOOLS

Tape measures, drills, and hammers are useful to framing crews, electricians, steam fitters, and just about everyone else. But there's a whole universe of tools that are exclusive to the practitioners of individual crafts. They include, of course, every homeowner-hobbyist game enough to give them a try.

A friend of mine likes to say about new challenges he's taken on, "Well, there's nothing magic about plumbing" (or about electrical work or tiling; you fill in the blank). He's right: A little tool sense and the investment of some time and patience becomes a little homework of a most constructive kind.

In the chapters in this section, we'll talk about tasks from piping to plastering and grounding to grouting. None requires the eyes of an eagle or the intellect of an Einstein. But the right tools, properly employed, make a great many tasks possible. We'll close with a few suggestions on how to carry and store your tools safely and securely.

A medium-sized toolbox, one that bears more than a few signs of good use over the years.

Chapter 13.
Plumbing Tools

Plumbing makes possible the cleanliness we know today. Yet solving some kinds of plumbing problems involves sink traps, soil pipes, and clean-outs most foul. Running new plumbing lines means shiny new copper, malleable and almost orange to the eye. But that backed-up toilet calls for the aptly named snake.

Plumbing tools are a diverse lot, as the trade requires cutting, fitting, and fastening, and even a bit of carpentry when installing new lines and closing up around them. A basic knowledge of the tools we'll talk about here will allow you to perform basic repairs, as well as install new fixtures. Other tools from other sections of this book, including the drill, hole saw, reciprocating saw, chisels, hammers, and numerous others, are often needed by the plumber, too. The homeowner-plumber must be able to move swiftly from one trade to another, depending upon the needs of the particular task immediately at hand.

Not all piping is copper these days. Iron pipes are found in older structures, and their thread fittings require different techniques from the soldered sweat fittings that join copper elements. In many places today building codes allow for the use of plastic pipe for waste lines or even for supply lines. We'll talk about copper, iron, and plastic, too.

Another essential tool of the plumber, the water-pump pliers, is discussed in the chapter devoted to pliers and wrenches (see page 160).

THE TUBING CUTTER

These clever tools make neat, square cuts of plastic, copper, brass, or thin wall steel or iron tubing. They resemble adjustable wrenches in that they have one fixed jaw and another that moves. The resemblance ends there, however, since these tools have cutting wheels and rollers instead of flat or serrated jaws.

The outside, fixed jaw has the cutting wheel, which is replaceable on most models. The lower jaw, which is advanced with a threaded screw and handle mechanism, slides along the back of the cutter. On most models, the sliding jaw has two rollers that hold the pipe squarely to the cutting wheel.

This pedestal sink (from a grand old Manhattan apartment building) is surrounded by the tools of the plumber, including water-pump pliers, drain auger, propane torch, plunger, basin wrench, pipe wrench, and a miscellany of plumbing fittings and pipe.

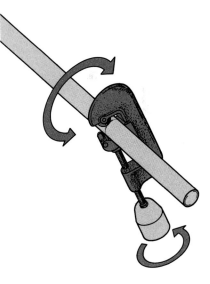

When the cutting wheel is snug to the pipe, the tubing cutter is spun around it. Then the adjusting screw is tightened a bit more, and the cutter is turned around the pipe again. Spin and tighten; spin and tighten; and, soon, the pipe will snap in two.

SOLDERING A SWEAT FITTING

Connections are made between sections of iron pipe using threaded fittings. The walls of copper pipe, however, are too thin and soft to be threaded, so a different sort

To sweat a copper fitting you need a tubing cutter (foreground), a means of polishing the pipe and fittings (a stripping pad, wire brush, and plumber's tape are at left), and a propane torch to heat the flux and solder. The square of flashing and the thick gloves are sensible precautions, too.

of fitting is used, called a sweat fitting. It's called that because the process of joining the various elements using solder involves heating them with a propane torch until they seem to sweat.

There's no particular magic required to solder a sweat fitting, though the very presence of a propane torch makes it a procedure that must be done carefully. Making a tight, leak-free joint is more a matter of careful preparation of the parts than of skill or experience.

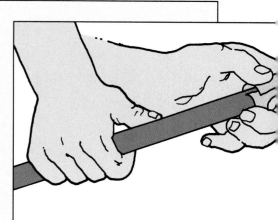

Polish the end of the pipe with an abrasive until it shines coppery bright.

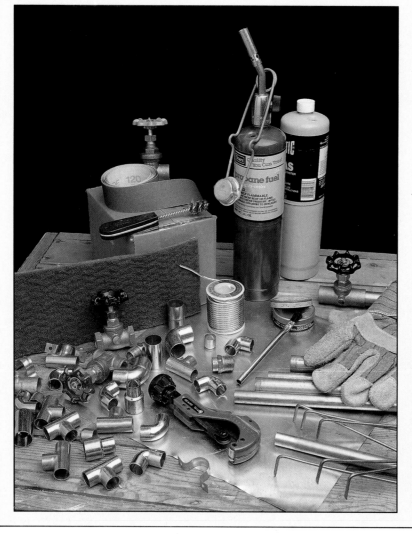

Polishing the Tubing and Fittings. The individual lengths of tubing that link the elements of the plumbing system are connected at fittings. The fittings come in a variety of configurations, including elbows, Ts, forty-fives, couplings, and others. No matter what fitting you are sweating, however, the first step to the process is smoothing and polishing the areas to be joined.

Lay out the arrangement of pipes and fittings, and cut the pipes to length. Make sure the ends are cut square. Use a utility knife to trim off any burrs from the cuts.

At each joint, polish the outside of the pipe using plumber's tape (also called emery cloth, it's sold in narrow strips). Another convenient option for shining pipe surfaces before sweating them is a synthetic, woven abrasive pad. Sold as stripping pads, they resemble those sold for scrubbing pots but will clean and brighten copper in a few easy strokes.

Polish the openings of the fittings, too, using a wire-brush pipe cleaner. Polishing both surfaces is critical: blemishes left on the connecting surfaces are likely to produce leaks later because the solder will not bond properly.

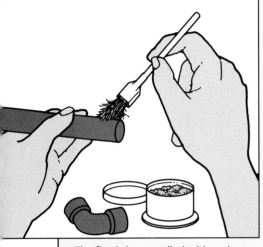

The flux is best applied with an inexpensive and disposable flux brush.

Flux the Fittings. Apply plumber's flux to the inside of each fitting to be soldered. Use one of the inexpensive flux brushes made for the task, as it keeps your fingers and hands clean. The flux has the consistency of a thin grease, and when heated will draw the solder into the fitting. Slide the pipe into the fitting, give it a twist to spread the flux evenly, and wipe off any excess flux that squeezes out.

Igniting the Torch. Now you are ready for the torch. I always wear gloves when using a torch. It's a small safety precaution, and all the work that requires lots of finger dexterity is completed by this stage.

To light the torch, open the valve slightly; you will hear a gentle hiss of the escaping gas. The nozzle is designed so that oxygen from the atmosphere of the room is drawn into intake holes, mixing with the propane. Light the flame using a sparking tool or open flame lighter.

Heating the Fitting. The hot point in a flame isn't closest to the nozzle, as many people erroneously think, but rather about halfway along its length. Position the torch so that the flame heats the fitting directly (not the pipe). There are almost as many approaches to this as there are plumbers, but my favorite technique is to hold the torch in one position, with the midpoint of its flame heating the section of the fitting that is farthest away from the joint(s) to be sweated. That helps insure that the entire joint is hot when the solder is applied.

One aspect about which there is little disagreement is the need to protect surrounding flammable surfaces. A sheet of fireproof material beyond the fitting should be positioned to protect them.

Applying the Solder. Let the flux be your guide: When it bubbles out and begins to steam, the melting temperature of solder has been reached. Touch the solder to the pipe. If it melts on contact, you can be sure it's sufficiently hot.

Remove the flame from the fitting before you apply the solder (it's the heat of the fitting that melts the solder, not the flame of the torch). If pos-

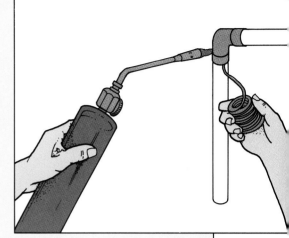

Heat the fitting, not the pipe. Then approach with the solder from the side opposite the one you have heated.

sible, apply the solder from above so that the combination of gravity and capillary action can draw the solder into the joint. You may need to apply the solder to several points around the joint.

Do all the joints on the fitting at once (as on a T, with three pipes, or an elbow with two). The pipe remains quite hot for some minutes, so avoid touching it with your bare skin.

After all the fittings have cooled, test the lines. If a fitting leaks, you can't go back and just apply more solder. I'm sorry to say that the joint must be reheated until the solder softens; then the joint must be pulled apart, the elements cleaned, fluxed, heated, and soldered all over again.

To use a tubing cutter, the jaw is opened to allow the end of the pipe to be inserted. The cutting wheel is positioned at the point along the pipe's length where the cut is to be made, and the adjusting screw tightened until the wheel and rollers grip the pipe. Don't over-tighten the jaws, since they can crimp the pipe.

The cutter is then rotated around the pipe. Check that the score line the cutter has made forms a complete circle, and doesn't tend to spiral off line, as it will if the pipe cutter isn't set squarely onto the pipe. To cut through the pipe, tighten the adjusting screw a fraction of a turn after each revolution; then rotate the pipe, tighten the screw further, and repeat the process until the cut is complete.

The inside of freshly cut copper and other soft pipe should be reamed clean of burrs and shavings. Most tubing cutters have a reaming device mounted on the back of the tool for this purpose.

Pipe cutters function in much the same way as tubing cutters do, but are made of steel and are designed for cutting pipes with thicker walls. Instead of having one cutting wheel and two rollers, like tubing cutters, pipe cutters have three cutting wheels. For those of us who run the occasional copper or plastic supply pipe, a simple and inexpensive tubing cutter is quite adequate, one that will cut copper, aluminum, or brass pipe of diameters up to an inch or an inch and a half.

THE PROPANE TORCH

One trick I've seen many plumbers use is to carry a piece of aluminum flashing in their tool kit, one perhaps twelve inches square. It can then be tacked in front of any flammable surface to prevent the propane torch from heating up the wrong material.

Sometimes called a blowtorch, this tool is small, light, and portable. Older models relied upon kerosene, but much safer and easier-to-use propane-fueled models are now the rule.

The propane torch can help perform a variety of tasks, but its principal use is to join metals by soldering or brazing. It is also used in stripping paint (the heat softens the paint; wear a respirator if you are in doubt as to whether the paint is lead-based) and in removing old putty from window sash when replacing a windowpane. Attachments can be fitted to the nozzle to focus the flame tightly for precision soldering or to spread it for paint stripping or removing resilient tile. The standard nozzle produces a flame suitable for sweat-fitting domestic water pipes.

Canisters of fuel can be purchased separately; in them the pressured, liquid propane is stored. When it is released via the valve and nozzle, the gas vaporizes and can be lit to form an even flame. The intensity of the flame is controlled by the valve, which allows more or less gas to escape.

Small canisters of propane have the brass burner and valve assembly screwed directly onto the mouth of the container. The tank then doubles as a handle during the heating process. Other models are available that have larger tanks that are connected to the nozzle via a hose. These are considerably more expensive, but the nozzle is

WORKING WITH PLASTIC PIPE

Plastic pipe requires a minimum of tools and experience. If you can use a tape measure and a hacksaw, you can probably cut, fit, and fasten plastic pipe.

There are a variety of types of plastic pipe on the market, most of which are joined using a gluelike solvent that, when applied to the pipe, actually dissolves the surface and fuses the pipe and fitting, producing a bond not unlike that of a metal weld but without requiring any heat.

Preparing the Pipe. Regardless of the type of pipe you are using, the layout and preparation of the pipe and fittings are all important. Before you cement any of the fittings together, lay out the entire job.

Cut the pipe to length. For some rigid plastic pipe you can use a tubing cutter, though a hacksaw will cut it easily as well. Be sure the cuts are square. Remove any ragged edges from the inside and outside of the cut, using a utility knife or plumber's tape (an emery cloth sold in narrow strips).

Don't remove so much material from the pipe that the fitting becomes liable to leak. To be sure, check the fit of each pipe into a fitting. It should be snug; if the pipe is loose or slides easily, try another fitting or cut another piece of pipe.

Here's one common variety of plastic waste piping, in this case Schedule 40 polyvinyl chloride. Plastic pipe is remarkably easy to use, though the glue exudes such strong fumes that it must be used with care and only in a well-ventilated location.

Cementing the Fitting. Use the solvent that was formulated for the type of pipe you are using (polyvinyl chloride or PVC; acrylonitrile-butadiene styrene or ABS; chlorinated polyvinyl chloride or CPVC; or one of the several other types). Follow the instructions on the container, which may require the use of a primer to clean and prepare the area to be bonded. There may also be temperature restrictions, as some solvents do not bond properly at cold temperatures.

In most cases, the primer is applied to the inside of the fitting and the outside of the pipe to be joined and, ten or so seconds later, the solvent is applied to the same surfaces.

The pipe is then inserted into the fitting in a twisting motion that helps assure the cement is spread evenly. Excess cement will squeeze out around the edge of the fitting, but there's no need to wipe it off.

lighter and easier to use in the cramped quarters that so often are the rule in plumbing.

When used and stored properly, propane torches pose few risks. But they must be used with care.

Always turn the torch off immediately after use. Never allow its flame to point in the direction of any flammable material. Store the torch carefully, away from any source of heat. Discard empty containers properly (many suppliers will accept them as returns).

Don't be confused if some of the old-timers call this tool a Stillson wrench. Whatever its name, it's still a pipe wrench.

THE PIPE WRENCH

The pipe wrench (recognizable to some as a monkey wrench) is an adjustable wrench generally used to grip pipes or rods. The head jaw is at the end of the handle, while the hook jaw hangs from a pivot that slides along the back of the handle.

What distinguishes the pipe wrench from other adjustables (and specifically from those more properly known as monkey wrenches) is the pivot. Unlike adjustable wrenches, the pipe wrench's serrated jaws are not fixed parallel to one another, but when pressure is put on the handle, the pivot causes the jaws to close slightly . This clenching action allows the tool to grip round workpieces. Pipe wrenches are made of steel with hardened jaws.

Pipe wrenches are intended to be used to turn a pipe or other round workpiece in one direction; in order to change direction, the wrench must be removed and the position of its jaws reversed.

The pipe wrench is also a tool of last resort for removing an otherwise immovable nut or bolt. However, once the serrated jaw of a pipe wrench bites into the metal, that nut or bolt will almost certainly have to be replaced. Exhaust your other alternatives first.

THE BASIN WRENCH

This is one of those specialty tools that has few uses – except at the moment you need the basin wrench and only the basin wrench will do.

The basin wrench has the head of a pipe wrench and the neck of a giraffe. It's designed to reach up behind the bowl of a sink and connect or disconnect the nuts that fasten the faucet or other fittings that provide water to a sink.

The pipe wrench jaw is mounted at right angles to the length of the handle; at the opposite end, there is a T bar for torquing the tool. The mechanical equivalent of a periscope, in a sense the basin wrench allows you to work where your hands can't reach. It's a relatively inexpensive tool that will quickly prove its worth when retro-fitting kitchen faucets or other sink fittings.

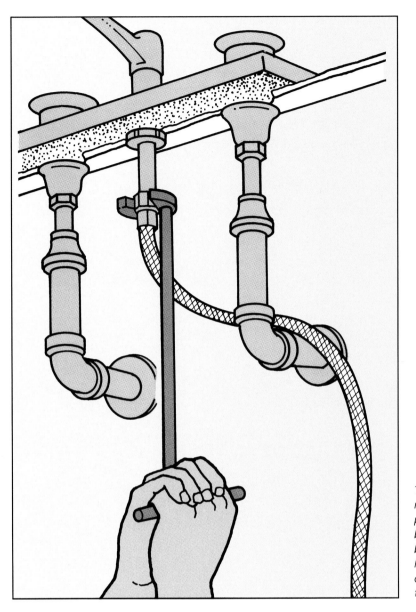

The basin wrench allows you to remove faucets that are awkwardly placed, often up in the narrow slot between the sink basin and the wall behind. Even with a basin wrench, however, you'll probably find yourself on your back, half in and half out of the vanity or sink cabinet.

THE PLUNGER

Even if you never plan to do any sweat fittings or plumb any plastic pipe, the plunger is a tool that may have a role to play in your household. It doesn't have anything to do with running new pipes; its job is to help clear blockages in old ones.

The plunger consists of a molded rubber cup mounted on the end of a wooden handle. Sink plungers have a simple, hemispherical cup; those designed to unclog toilets have a conical extension at the mouth of the cup that inserts into the throat of the toilet. This helps assure a tight fit and adds force.

To use a plunger, position its cup over a sink, tub, or toilet drain. Fill the sink or other receptacle to a depth that covers the cup. If

TEFLON TAPE

In the past, threaded fittings required pipe-joint compound, a thick, oily paste that was applied with a small brush. Often, a stringlike material called wicking was then wound into the threads. The process was dirty and time-consuming.

Today, teflon tape is the simpler, more efficient material used for threaded fittings. This extremely thin tape comes in rolls, and is applied clockwise over the threads at the end of the pipe, in one and a half or two rotations around the pipe. The fitting is then simply threaded on over the tape, and tightened. It's quick, clean, tight, and really just that easy.

there is an overflow drain in the sink or tub, block its opening with a rag or a strip of duct tape.

The cup must make contact with the sink around its entire perimeter. A coating of petroleum jelly around the rim of the cup may help insure an airtight seal.

Pump the handle downward, collapsing the cup. This forces air into the pipes, increasing the pressure on the blockage, which may break up the material that is clogging the pipe. Work the tool up and down five to ten times. Repeat again if necessary.

If the material still has not been loosened, you may need to resort to the drain auger (see below).

THE DRAIN AUGER

The drain auger is used when a plunger is unable to open a blocked drain line. It consists of a twisted wire hook and auger fastened to the end of a steel spring coil. More expensive models come with a crank and with a storage canister into which the length of the coil can be withdrawn, while simpler varieties are wound by hand into a coil. Coils of various diameters are sold, but three-eighths and half-inch coils are usual.

To use the drain auger, the end is inserted into the pipe. If your blockage is in a sink, remove the trap beneath the sink first. That way you can be sure the clog isn't simply at that point and easily removed by hand. By removing the trap, you also open up a more direct access to the drain lines beyond. (One suggestion: when you remove the trap, position a pail or other watertight receptacle beneath it to catch the water contained within.)

Push the auger in until it reaches the blockage. One of this tool's nicknames, the snake, describes the way it twists and weaves, following the bends in the pipe.

At one or several points, it may refuse to travel any further into the pipe. That doesn't necessarily mean you've reached the blockage, but the end of the snake may have reached angled fittings and may need a little persuading to continue its journey.

Try twisting the snake in a cranking motion, using the built-in cranking handle that can be tightened (using a set screw) to the length of the coil. If your snake doesn't have a crank, position one hand on the snake where it enters the trap. With the other, grip the snake about eighteen inches further along its length. Then crank it, rotating your hands as if you were pedaling a bicycle.

The cranking motion should be in a clockwise direction (when looking into the end of the pipe). If you have reached the blockage, the turning snake will engage the blockage, and the twisted steel auger at its end will bore into the material, either causing it to break up or allowing you to pull it back out. If the resistance you felt was not the blockage but a fitting, the cranking motion, together with some pushing pressure, will allow the snake to advance in the drain line.

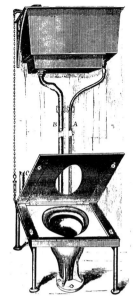

I personally have never come across one of these in any of my renovations. But if you do, you can be sure of two things: today, the "drip tray slop-hopper," as it was known in its own time, is certainly a classic and it is definitely a plumber's nightmare.

Chapter 14.
Electrical Tools

For many people, electrical work is daunting, to be feared and avoided. If you feel that way, then you should remain in your comfort zone, and keep away from tasks that make you anxious.

On the other hand, if you've always suspected that many basic tasks around the house involving electricity are within your ken – well, take your time, do your homework first, and give it a try. Of course, that's *after* you've made sure the power is off on the circuit you want to work on.

A handful of basic electrical tools are described below, enough to enable you to run a new line to power the light over your workbench, or replace that burned-out receptacle in the guest bedroom. Two valuable tools not included in this chapter are the linesman's and needle-nose pliers; both are discussed in the chapter devoted to Pliers, Wrenches, and Sockets (see pages 161 and 163). A number of other tools that are used by many sorts of tradesmen, including electricians, are screwdrivers, drills, tape measures, saws, and hammers, and they, too, are found in other sections of the book.

In the pages that follow are the extension cord, droplight, and flashlight, sources of power and light. We'll start with those since, even for those with trepidations about strapping on an electrician's pouch, these tools will often prove essential.

Wiring, anyone? Here are some basics of the electrician's trade, including a cable ripper (center), wire strippers (front left), and an electrical meter (rear center). Whether you take on electrical tasks or not, you'll probably find good use for an extension cord, droplight, and flashlight.

THE EXTENSION CORD, DROPLIGHT, AND FLASHLIGHT

Although you may intend never to do a single wiring job, there are several electrical tools that are still basic requirements for anyone involved in home maintenance tasks. No toolbox is fully equipped without a flashlight, extension cord, and droplight.

Flashlight. You can buy flashlights that fit in your pocket or attach to your head, that can spotlight an entire roadway or peek through a keyhole. You can spend a lot of money or a little. It's your call.

Let me recommend a minimum. Purchase an inexpensive flashlight that takes two D-cell batteries. You're familiar with the variety I have in mind – it's a bit thinner and longer than a twelve-ounce soda

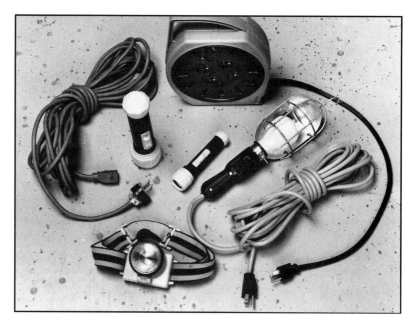

I find that extension cords with more than one receptacle are very handy. I like headlamp flashlights, for those unexpected repairs in the attic or a crawl space, when you need both hands for tools.

can. Keep it in your toolbox: it'll prove invaluable in the attic or for peeking behind or around your furnace or water heater.

Better yet, buy several, and keep them handy (one in the kitchen, one in the car, one with your tools, and so on).

Extension cords. A twenty-five-foot-long extension cord is ideal: Its length will not produce a significant voltage drop but will be enough to get you into the further reaches of your house. The wire should have three conductors; extensions made of two-conductor lamp cord are inadequate or even unsafe for running power tools. The plug and receptacle at either end should be grounded (three-pronged).

One design I favor features three or more plug receptacles. This allows you to keep, say, a drill and driver and portable circular saw plugged in at one spot, saving you the time and trouble of unplugging and replugging various tools. A number of variations on this theme are sold, including the one pictured above.

Droplight. This is just a long cord that has a light socket at the end, with a cage or housing to protect the bulb. Flashlights can provide only limited illumination; a droplight can bring bright light into almost any dark corner.

A droplight can be purchased with either fluorescent or incandescent bulbs, though the incandescent models are more popular. When using the droplight, you'll probably find it necessary to hang it conveniently over your work area. Don't leave it to roll or get kicked around on the floor.

Given its portable nature, the droplight is subject to bangs and blows that will abruptly end the life of its bulb. Buy construction-grade bulbs, as they have stronger filaments than standard bulbs and will survive some of the inevitable knocks and abuse.

When attaching a wire to a screw terminal like that on a wall switch or plug receptacle, shape the stripped conductor into a little crook. Hook it beneath the screwhead, with the crook wrapped clockwise, so that as you tighten the screw it draws the wire tight.

STRIPPING WIRES

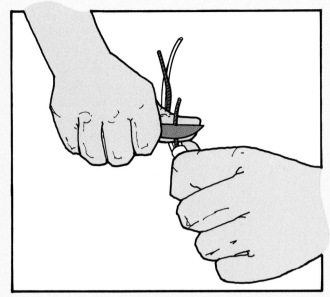

When stripping wire insulation with a knife, keep the knife steady in your hand, turning the wire or pivoting your entire hand around the wire end. That way you're less likely accidentally to slice into the pad of your thumb.

When stripping with a wire stripper, it's mostly a matter of squeezing the correct notch around the wire and twisting off the insulation.

Stripping insulation from electrical wire is most easily done with a knife and a pair of pliers (preferably linesman's pliers), and it's *always* done after you've unplugged or turned off the power in the line you are working with.

Hold the knife blade perpendicular to the wire at the point you wish to remove the insulation (that's usually three-eighths or a half inch from the end). Pinch the wire between the knife and your thumb. Be sure the pad of your thumb is not in contact with the blade of the knife.

Rotate the wire with the other hand. The knife will cut into the insulation, and when it reaches the conductor, you'll feel the blade begin to scrape the metal. Cut all around the wire.

Using your linesman's pliers, you can now pull off the insulation from the end of the wire. Use a twisting motion.

If the wire you are stripping is stranded (rather than solid-core wire), you will have to be careful not to sever any individual strands. You'll find that, with a little practice, this is a simple procedure. Practice on scrap wire first.

A tool called a wire stripper can also be purchased to remove the insulation from wire ends. Shaped like pliers, this is actually a multipurpose tool, with a pair of wire cutters at the mouth of the jaws and a small opening behind designed for crimping terminals. Further back on the tool, adjacent to the pivot, is a set of incised holes, each of which is labeled with a wire size. When the stripper is closed around the correct size of wire, the tool is then twisted around the wire and the wire is pulled out, with the insulation being stripped away in the process.

Wire strippers are most useful for removing insulation from small-gauge wire, especially stranded cord.

THE CABLE RIPPER

This simple, inexpensive tool is used to slice open the plastic sheath that protects the wires in cable that contains two or more conductors. The tool fits over the end of the wire; its single, triangular tooth is pressed into the plastic covering, and then the tool is tugged off the end of the wire. The result is a tear in the sheathing that makes the conductors within accessible.

This tool is not essential: A knife can be used to slice the insulation; or two pairs of pliers, gripping the conductors, can rip the covering away. But the cable ripper is quicker, safer, and easier. And quite inexpensive, too.

THE LINE TESTER AND THE ELECTRICAL METER

Everyone who does any electrical work needs to have a line tester at hand. It costs only a couple of dollars, is small enough to fit into a pocket protector (supposing you're willing to wear one), and may save you the shock of your life.

The line tester is really just an indicator light with two leads. Keeping your fingers on the insulated portions of the tester, you press the metal electrodes into a receptacle or onto the terminals you wish to test. If the light comes on, there's power there; if there's no juice, as they say in the trade, the indicator light will not illuminate.

Get yourself a simple tester and use it as often as you need it.

For joining wires, a wire nut does the trick safely. Inside the plastic cap is a conical metal spring into which the twisted wires are tightened, thus both fastening them together and insulating them.

The electrical meter (right) will read out lots of things you never knew you had to know about ohms and watts and volts. The simple line tester at center is quite adequate to tell you whether a line is hot or not – and, therefore, whether you're about to get a shock or not.

If you want to get beyond that most basic determination (whether there's power in the line or not), the line tester won't be much help. Enter the electrical meter.

Meters come in big packages and little ones, with small price tags and hefty ones. The fancy ones have clamp-on ohmmeters and voltmeters, can measure frequency, and capacitance, and will test transistors and diodes. Your needs should dictate which device to buy, but these tools are very useful in troubleshooting electrical problems, especially when repairing appliances.

THE GENERATOR

In new construction, the excavation and foundation contractors, electrician, and carpenters often appear on the scene before the power company can put in a temporary feed. In such cases, a generator may be a valuable or even essential on-site presence. A gasoline-powered engine drives the generator, providing 120- or 240-volt alternating current to run saws, drills, and other power tools.

The output of a generator is measured in watts. Some portable generators have wattage as high as 8,000, while smaller models have as few as 2,400. What you require is calculated using the formula we learned back in high school: *volts* times *amps* equals *watts*. Thus, a table saw that surges at start-up to 18 amps at 110-volt house current uses about 2,000 watts; a portable circular saw might need roughly two-thirds that wattage. So if you plan on having both plugged in and, at least occasionally, running simultaneously, you probably need a capacity of about 3,500 watts. If you plan to run a compressor, pump, or other tools, too, a larger capacity will be required. Most manufacturers also recommend allowing a safety margin of an extra 25 percent on top of your anticipated total wattage needs.

Many models come with wheels to make the machines easier to move (generators are heavy, with some models weighing two hundred pounds or more). On most models, a metal frame protects the motor, fuel tank, and electrics. Generators are expensive tools, but on a work-site where time translates quite directly into money, they may well be worth the investment.

For the work-site without electrical service, the generator is indispensable for running saws, drills, and other power tools that seem essential today.

Chapter 15.
Tiling Tools

For many years, ceramic tiling was regarded as arcane. It was a specialized vocation best left to the gifted few who, with their years of apprenticeship, were masters of the trade.

That perception has certainly changed. There are chains of retail stores today that sell only tile and tiling supplies, and most of their customers are homeowners. Tile is now widely used not only in bathrooms, but in kitchens, entryways, and other locations in the home and office where durable, water-resistant surfaces are required. Increasingly, the installation is done by novices, those of us who want the look of tile but don't want to pay virtuoso fees for the privilege.

Enter the simple tools of the tiler. This doesn't have to be a long chapter, because the tools are relatively few and fairly easy to use. There's the tile cutter (it's essentially a sophisticated version of the glass cutter) that scores and snaps tiles along straight lines. The nipper, a cutting tool with jaws, handles, and a pivot, resembles a pair of pliers but allows the picking and nipping of little bits from a curve or compound cut. The notched trowel is used to apply the adhesive or cement for affixing the tile, and the grout float spreads the coarse mortar that fills the joints between the tiles.

You'll need a few other familiar tools, like a tape measure, chalk box, framing square, and a level. These days, tiling is no longer solely the domain of the tilers' guild.

THE TILE CUTTER

Also known as a snap cutter, this tool consists of a platform topped by a frame along which a cutter wheel slides. The tile is positioned on the padded platform, with one side flush to a fence at the head to hold the workpiece square.

The cutting wheel, quite like the wheel on a glass cutter, is mounted on a lever mechanism that allows considerable leverage to be applied. The wheel is pressed against the tile to score its glazed surface. The tile is then pressured with the cutter lever to snap the tile apart (see *Cutting Tile*, page 190).

Tile cutters vary greatly in price. Some have hardened steel cutter wheels, others have carbide cutters (these cost several times as much,

Surrounding the tile cutter (moving clockwise from right) are a pair of nippers, a notched trowel, and a grout float. There are sponges and both trim and field tiles, too.

If you are buying flooring tile or any large tile (ten or more inches square), take your tile cutter with you to the store. Some tiles are difficult to cut with snap cutters, and most suppliers will let you test your cutter with a piece of scrap tile. This little experiment might save you added time and expense later.

LAYING OUT TILE

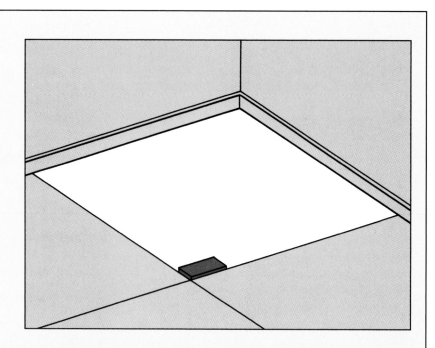

Snap perpendicular chalk lines to guide you as you lay out the tile.

A little layout sooner can save a lot of frustration later. You want to be sure the finished product looks as neat and regular as possible . . . and to save yourself unnecessary cutting and nipping chores that can double the time required to complete a job.

First Find the Center. When tiling a floor, you want the finished surface to appear symmetrical (even if it isn't). To accomplish this, you need to find the center of the surface first, measuring in from the sides.

This is especially important in small areas, where wide tiles at one edge and slender ones at the other will make the whole job look out of balance.

Squaring Up. Particularly in a house of a certain age, you may well discover that the floor area isn't square. That makes the job a bit more complicated. Most often, the best strategy is to use as a baseline the wall that is most obvious.

Then when your guests walk into the room, they'll see tile lines that are parallel to that wall, and you'll get credit for a nice even job.

If their first view is of lines that aren't aligned, the whole job may look cockeyed, even if it isn't.

Quartering the Job. Once you've identified the center and the baseline from which you will work, snap a pair of perpendicular chalk lines. These will divide the room into roughly equal quadrants. You'll want to work outward from the center point in each of the four sections.

When tiling a wall, your first concern is not a center point; you'll want to establish a top line that is level. Few walls are truly plumb (or floors true level) so use a level to mark the top line.

Establish its height so that you won't have to cut very thin tiles (or cut very thin shards

from nearly full tiles) to come flush to the floor. Snap a top line on your walls; then snap a center line, too, just as you would for the floor. And be sure to lay out all the walls you plan to do *before* you begin tiling.

Stepping Off the Pattern. One last, essential step: After you've found the center point, squared the room, and are ready to go, position rows of tiles (do it dry, before you mix the adhesive or mortar) within each quadrant of the grid. Take the rows to each wall. This last step should warn you of any trouble to come.

Follow the same procedure for the walls, too, stepping off horizontal and vertical distances.

One problem you might encounter, for example, is if you made an arithmetical mistake and your center line isn't your center line at all. This can easily be corrected at the layout stage but could create

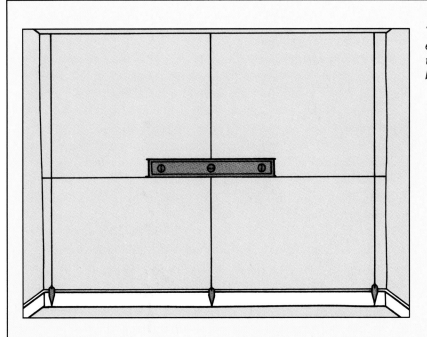

Your first concern in tiling a wall is to establish level: even if the floor isn't true, the top edge of the tile should be level.

major headaches later on.

Another example: You might discover that the last tiles you laid to butt to the walls (or floor) are so narrow as to be impossible to cut (cutting a ceramic tile to a width of less than about three-quarters of an inch is difficult and should be avoided if at all possible). You could decide to go back, and cheat the whole grid an inch or so one way or another, even at the cost of

losing your perfect symmetry. Only you will know.

You may also opt to make a variation on the story pole (see page 10) that is called a jury stick. If you mark on a straight piece of plain wood stock the width of a particular series of tiles (and don't forget the grout joints, too), you can hold it to the surface to be tiled and identify potential difficulties easily without having to set whole areas of tile in place.

When it comes to the actual tiling, work across to the outside edge of one quadrant, then to the top or bottom one row or course at a time. Fill in as you go.

Successful tile jobs are a direct result of good planning and a methodical approach. Doublecheck every step; measure at least twice with a tape and a second time by stepping off.

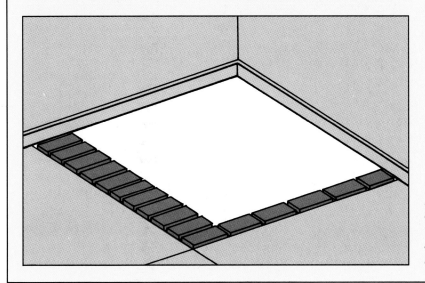

Position dry tiles (without mortar or cement) to be sure your layout will work. Moving your chalk lines is easy at this stage; lifting and cutting tiles later is messy and time-consuming.

but last much longer). Some have larger tables, others can be set up to make accurate miter cuts.

A much more expensive option is a wet saw, which is essentially a portable circular saw mounted onto a special frame and water-filled trough. A movable cutting table with an adjustable fence allows the tile to be presented to the cutting blade, which is in turn kept cool by jets of water.

The wet saw is invaluable for working with thick and shaped tile, and for shaping curves from tile. It makes smooth, regular cuts, when used with both skill and care. If you have used a circular saw, similar safety rules apply. Wet saws can usually be rented for reasonable fees on a daily or hourly basis.

For most simple tiling jobs, however, a snap cutter will do quite nicely, at a reasonable cost, and with no exposure to the risks of the power saw. When you buy tile, it may be worth asking suppliers whether they have cutters they are prepared to rent or loan to their customers.

CUTTING TILE

A little patience, along with a little practice and a score and a snap, and you're a tile cutter. You do it this way.

Measure and Mark the Tile. Measure the size of the tile you need to cut, and transfer the dimension to the glazed surface of the tile, using a felt-tip marker.

Position the tile on the cutter, aligning the center line of the cutter with the axis on which the tile is be cut. The top of the tile should be held flush to the fence at the top of the cutter to keep it square to the cutting wheel.

Score the Surface. Using the lever to which the cutting wheel is attached, draw the cutter across the surface of the tile, exerting a firm, even pressure to cut through the glaze. Make only one pass with the cutter.

Snap the Tile. Different snap cutters have different means of snapping tile. Some have a heel at the rear of the lever that has the cutting wheel at its toe, others the reverse. Whatever the design of your cutter, use the surface to apply pressure to the score line. In combination with a bead built into the base of the cutter, the pressure will cause the tile to snap in half.

This sturdy tile cutter makes short work of cutting even large tiles. The adjustable fence and miter gauge in the foreground can be fastened in place for repeat or angle cuts.

THE NIPPERS

This is the second of the two essential tile-cutting tools (along with the tile cutter). Like the pliers they greatly resemble, nippers can be purchased in many sizes and configurations. A basic model will suffice for most jobs.

Nippers are used to cut curved or irregular tiles, or to nip away very thin strips from the edges of a tile. They work best when the area to be trimmed has been scored with a tile or glass cutter; the nippers are then used to clip off small sections at a time. Some nippers have one flat jaw that is held flush to the glazed surface of the tile; the other has a curved cutting edge that is designed to bite into the unglazed vitreous base (called the bisque). Others have two cutting edges. Both designs work well.

Cutting curves into tiles isn't difficult with the proper tools. The nippers do most of the work of nibbling off small bits of tiles, but the area to be removed should first be scored in a crisscross pattern. A purpose-made tile scorer can be purchased, but a glass cutter will also do the job.

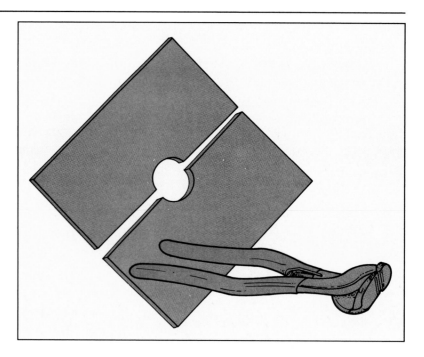

When a faucet or pipe hole falls at the middle of a tile, you may wish to drill the opening using a hole saw. Another option is to snap the tile in half and nip out the necessary hole.

THE NOTCHED TROWEL

This tool is used to spread adhesive over walls or floors in order to apply surfaces such as ceramic tile. Also called a serrated-edge, adhesive, or mastic trowel, the notched trowel has a flat rectangular blade and a wooden handle mounted along the center of its back. The edges of the blade are notched, sometimes in two different profiles.

When you have finished laying out the job (see *Laying Out Tile,* page 188), you apply the adhesive to a small area of the wall or floor (say, a three-foot square) using the notched trowel. Smooth the adhesive or mortar evenly onto the surfaces, then draw the notched edge through it on a final pass, holding the trowel at a low angle. This will create a uniform series of ridged lines in which to bed the tiles.

The tiles can then be set in place, one at a time. They are pushed firmly into the adhesive, perhaps with a slight twisting motion to bed them thoroughly. As you finish each section, check the areas for plumb and level.

THE GROUT FLOAT

After the tile is in place and the adhesive or cement has set for twenty-four hours or longer (follow the instructions on the adhesive or mortar package), a thin, coarse mortar called grout is applied to fill the joints between the tiles. A sponge can be used for this purpose, but the job is made a good deal easier if you have a grout float.

(You'll still need a sponge, though, to clean the surface of the tiles after the grout is applied.)

The grout float looks rather like a trowel, with a hardwood handle at the center of its back. However, the body of the tool is also wooden, and its working surface is made of rubber (hence another name by which it is known, the rubber float).

It is used like a trowel, in that it is held with a long edge at a low angle to the tile, and swept across the area, with the pressure from the flat surface working the grout between the tiles. Follow with a sponge to remove the grout residue from the tile surfaces.

SOME TILING TIPS

Preparation. Wallpaper, loose plaster, flaking paint, peeling tiles, or unsecured sheet flooring must be removed from the walls or floors that are to be tiled. Make sure your tiling surface is flat, rigid, and dry.

Layout. Proper planning is every bit as important as careful cutting. Establish a precise strategy for the process before you begin (see *Laying Out Tile,* page 188).

Adhesives. If you are using tile, chances are that it's to be in a setting where moisture is a given, whether it's a kitchen, bath, or entryway. Make sure you use a waterproof adhesive.

You can use a premixed adhesive or a mortar, but if you choose the latter, make sure it's a thin-set variety. The thick-bed mortars require some practice and skill at smoothing to get the tiles to sit flat, and the additional mortar isn't necessary for a watertight finish.

Grouting. Grout is usually purchased as a powder, then mixed with water or a recommended additive (read the instructions on the package, or ask advice at the tile store to be sure the mix is appropriate). One simple way to enhance your color scheme is to add a dye or pigment to the grout. Adding a color can be especially important if you've tiled a floor because white grout, even after it has been sealed with a grout sealer (which is to be recommended, especially for floors), may prove difficult to keep looking clean and white.

Make sure you sponge off the residue on the surface of the tiles before it dries. This will require several passes over a period of an hour or more. This is critical when you're working with tiles that have a porous or variegated surface. Dried grout can be almost impossible to remove from the indentations.

The grout saw is indispensable when renewing grout. It can remove the old grout below the level of the tile, providing the new grout with enough area to bond to the tiles.

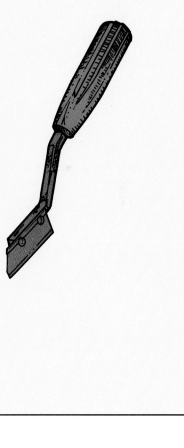

Chapter 16.
Plastering and Wallboard Tools

Hanging drywall is often one of the first tasks taken on by the novice renovator. Plasterboard or Sheetrock, to call it by one well-known proprietary name, has become perhaps the most common walling material in this country. It's easy to use, relatively inexpensive, offers some soundproofing and insulation, and, when properly installed, results in a smooth and handsome surface.

Drywall comes in sheets. It consists of a core of a plasterlike material (usually gypsum) sandwiched between layers of paper. The sheets are four feet wide and of various lengths (eight-, ten-, and twelve-foot lengths are common). Thicknesses vary, too, but most building supply yards will carry three-eighths, half-inch, and five-eighths-inch sheets.

The sheets of wallboard are attached to the structure of the walls with specially designed drywall nails or screws and sometimes with adhesives. Then the joints between the sheets are hidden with a specially made drywall tape (either a fiberglass mesh or paper tape) followed by several layers of a premixed, plasterlike material called joint compound. Or, in some cases, the entire surface is coated with a skim coat of joint compound or even of traditional plaster.

The kind of drywall used varies, depending upon the location and eventual finish to be applied. Standard wallboard has a smooth, gray surface. Sheets with a greenish hue have a vapor barrier of fiberglass within for installations (like bathrooms) where the amount of moisture will be high. The blue-tinted wallboard is designed to be skim coated. Fire-resistant wallboard is also available.

Here are the tools of the trade, and some basics on how to use them to patch and finish wallboard surfaces. I've included a quick introduction to skim coating, too, a skill that I believe is too little employed, considering its most satisfactory results.

THE SURFOAM

This tool is a relative of the file. It has a hollow aluminum frame with a steel blade. The replaceable blade is perforated, with individual raised teeth called rasp teeth.

The tool can be used to smooth wood but is particularly useful when hanging drywall. It will remove irregularities from the edge of

Those are surfoams at front left, and taping knives on the right. The plasterer's tools are in the rear to the right of the drywall T square. Above the drywall hammer and the two wallboard saws is a corner-bead clincher, a tool designed to fasten corner bead to drywall in a few strokes without nails or screws. The mallet beside it is used to drive the tool.

After scoring, snapping, and cutting a piece of wallboard, run the surfoam along the edge. It will remove high spots, resulting both in neater work and less time spent lowering sheets of wallboard to trim them that last fraction of an inch.

a piece of wallboard that has been scored and snapped. It can also be used to shave down a piece slightly, or to finish a hole or slot cut in the board.

Surfoams are sold in one-handed and two-handed sizes. The smaller surfoam is about the size of a block plane, five or six inches long. It's held in one hand, freeing the other to hold the workpiece. The longer surfoam (its blade is ten inches long) is most effective when used with two hands. The extra length helps flatten out long, wavy cut lines.

THE DRYWALL T SQUARE

Also called a wallboard T square, the drywall T square has a four-foot blade in order to reach across the width of a standard sheet of gypsum board. The crosspiece at the head is shorter than the blade (typically less than two feet), but it resembles a draftsman's T square in being off-set slightly so that its lip butts to the edge of the wallboard. The length of the blade and the crosspiece are marked with dimensions in inches.

The T square is intended as a cutting guide, though it is also useful for marking holes to be cut in the interior of sheets of plywood as well as wallboard. When used for marking gypsum board, a utility knife is positioned flush to the side of the square and cuts a score line through the top layer of paper on the wallboard. The core of the piece will then snap when it is bent away from the score line, after which the backing paper is sliced with the utility knife.

While wallboard can certainly be marked using a chalk box and cut freehand, using a drywall T square makes both marking and cutting faster and more accurate. The two-inch wide blade is exactly the same width as plug boxes, so both sides can be cut without the square having to be moved.

Though primarily intended for marking and scoring wallboard, the drywall T square can also double as a panel gauge, helping to lay out holes or cuts in sheets of plywood.

DRYWALLING HINTS

You've probably hung some 'rock over the years, either at home or helping a friend refurbish a room. So you probably know it isn't particularly difficult to score, snap, and cut sheets of wallboard, and to nail or screw them in place.

What about getting a truly professional look at the end of the process? Well, that's not quite so automatic. We've all seen sloppily taped joints, poorly supported sheets of drywall that are floating free

(causing cracks here and there) and moldings that aren't sitting flush to the wall surfaces.

Limitations of space don't allow for a lengthy dissertation here on all the intricacies of hanging wallboard. But let me offer a few advisories to consider before you tackle your next drywall job.

Nailing Surfaces Are Necessary. Every edge of a piece of wallboard needs to be attached to a rigid structural member. Add scrap pieces behind all joints to insure that

seams become part of a seamless surface, and not unsightly cracks.

Planning and Plumbing. Before you cut your first piece of wallboard, devise a plan whereby you use the largest pieces of wallboard possible. The larger the pieces, the fewer joints there'll be to feather and finish later.

Another important consideration is finding a corner that is square and working from there. You should also make sure that the first piece applied to each wall is precisely

It's an ongoing debate among professionals: which is better, the taper's finishing knife or the finishing trowel? To my way of thinking, the answer lies in the individual hand of the holder.

plumb. That'll help you line up the rest. Seeking square and starting plumb save you having to make trapezoids out of rectangles.

Mark It a Mite Short. Measure the space into which you want a piece to fit. Then mark and cut the piece an eighth of an inch narrower and shorter than the space to be filled. This will insure that it will fit, and the compound or plaster you apply later will fill up the space at the seam.

Wallboard Screws Are Stronger. Drywall nails, with rings along the shaft for added holding power, are a must if you want to use nails. But if you have a power driver, drywall screws are a faster and stronger alternative. (Note that they also allow for the removal of a piece without doing it a lot of damage.)

Ceilings Come First. If your project involves ceilings as well as walls, do the ceiling first. Then you will be able to butt the wall panels to the ceiling for tighter fit.

Employ the Tools of the Trade. The surfoam and drywall T square are good investments. Equally valuable are the utility knife (with plenty of spare blades; change them frequently), the chalk box, the drywall driver, a drywall or keyhole saw, and a retracting tape measure. With those tools, a strong back, and a willingness to go hard at it, a remarkable transformation can be wrought in a room in a day.

TAPING KNIVES

At first glance, taping knives look like oversized scrapers (see page 114), with wide blades and wood or plastic handles. They are known by several names (drywall knives, taping knives, filling knives, finishing knives, and so on) and come in a variety of sizes.

Taping knives differ from scrapers in that they are more flexible. They are used to apply joint compound, the premixed plasterlike substance, purchased in tubs, that is used to finish the taped joints between sheets of drywall. The application process varies from tradesman to tradesman, but typically two or three coats of joint compound are applied, each being allowed to dry before the next is put on. The first coat is applied with a narrow blade (perhaps four inches), the later coat or coats with blades of increasing width (see *The Seamless Wall*, page 200).

To make explanation easier, I've divided the drywall knives into three categories distinguished by blade shapes and sizes.

Broad Knives. The flat drywall knives with narrow blades (in the four- to six-inch range) tend to have blades that curve into a roughly triangular shape. They're used for the first coat of joint compound or for patching jobs.

The Finishing Knives. The flat knives with wider, rectangular blades (eight to fourteen inches wide) are used for finishing. Also called taping knives, these are usually sold with blue steel or stainless steel blades to resist rust.

An alternative to a scraper-shaped finishing knife is a purpose-made finishing trowel. It resembles a plaster trowel (see *The Skim Coat*, page 200), but has a slight bow in its blade to allow for the build-up of compound at the seams between sheets of wallboard. The trowel design is more expensive than the knife; which configuration is better is largely a matter of the user's personal preference.

Corner Knives. As the name suggests, these tools are for corners. They have flexible blades that are bent at a ninety-degree angle, permitting the application and smoothing of compound to corners; different models are sold for inside and outside corners. (Without such a knife, inside corners in particular must be done in two steps, with an overnight wait for the compound to dry.) In practiced hands, these knives produce smooth, finished corners.

PATCHING
PLASTER

Finishing a new wall or room with plaster or joint compound takes practice. If you have no experience with plaster or its near relation, joint compound, don't learn in your living room. Experiment first in a closet, the attic, or a workroom area where you can glean valuable dos and don'ts from the inevitable imperfections.

Another good approach is to try patching first.

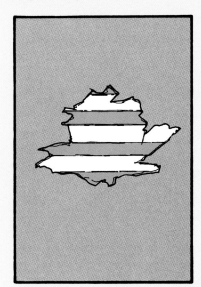

Preparation. Remove all the old, loose plaster. When working directly on a masonry surface, use a club hammer and cold chisel; rake out the joints to a depth of a quarter inch so that the plaster can form "keys" in the joints, adding strength to the new surface. Replace damp or molding wallboard that sags. If necessary, add wooden nailing surfaces at the edge of the wallboard patch to be certain it remains flat and stable.

Reinforce the Patch. At the joint between the existing wall and the new patch, apply self-adhesive fiberglass mesh tape. This will help bond the old and new together. For large holes, you may wish to use a sheet of aluminum or galvanized screening.

Putting on the Plaster. Most commercial patching plasters require a thorough wetting of the surrounding plasterwork, though some do not (read and

follow the instructions to be certain). If you are patching a larger void, a two-coat approach is probably best. Fill the edges of the hole with plaster, covering the tape or screening. Use a small filler knife, and bring the plaster just shy of the surrounding finish plaster. Let the newly applied patch set overnight.

Some shrinkage and cracking is likely, especially in large patches. After the plaster has set thoroughly, apply a second coat, using a wider knife or trowel, preferably one wide enough to sweep over the entire width of the patch. Some plasters set quickly, so don't delay in feathering the plaster surface flush to the surrounding surface.

If you are using a two-stage patching plaster, you may be able to sponge on a small amount of water to gain added working time for further smoothing.

In order to patch a plaster surface, first remove loose plaster. Insert screening or fiberglass mesh tape to reinforce the area to be patched; then fill the area with patching plaster, using a narrow filler knife. Be careful not to leave any areas that stand out beyond the plane of the wall. Come back for a second, and, if necessary, a third coat, smoothing the area flush to the surrounding plaster, using a wider knife.

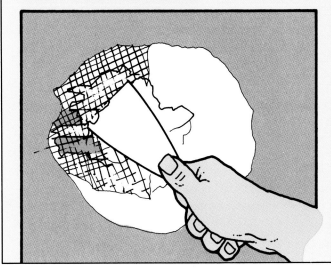

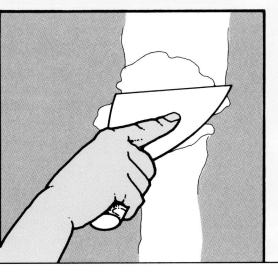

THE SEAMLESS WALL

I won't attempt here to tell you in detail how to hang wallboard or to tape joints; there are a number of book-length publications out there that offer excellent advice and guidance. But there are a few basics that always bear repeating. I've also picked up a few tricks over the years from the pros.

Preparing the Surface. The wallboard must be firmly attached, nailed, or screwed to the studs, joists, and other wooden structural members. The edges, in particular, need to be supported.

Be sure all nail or screwheads are set below the surface of the wallboard. Large holes or openings should be patched before you begin (see *Plaster Patching*, page 199). You can't expect joint compound to fill more than seams and nail dimples.

Tape must be applied to each of the seams, both on flat walls and in corners. I prefer the self-adhesive fiberglass mesh tape, though some professionals still insist that paper tape is better.

Narrow Knives First. Sequence is everything in finishing wallboard joints. Start with a narrow knife, say, four inches wide, and apply the first coat. Center the blade on the joint, and cover the taped seam with joint compound.

The purpose of the first coat isn't cosmetic, but structural: you're filling the gaps, not smoothing the surface. Don't worry about keeping it perfectly smooth, but do be sure that there are no high spots that stand proud of the surface of the wallboard.

The second coat of joint compound is applied in a thinner, broader band, using a broad knife, perhaps six inches across. The approach is the same, as you should center the blade on the seam, but this time you should take care to keep the surface as smooth as possible. It'll make the next pass (and the sanding thereafter) easier.

The third coat is the one that really counts. This one is applied with a wide taping knife (ten inches or so), and should be quite thin. If the first two coats were applied carefully and evenly, a third coat should do the job, though in some cases a touch-up with a fourth coat may save a lot of sanding time.

Sanding the Wall Smooth. Some professionals are so proficient with their taping knives that they can trowel their joints smooth: A few easy strokes, and the wall is done. For most people, however, there are bumps and beads and trowel marks that must be sanded off.

Buy drywall sandpaper to do the job. It resembles wire mesh screen, with an open weave that doesn't clog as easily as regular sandpaper. You can also buy specially made devices to which sandpaper is clamped. These

THE SKIM COAT

Traditional plastering consists of three separate coats of plaster. The first two, called the brown and scratch coats, are coarse, often with sand, horsehair, and other binders added to the mix. The third or finish coat is a smoother blend, made of water and finely ground lime and plaster.

The three-coat method, which requires strips of wood or metal lath for reinforcement, is relatively rare today. Its advantages remain, as it's durable, adds significantly to soundproofing, and, in the opinion of many people, has more character. Yet because it is both labor- and material-intensive, it can be prohibitively expensive.

sanders have a flat, trowel-like bottom and handles, so they can be used like sanding blocks. Broom-handle and swivel attachments are also available for sanding ceilings and wall surfaces beyond easy reach.

Take special care when sanding the feathered edge of the compound where the paper surface is exposed. The paper can very easily be abraded and torn, so keep your sanding there to a minimum.

Be sure you wear a mask when sanding drywall. The dust generated isn't toxic, but it's only sensible to avoiding inhaling the powdery residue.

Wet sandpaper and wet sponge sanders are available for drywall work. Wet sanding limits the amount of fine dust that gets into the air.

Other Options. There are also a range of new tools on the market for applying joint compound. One, called a bazooka, contains a reservoir of compound that feeds dir-

ectly through the tool onto the joints being taped. Tools for applying tape (called banjos) are time-savers, especially in the hands of professionals. For one room, such machines probably aren't sensible investments. On the other hand, if you are planning to do the taping work in an entire house, consider buying the more sophisticated equipment.

The layers of joint compound on wallboard seam don't have to be limited to three, but typically the first layer is a bed for the tape; the second broadens to four or five inches, covering the tape and most of the beveled edge of the drywall; and the third feathers off to the finished surface.

There is, however, a middle ground between three-coat plastering and simply taping and coating the seams between sheets of wallboard. The skim-coat approach, which involves the application of a single, eighth-inch-thick layer of plaster over the entire wall or ceiling surface, is a compromise, offering something of the character and quality of real plaster with the economy and speed of wallboard.

Skim coating requires some skill with a trowel, so if you've never held a trowel in your hand, you would be well advised to start out with a little patching work first. But you don't have to apprentice to a professional plasterer for a year and a day to be able to produce a quite satisfactory finish.

You will need the same tools as the professional plasterer. The key ones are the plasterer's trowel; a carrier called a hawk, with its square top surface and handle below; a narrow trowel (or wallboard knife) for smoothing small areas and finishing around pipes; and a brush for applying water during final smoothing. Mixing equipment will be required, too, including an empty joint compound bucket or the equivalent, and a mixer bit for your drill.

Plasterer's Trowel. This tool has a flat, rectangular steel blade, with a wooden handle mounted along the center of its back. It can be purchased in a number of different sizes, but a four- by-ten-inch trowel is a manageable size for beginning plasterers. If you've used a similarly shaped trowel to smooth cement or apply mortar, the heft and feel of the trowel will be familiar. If trowels are new to you, however, some practice will be required to master the coordination required in manipulating plaster with the tool.

Other Trowels. There are many purpose-made plastering trowels available, with short blades and narrow blades, trowel handles and scraper handles, at inexpensive prices and higher ones. To begin with, a pair of tools, one perhaps two inches and another four inches wide, will be sufficient. Corner trowels are also valuable; to start with, though, a joint-compound corner trowel, if you have one on hand, will prove quite adequate.

The Hawk. This tool acts as a reservoir for the plasterer as he or she applies the material to the wall or ceiling. The hawk is held in one hand, a trowel in the other. The hawk has a flat top surface made of magnesium or aluminum, with a wooden or plastic handle beneath. The top is square with rounded corners; several sizes are available (twelve, thirteen, or fourteen inches square), but to begin smaller is probably better.

The Water Brush. Any high-quality brush will suffice for splashing water onto a plaster surface to be smoothed, but I favor a purpose-made blister brush. It has a pair of felt pads and sponges a surprising amount of water. It will outlast most other brushes, and will help in the smoothing process when applied directly to the plaster, because it has no bristles to fall out or to mark the surface.

The Preparation. Prepare the surface as you would for taping wallboard joints. However, use the less expensive variety of drywall that is designed for skim coating (it's often called blueboard because of the color of its paper surface). You can skim on regular wallboard, too, but you will need to apply a bonding agent first. This is put on with a roller, and is available at most building supply stores.

Apply fiberglass mesh tape to all joints between sheets of drywall and at all junctions of wallboard and molding. This will help prevent cracking. While not every professional insists on it, I also recommend covering the joints first with a base coat of a perlited plaster.

Wet the area first, then apply the coarse plaster as you would a first coat of joint compound, covering the tape but taking care to avoid leaving lumps or ridges that stand beyond the plane of the wallboard.

Making the Gage. I favor a mix of lime and finish plaster blended by hand in a gage (or gauge). The lime is mixed first in a bucket: pour in the water, add the plaster, and mix, preferably with a half-inch drill and mixing bit. The lime should have the consistency of heavy cream.

The gage, ready to mix, with plaster at the vortex of the lime.

Now for the gage. Pour a mound of the lime onto a mixing surface (a four-foot-by-four-foot sheet of plywood works nicely). Using a plasterer's trowel, shape it into a circle, empty in the middle, that resembles the mouth of a volcano. Pour water into the ring to a depth of an inch or more, then ladle in a mound of plaster, using a cup or other convenient receptacle. The amount of plaster and lime should be roughly equal.

Once the plaster is dampened, the mixing is done in a modified rowing motion, first pushing the two trowels away, then working the mixture back toward yourself.

Use two trowels to mix the ingredients, wetting the dry plaster first, then working the blend away from you, then back, in a modified rowing motion. When the concoction is uniform, you're ready. And you now have fifteen or twenty minutes before the plaster sets.

Applying the Plaster. Load up a hawk: Not too much at first, no more than you can handle. Don't attempt to do too big an area at first, either. Start with an area no larger than three feet square.

Working with a small amount on the trowel, apply the plaster to the wall with the tool held at a low angle to the surface. Push the plaster gently along the surface, with one long side of the trowel flush. Cover the area thoroughly, without worrying a great deal about smoothing it.

The first pass involves applying a thin (roughly an eighth-inch-thick) coat of plaster.

Once it's covered, go back over it with a small amount of plaster on your trowel. Apply more pressure this time (you may, in fact, remove as much plaster as you are applying in this pass). Work the surface over in parallel strokes, then do it again perpendicular to the previous pass. A third pass on the diagonal may be necessary. The surface should be fairly smooth, but don't worry about a mirrorlike finish, as the final smoothing is done with the assistance of a little water (see facing page).

As you proceed to apply plaster to adjacent areas, keep in mind that plastering shares with painting the old rule, "Keep a wet edge." Work in one direction, picking up where you left off.

The blister brush applies a little water to soften the surface . . .

Smoothing the Plaster. For smoothing, the plasterer's trowel is again held at a low angle to the fresh plaster surface. If the plaster has set up (hardened), you may need to add some water. Wipe the blister brush over the surface, and try again (a paintbrush dipped in water can also be used to splash the area).

As you smooth, your trowel will accumulate a fine paste as it scrapes the plaster. Use that to fill holes, scratches, trowel marks, or other indentations.

. . . allowing a smoother finish to be troweled.

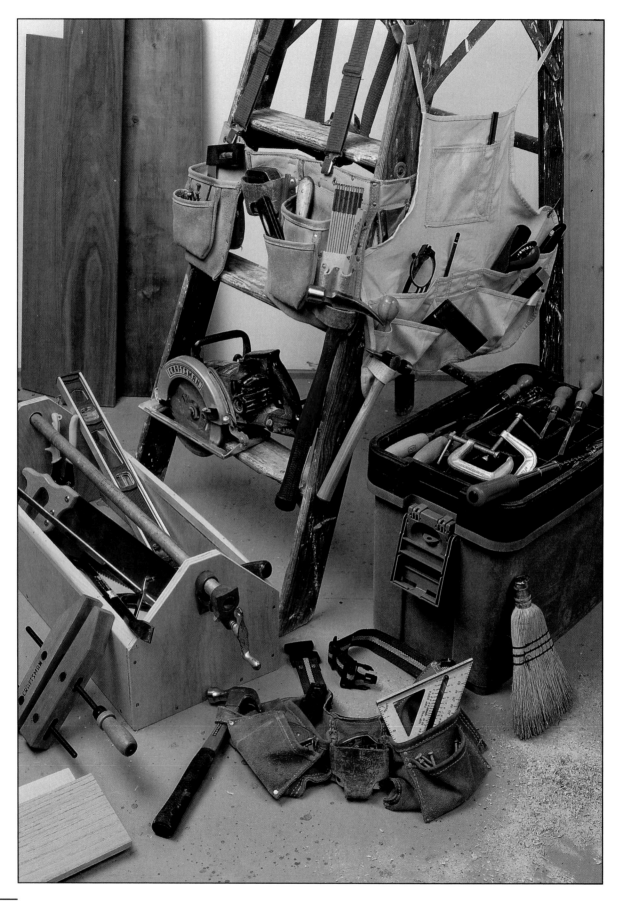

Chapter 17.
Storing and Transporting Your Tools

Too often, tools are taken for granted. A job gets done, and the tools get left behind in the attic or crawl space. Two months after you last used it, you find that wrench you were looking for two weeks ago. I know it's a homely truth, but still one that's beyond argument: A tool you cannot find is a useless tool.

The way to avoid the I-can't-find-it syndrome is to have appropriate containers for tool storage and transport. Several varieties of toolboxes and bags and belts are described below, but there are many other kinds, too. Like specialty toolboxes designed to lock securely into the bed of a pickup, or enormous storage cabinets for workshops, which are essentially closets that are built in or are too big to move readily.

However many tools you have, there's certainly a suitable container (or containers) that will store your tools safely and securely, yet provide you with easy access when needs arise. Remember, storing and transporting your tools is every bit as important as using them with respect and care in order to avoid breakage or loss.

TOOL CHESTS

The traditional tool chest – the size of a footlocker, with trays of neatly organized tools – is still to be found in antique shops, museums, and in the hands of craftsmen who consciously work within the hand-tool heritage. But for most people, such toolboxes are heavy, awkward, and less practical than some other designs.

The nature of the work you do with your tools must determine what sort of tool containers you require, but one practical option for a medium-sized selection of tools (that is, one with a couple of power tools, saws, hammers, framing square, a few dozen other tools) (see *The Basic Tool Kit,* page xviii) is an all-weather plastic toolbox. One popular design has an open area in the base that functions rather like a bin for storing your electric drill and portable circular saw, and has a tray for pliers, drivers, a chisel, and a variety of other tools.

There are many tool chest options. Consider carefully what you need – not only to contain and carry your tools, but for ease of use in the spot where you'll be using them. You will want a box that will fill all your needs, and prove durable as well.

A turn-of-the century tool chest, complete with hammer, mallet, chisels, brace, and planes.

MAKING A BASIC
CARRY-ALL BOX

The tool carrier is easy to see into, and easy to pull tools out of.

the attic or garage, or even across the street for a job.

This one was made from pieces of scrap plywood left around the shop after a cabinet making job. But you may wish to make yours from a plywood made from waterproof glue, or from solid wood stock. Whatever the material, it should be at least three-quarters of an inch thick.

As for overall size, I made mine large enough to accommodate a framing square, a two-foot level, and a number of other tools; smaller versions are very handy, too, especially if your storage space is limited. Amend the dimensions as you see fit to suit your needs.

In joining the sides to the bottom, I ripped rabbets into which the bottom and sides are set (see *Table-Saw Techniques,* page 76). That isn't necessary, but does add strength to the whole carrier.

One alternative to a commercially made toolbox is to make a tool carrier of your own. The tool carrier described here isn't designed for storing your tools in – it's open to the elements and to sticky fingers. But I've found that carriers of this design are very handy for taking the tools I need into

I finished off the box with a pair of holes, centered, in the end pieces, through which I slid a pipe clamp. It's amazing how many times that pipe clamp finds itself leading a double life, acting as a handle on the way to the job, only to be put to use as a clamp once we get there.

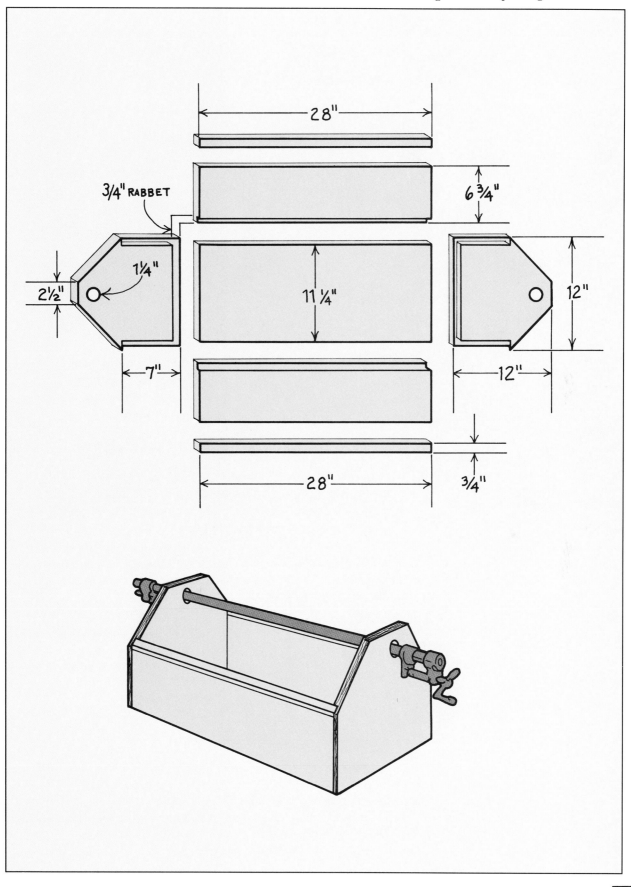

Here are two smaller alternatives to a full-sized toolbox. I find the tool bag is perfect for tools, like plastering trowels, that you remove from the bag when you get to the work-site (rummaging through these bags when full to find a nail set or other small tool falls somewhere between irritating and impossible). On the other hand, a small carpenter's toolbox is very suitable to work out of: it's easy to see into it and to remove (and return) tools to its trays and bottom bay.

TOOL BELTS AND POUCHES

When it comes to performing many jobs, a tool belt or tool pouch can provide easy access to the tools required. Carpentry and electrical work, in particular, have specially adapted tool carriers that fasten immediately on your person, like a carpenter's belt or an electrician's pouch. Then you don't have to hunt around for that pair of pliers or your tape measure; they're right there where they belong, and come to hand like the marshal's six-gun from its holster.

Like toolboxes, tool belts, pouches, and aprons can be purchased large and small, for light or heavy duty. You may find it necessary to have two or more for different kinds of jobs, or one of average size that you adapt for varying tasks. Tailor your purchase to your needs.

THE PORTABLE WORKBENCH

This small, portable workbench has been around for barely thirty years. Created by Englishman Ron Hickman, an automobile designer by trade, it has sold in the tens of millions of units under the trade name Workmate.

One reason for its popularity is that this device fits many different needs; another is that it can do so in many, many different places. Its aluminum and steel frame folds, so it can be easily stored and transported. The Workmate is adaptable, too, as its legs can be folded up or down to provide the option of two steady working surfaces, one at workbench height (thirty-two inches), the other adapted to sawing at a lower, twenty-four-inch height. A foot board at the front allows for the worker's weight to stabilize the bench when heavy workpieces are being worked or considerable force employed.

The Workmate's ancestry is ancient, even if its space-age plastic hardware and laminated plywood worktop are not. It's really a simplified workbench, one that folds up and down. The holes in its surface accommodate pegs or stops at a variety of locations, allowing

The Workmate can be adapted at the work-site to perform many tasks, including serving as a clamping or sawing surface. Here we put it to use as a stand for a portable table saw.

for clamping of a multitude of regular or oddly shaped objects.

The top surface consists of two sturdy plywood boards that can be moved into a range of positions with one another. Cranks at each end transform the boards into jaws that can grip workpieces of a variety of thicknesses, ranging from a fraction of an inch up to about eighteen inches. The edges of the plywood surfaces have V-shapes, allowing for pipes to be gripped for cutting.

The Workmate isn't a magic solution in every workplace, but it is light, quite durable, and surprisingly flexible. Its portability is perhaps its greatest asset, as it makes it possible to perform a number of different cutting, shaping, clamping, and other tasks just about anywhere there's room to set it up.

Keep in mind, however, that it isn't designed to be stored outdoors, as the plywood jaws on its surface will delaminate if exposed to dampness over a period of time. The Workmate also works best if, like Dorothy's Tin Man, its joints are given an occasional dose of lubricating oil.

Around the shop, I find that a cloth apron works best, one with pockets for a few nails or screws, one for my tape, a hammer loop, and a narrow pocket for my utility knife. For light-duty on-site work, I have a medium-weight belt with four pouches, a tape measure holder, and a hammer loop. But for framing, a sturdier belt is necessary, in order to handle the larger nails, heavier hammer, and more athletic demands of the work.

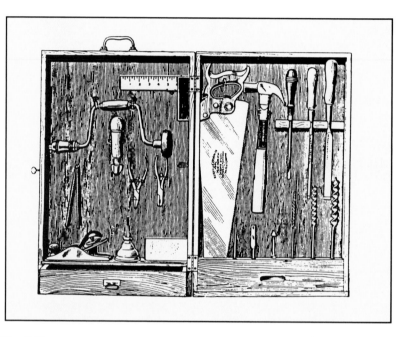

STORAGE BACK HOME

In the companion volume to this book, *Bob Vila's Workshop*, I'll talk at length about stowing your tools properly and safely back home. But a few of the basics are as follows:

Keep Your Tools Dry. That's the first rule. A damp cellar is not appropriate: metal tools are inclined to rust, and no wood or electrical component benefits from dampness. Keep all of them off the floor of the garage or other potentially wet areas.

Keep Them Organized. Keeping track of your tools needn't be time-consuming. One short session on a Saturday morn-

ing – and an accompanying resolution – is all it takes. Just assign your tools proper storage spots, and put each one back in place when you finish using it. Believe me, getting in the habit will save you time, money, and stress.

Keep Them Secure. One important factor in keeping track of your tools is monitoring their use by others. If you have young children in the house, be sure your tools are stored securely so that they are not within reach of little hands – hands that can misplace tools in an instant or, worse yet, harm themselves. High shelves, locked closets, off-limits lockers, or

good toolboxes can help insure safety and security.

Other Suggestions. There are as many guidelines as there are tools (and sets of instructions). But do keep in mind that power tools are expensive, dangerous, and subject to damage from moisture, so they should be stored with special care. High shelves or a covered toolbox or carrier are good storage spots. Never leave power tools plugged in.

Another important consideration is that shaping tools, like planes and chisels, have sharp blades that are easily nicked if they are carelessly stored. Designate areas for their storage that are safe and appropriate.

APPENDICES

CONTENTS

The purpose of this book is to offer some basic guidance about the uses and usage of tools that a typical homeowner might require in maintenance and construction projects. Given space limitations, it simply isn't possible to discuss at length many, indeed most, of the remarkable array of building materials now available. Yet I believe it is necessary to offer some rudimentary information about the principal material from which most homes are built and the fasteners most often put to use in the building process.

In the following pages, then, you will find a brief introduction to wood and its terminology as well as to nails, screws, and bolts.

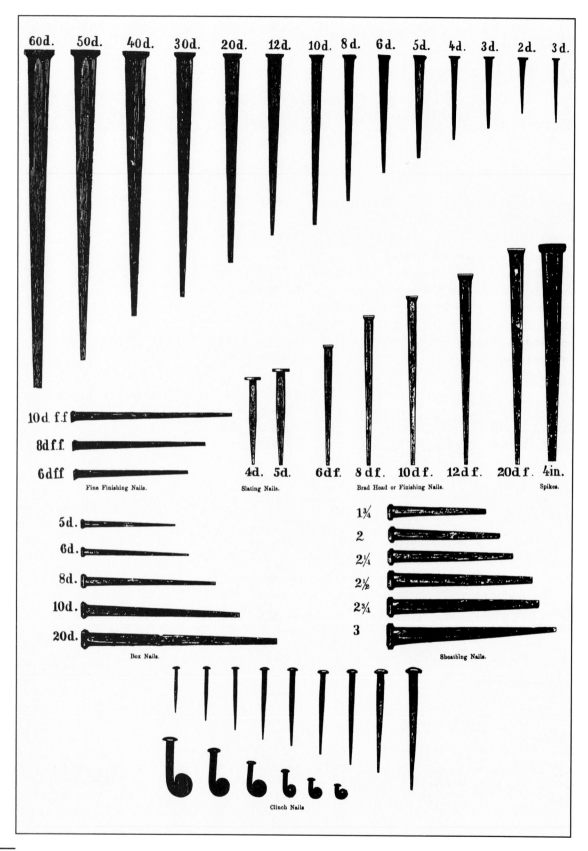

60d. 50d. 40d. 30d. 20d. 12d. 10d. 8d. 6d. 5d. 4d. 3d. 2d. 3d.

10d. f.f
8d f.f.
6d ff
Fine Finishing Nails.

4d. 5d.
Slating Nails.

6d f. 8d f. 10d f. 12d f. 20d f. 4 in.
Brad Head or Finishing Nails.   Spikes.

5d.
6d.
8d.
10d.
20d.
Box Nails.

1¾
2
2¼
2½
2¾
3
Sheathing Nails.

Clinch Nails

214

Appendix I
Mastering Lumber Numbers

Entire books have been written about wood. As a matter of fact, whole *shelves* of books exist on the subject.

Wood is a diverse material, given the many species of trees that are harvested, milled, and processed. It comes in a tremendous assortment of colors, in an amazing array of sizes, and all in all is an extraordinarily good bargain. Maybe you've guessed: I'm among those people for whom wood is a friendly, familiar presence. I trust it to do a multitude of jobs and I get pleasure from working with it.

When first cut down, wood contains a high percentage of moisture and must be properly dried or "seasoned." The strength and elasticity of the material increases as it dries, whether the process is done slowly by exposure to the sun and air or more quickly by such artificial means as kiln drying. There is a continuing debate among professional woodworkers as to which is best (most look down their noses at kiln drying), but for most construction purposes it really doesn't matter as long as the wood is relatively dry.

Wood can be processed in countless ways to produce products (methyl alcohol, for example, as well as turpentine, charcoal, and wood tar). But for construction purposes, the trunk of the tree is generally cut into timber, lumber, or boards. Some woods are cut into very thin layers for making veneers or plywood.

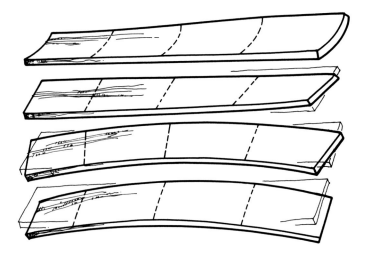

One risk of wood that isn't properly dried is that it will (top to bottom) cup, twist, crook, or bow. As this drawing illustrates, each of those terms connotes a distinct flaw.

A BOARD IS NOT A BOARD IS NOT A BOARD

That's dimension lumber on the right (one two-by-three, atop a two-by-four, six, eight, and ten, respectively). The boards on the left are a one-by-ten, eight, six, and four, in ascending order, with a piece of five-quarter-by-six on top.

Lengths of wood that emerge from a sawmill are not all boards – even if they are to be measured in board feet.

The largest sawmill products are called *timber*; *lumber* is next; and *boards* the smallest of the categories. Technically, timber is wood of a dimension greater than five inches by five inches; boards are of a thickness of one inch or less; lumber falls in between.

Keep in mind, however, that those are the dimensions before planing, so the milled lumber you buy as building materials today has been planed to a smaller dimension. Thus, a two-by-four is actually one and a half inches by three and a half inches, having had a quarter inch milled off each side (though it's still called lumber); one-inch boards are actually three-quarters of an inch thick.

When wood is milled, it is also sorted and categorized. The system is relatively complex, particularly when both hardwoods and softwoods are considered. In practice, however, the vast majority of construction projects undertaken will use one or another variety of softwood, typically pine, fir, or spruce.

The grading system for white pine alone consists of about ten levels. If you are going to work with wood professionally, I'd suggest you consult a basic reference work on wood and master some of the subtleties. But most of us need to know only a couple of basic facts.

First, "clear" means free of knots; the fewer the knots in a piece of stock, the more expensive it is likely to be. Second, when looking for boards to do high-quality finish work, you might want to mumble the simple epithet "Number 1" in the general direction of your lumber supplier. That will generally get you high quality, relatively clear wood for moldings, casings, and projects that require a fairly high level of finish. Number 2 boards will have more knots, be of quite good quality, but cost a great deal less. Boards are sold in nominal one-inch thicknesses (actual thickness: three-quarters of an inch) and in so-called five-quarter (5/4; actual thickness: one inch). Four-inch, six-inch, eight-inch, and ten-inch-wide boards are generally available (actual widths: three and a half, five and a half, seven and a quarter, and nine and a quarter inches). Lengths vary, but eight- and sixteen-foot stock is usual.

In buying dimension lumber for framing, the terminology is a lot less important than how straight the two-bys are, whether they have knots that will weaken them, and whether there are splits. You'll also find when you move into larger stock that fir, for example, is much stronger (and more expensive) than spruce or pine, but better suited to wider spans for floor joists or longer rafters. When building outdoor or damp-area structures, pressure-treated lumber is another choice. This is regular lumber that has been injected or soaked in chemicals to prevent decay and rot.

Standard dimension lumber, as well as pressure-treated stock, is sold in a wide array of two-inch pieces (again, the dimensions refer to sizes before planing, so nominal two-by stock is actually one and a half inches thick). Two-by-threes, fours, sixes, eights, tens, and twelves are standard (actual widths: three and a half, five and a half, seven and a quarter, nine and a quarter, and eleven and a quarter inches). Common lengths are eight, ten, twelve, fourteen, sixteen, twenty, and twenty-four feet. Four-inch thicknesses are also sold in some widths.

Whatever the kind or size of wood you're buying, the unit of measurement is usually the board foot; one board foot is the equivalent of the cubic content of a piece of wood twelve inches by twelve inches square and one inch thick. Wood is usually priced on a board-foot basis, though some specialized stock like moldings is sold by the linear foot.

Plywood. Plywood is made of thin layers ("plies") of wood that are glued together to form panels. Each ply is glued with its grain perpendicular to the adjacent plies for added strength. Many varieties of plywood are sold. Finish plywood has at least one quality surface, while sheathing plywood, intended for use beneath siding, has rougher surfaces. Most plywood is stamped with a letter designation that indicates the quality of its surfaces. The gradation extends from A to D, so a sheet graded A-A, for example, has quality surfaces on both sides, while A-C has one good surface and one rougher one.

Inspect the wood you are going to buy before you buy it. In many lumberyards, the boards sold are all essentially what the old cliché "run of the mill" was coined to describe. Which is to say: Nothing special, average, or worse. If your supplier will let you, cherry-pick the pile and select the clearest, least blemished stock. At the very least, however, make sure that what you're paying for at the counter is worth putting in your truck or on your roof rack.

hardwood (har-dwud) n. *The wood of a deciduous tree, as distinct from that of a coniferous tree ("softwood"). Hardwoods include oak, maple, cherry, walnut, ash, and birch; pine, fir, redwood, and cedar are softwoods. N.B. The terms softwood and hardwood do* not *in every instance indicate hardness of the wood, as some wood from evergreen trees is harder than that from some leaf-bearing trees.*

In brief, Grade A means the surface is blemish-free; Grade B may have plugged knotholes; Grade C may have small knotholes and splits (checks). Relatively larger knotholes are permitted in Grade D.

Plywood is sold in a variety of thicknesses, commonly from a quarter to three-quarters of an inch. Some plywood is cemented using waterproof glues for exterior applications, and graded using the code "EXT" for exterior use (conversely, plywood marked "INT" is intended for interior use). Four-foot by eight-foot sheets of most plywood are standard.

Appendix II
Nails for All Occasions

If a child's first real tool is a hammer, then, most likely, his or her first fastener will be a nail. There's something quite elemental (and, for that matter, elementary) about banging nails. A lot of us grown-ups find it therapeutic at times, so why shouldn't a youngster?

Nails are used to fasten pieces of wood together. There are exceptions to that statement, of course, like roofing nails that attach asphalt shingles to a wood frame or masonry nails that affix wood and other materials to masonry surfaces. But nails, for the most part, are wood fasteners, used by the thousands in constructing not only wood-frame houses but in assembling and attaching the constituent parts in almost anything made of wood.

Nails are generally available and inexpensive. Yet that hasn't always been the case. Until the nineteenth century, nails were made entirely by hand, individually shaped by a blacksmith wielding a hammer he brought clanging down on a length of hot iron rod. Since the points and heads alike were the product of many hammer strokes, nail-making was labor-intensive– and every nail was to be cherished. As a result, many wood joints in antique homes and wooden objects were joined by other means, such as wooden pins, rather than with nails or screws.

In the nineteenth century, cut nails were the rule. Made from a sheet of iron, usually about an eighth of an inch thick, cut nails were sliced off the sheet by a machine that resembled a paper cutter. As a result, cut nails are rectangular in section, little more than narrow strips of iron. The oldest have handmade heads, too, though by the second quarter of the nineteenth century the technology had advanced enough that machines could head the nails.

About 1890 the round-shafted nails we regard as the norm (the wire nail, as it is more precisely known) came to dominate in construction. The wire nail owes its popularity in large part to the fact that it is inexpensive to manufacture and easy to use.

When selecting nails for a given job, you must consider the type of work (flooring? framing? finish trim?) and the weight of the nail required (strong enough to do the job, but not so sturdy that it splits the wood). But don't forget the length factor: An easy rule of thumb is a nail should be roughly two and a half times the thickness of the piece to be fastened.

When buying nails, be sure to specify size, kind, and whether they have been treated in any way. For example, in framing a deck you might order ten pounds of galvanized twelve-penny common nails (abbreviated as "10# of 12d common, galvanized"). If you forget the word "galvanized," the nails will rust; omit the "common" and you may get small-headed finishing nails. Make sure you order what you want.

THE NAIL AS WE KNOW IT

The parts of the nail are the head, shank or shaft, point, and the gripper marks – slight grooves incised into the shank near the head of most (but not all) varieties of nails.

The nail functions by displacing wood fibers when it is pounded into the workpiece, and the pressure exerted against the shaft by the displaced wood provides the holding power.

Nails are sometimes referred to by their length in inches, but more often the traditional terminology of the penny is used. Dating from the days when nails cost a lot more than they do today, the term *penny* identifies the size of a nail. In an earlier era, one hundred nails of a certain size cost three pennies; hence the name "threepenny nail." One hundred nails of the next size cost four pennies, and so on. The pricing structure has long since been abandoned (today, nails are sold by the pound), but the nomenclature of the penny survives.

The word penny is often abbreviated in the British style by the letter **d** (for *denarius*, a Roman coin) — as in "3d nails," for example, to identify "threepenny nails." Nails shorter than one inch are generally identified by fractions of an inch rather than by pennies.

Wire nails are indeed the rule today, but not all wire nails are the same. They vary in size and in other ways as well. Various nails are manufactured for specific purposes, with differently proportioned and shaped heads and shafts.

Nails are made of brass, aluminum, and copper, though most often of steel. The steel may be plain or galvanized, the latter being the right choice for damp applications where a rust-resistant nail is required.

The following are eleven of the most common kinds of nails.

Common Nail. As the name suggests, these are your everyday nails. Used for rough construction work, the common nail can be purchased in lengths varying from one to six inches (2d to 60d). The largest common nails are colloquially known as spikes.

Box Nail. These look like common nails, but are thinner. This means they are less likely to cause splits in the wood; as they displace less wood, they also have less holding power, so are not generally used where structural strength is critical. Box nails are generally available in lengths from one inch to three and a half inches.

Finishing Nail. Finishing nails are (surprise, surprise) used for finish work. When the nailhead will show in the final product (as with moldings, for example), finishing nails are often used because their barrel-shaped heads are small and can be driven below the surface of the wood using a nail set (a technique called *countersinking;* see page 139). Finishing nails are generally available in lengths ranging from one to four inches (2d to 20d).

Casing Nail. A near relation of the finishing nail, the casing nail is slightly larger and has increased holding power. It is most often used for attaching moldings such as window and door casings where added strength is required.

Brad. Brads are essentially diminutive finishing nails, proportionately smaller in diameter and length (one inch or less). They are used in making frames, attaching plywood paneling, and in cabinetwork.

Roofing Nail. Roofing nails have disproportionately large, round heads and heavier shafts for their length. They are designed to hold roofing materials in place, in particular composition and asphalt-based materials. In order to resist rust, roofing nails are heavily galvanized or made of aluminum. Three-quarter-inch to one-and-three-quarter-inch sizes are usual; the penny system is not used in reference to roofing nails.

Masonry Nail. Several types of masonry nails are sold; all are designed to be driven into brick or concrete walls. These hard nails may be rectangular in section or have fluted shafts, but all are hardened to resist bending and breaking as they are driven into almost rock-hard materials. Given the nature of masonry materials, be sure to wear safety glasses or goggles when nailing masonry nails, as flying chips pose a danger to your eyes.

Cut Flooring Nail. The lone surviving direct descendant of the once-dominant cut nail is the flooring nail. These nails are large, strong, and are often used in a nailing machine.

Spiral Flooring Nail. Spiral flooring nails feature a spiraled shaft and were traditionally used for nailing subfloors. Nail guns and the specially designed nails used in them have superseded these nails in much construction work today.

Annular Ring Nail. Often sold in galvanized steel, annular ring nails are commonly used as siding nails, to hold clapboards or shingles in place, or for underlayment or paneling. They are thin, lined with rings for added holding power, and resistant to rust.

Duplex Nail. This is a variation of the common nail. Featuring a second head formed a short distance down the shaft from the end of the nail, the duplex nail is used for temporary construction (like scaffolding and staging) because it can be driven snug, yet be easily removed.

Other Nails. Drywall nails, which feature rings on their shafts, are sold for hanging wallboard; their heads are traditionally driven

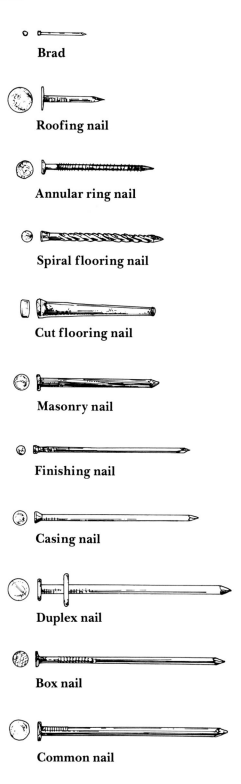

Of the many varieties of nails sold today, these are the most commonly used.

Brad

Roofing nail

Annular ring nail

Spiral flooring nail

Cut flooring nail

Masonry nail

Finishing nail

Casing nail

Duplex nail

Box nail

Common nail

slightly below the surface of the plaster panel (the hammer stroke creates a dimple that is then filled in with joint compound or plaster). Cement-coated nails are roughly the size and weight of box nails, but are coated with a resin for added holding power. They're used to nail outside sheathing.

Many of the varieties of nails discussed above are also sold in magazines for use in air-powered nailers. Framing, finishing, and roofing nails, as well as brads and flooring nails, are commonly available for such equipment.

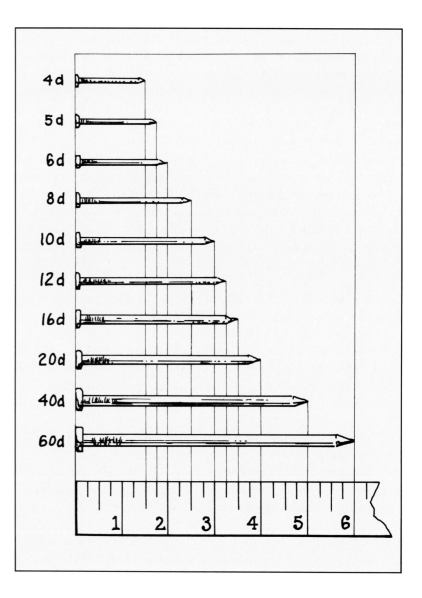

Nail sizes: One inch to six inches, 2d to 60d.

Appendix III
A Miscellany of Screws and Bolts

If you were surprised by the number of different kinds of nails, you may be equally amazed to learn of the remarkable variety of screws and bolts. Again, we can't cover them all, but I will discuss here the types that you are most likely to require in doing construction and renovation work.

Like nails, screws haven't always been the inexpensive and commonplace fasteners that they are in our time. Until 1846, in fact, screws didn't even have points (in that year a screw-pointing machine was patented). Early handmade screws were expensive, of course, and harder to use than their modern counterparts (not least because a pilot hole had to be drilled, no matter what the material, because of the blunt screw ends).

Screws, now, as then, are used to fasten wood or metal parts together. The threads on their shanks grip the workpiece directly. Bolts, in contrast, thread into nuts and indirectly bind the workpieces together. Both bolts and screws can be withdrawn from the workpiece at any time, which gives them an advantage over nails. They also pull workpieces together, hold them tightly, and in general have a neater, more finished appearance than nails.

The parts of the screw are the head, shank, threads, and (these days) the point. The parts of an individual thread are referred to as the crest and root, for the raised and incised portions of the thread. Screws are made in varying thicknesses, ranging from less than a sixteenth of an inch in diameter to three-eighths of an inch or more. However, diameters are specified by the gauge of the screw, with the smallest common size being Number 5 (about an eighth of an inch in diameter) ranging up to Number 24 (about three-eighths of an inch). Thus, a fourteen-gauge screw, for example, has a quarter-inch shaft.

Screwheads come in several different designs. In addition to variations in their openings and the tools used to drive them (see *Screwheads,* page 143), screwheads differ in profile, as some have flat heads, others round or oval ones. Flat screwheads require a countersunk hole in order to lie flush, while the heads of round-head screws remain above the surface of the workpiece (typically, round-head screws are used for fastening hardware or other metal components to wood). So-called oval-head or dome-head screws have curved heads with lower profiles, so they protrude less from the workpiece. Like flat-head screws, they require countersinking. Lag screws and some others have hexagonal heads, designed to be turned with a wrench or sockets.

When buying bolts or screws, you must specify the kind you desire, their gauge and length, and the material from which they are made. For example, in assembling a set of book-shelves, you might wish to use twelve-gauge, inch-and-a-quarter-long wood screws with flat heads.

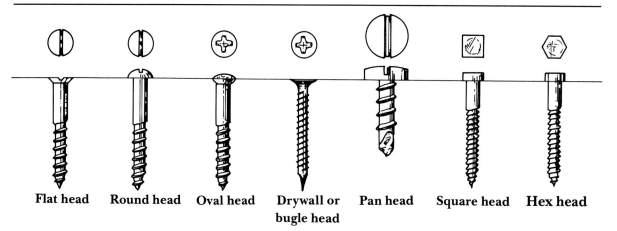

Flat head **Round head** **Oval head** **Drywall or bugle head** **Pan head** **Square head** **Hex head**

In general, a screw is driven by a screwdriver, allen wrench, or other device whose tip fits into an opening in the head of the fastener. The shaft may be cylindrical or conical, but whatever its shape it has helical ribs called threads. A bolt, in contrast, is a threaded metal rod or pin with a wrench head (typically hexagonal or square) around which a wrench or other device is fitted for tightening or loosening; the other end is secured using a nut. Wood screws have pointed (or gimlet) tips; bolts are blunt-ended.

The basic varieties and screws and bolts are these:

Wood Screw. A wood screw, as its name suggests, is intended for use in fastening wood or other materials to wood. Wood screws have tapered shanks, and are often threaded for roughly two-thirds of their length. They may be purchased in flat-, round-, or dome-head profiles. Lengths vary greatly, from fractions of an inch to five inches or more.

Phillips-head, slotted, and other drives are all commonly available. Brass, steel, aluminum, stainless steel, plated steel, and corrosion-proof materials are all used in making wood screws.

Drywall Screw. In profile, the drywall screw has a bugle-shaped neck, its head usually a Phillips slot (although finer-headed varieties are also available with a square drive). The thread generally runs the full length of the screw. Various sizes are sold, including one inch, inch and five-eighths, and three inches. The drywall screw is most often used to fasten wallboard, but is also suited to fastening softwood and man-made woods.

Machine Screw. Used to assemble metal parts, machine screws are usually made of steel or brass, with flat, round, oval, or cylindrical (called fillister) heads. Though it may also be used with a nut, the machine screw most often threads directly into a tapped hole in a metal workpiece.

Like other screws, machine screws are sold in varying lengths and gauges, but also with differing thread pitches. Thus, in buying machine screws the length, gauge, and pitch must be specified, as in

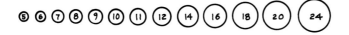

"I need a box of 8-32 x ½ screws, please." The 8 is the gauge; the 32 refers to the threads, namely that there are thirty-two threads per inch; the one-half to the length of the screw.

Sheetmetal Screw. Sheetmetal screws are designed to fasten together metal elements, like stovepipe, flashing, and other metal components. They are self-tapping screws, available in brass or steel, and with flat, round, oval, or fillister heads.

Lag Screw. Referred to interchangeably as a lag screw or a lag bolt (lag bolt is perhaps a more precise name), this fastener has a tapered shaft, with coarse threads that run about half its length. Lag bolt heads are hexagonal or square.

The lag bolt is essentially a longer and stronger version of the ordinary wood screw, though its head is driven using a wrench or socket. One common household use is in deck construction. Typically, lag bolts can be purchased in three-inch to six-inch lengths, though longer lags of up to a foot or more in length are to be found.

Stove Bolt. At one time, the name stove bolt distinguished bolts with coarse threads (machine bolts typically having finer threading). However, the term as used today generally means a bolt intended for use with a nut (as distinct from a machine screw or bolt). The entire length of a stove bolt's shank is threaded. Stove bolts are usually found in lengths ranging from three-eighths of an inch to four inches, in diameters from about an eighth to three-eighths inch.

Carriage Bolt. Carriage bolts most often have rounded heads, with a shaped shaft immediately beneath the head. Usually the shape is square (though finned and ribbed varieties are also sold). Whatever its shape, the shaft neck is set into an opening in the workpiece, and prevents the bolt from turning as the nut is tightened or loosened. Typically, only a third to a half of the bolt's length is threaded.

Carriage bolts are sold in a wide variety of lengths, from an inch or less to twenty inches or more, in diameters from about three-sixteenths to three-quarters of an inch. Flat washers are generally used between the nuts and wood surfaces (see next page).

Machine Bolt. These are rodlike threaded bolts with wrench heads that are square or hexagonal in shape. (See also *Machine Screw,* page 224.) When used with a nut, two wrenches are required to tighten the machine bolt.

Washers and Nuts. Flat disks called washers are used to prevent the marring of the material being fastened, to help secure the bolt or nut, or to cover a hole that is larger than the head of the screw or bolt. Nuts, like screws, come in a vast array of shapes and sizes, including those with hexagonal, square, wing, and acorn (or cap-head) shapes, with a flange attached (flanged nuts look as if a washer is an integral part of the nut), and other varieties as well.

Hangers, Wall Fasteners, and Anchors. As many types of screws and bolts as there are, there are even more hangers, anchors, and fasteners. There are molly bolts and toggle bolts; screw eyes and shoulder hooks; lead, hollow-wall, nylon, and plastic anchors; and a considerable number of other options.

I can't introduce you to all of these miscellaneous bits and pieces here, but I can offer you one piece of advice that, if you follow it, will save you time and money dozens of times in the future.

Find yourself a well-stocked and — this is just as important — well-*staffed* hardware store. Get acquainted with a clerk or two who really knows his or her stuff, and make it a habit to consult with that person when you're taking on a job around the house. With the many products available and the new ones that are appearing with regularity, having an ally at the hardware store is essential.

If the length of a nail should be two and a half times the thickness of the piece to be fastened, then a screw should be roughly three times its thickness (yet not so long that it protrudes from the opposite side of the workpiece). The screw's diameter should not represent more than about 10 percent of the wood's thickness, so as to lessen the possibility of splitting the stock.

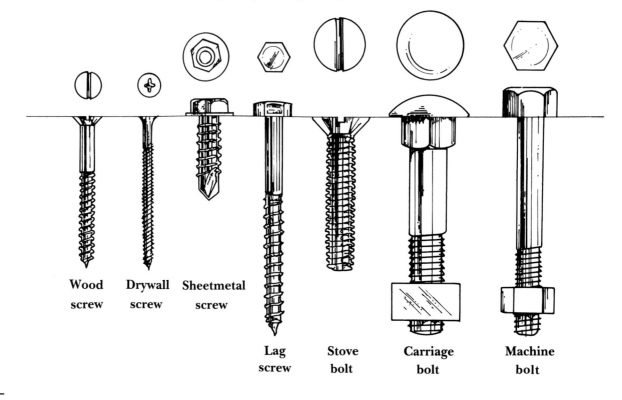

Wood screw   Drywall screw   Sheetmetal screw   Lag screw   Stove bolt   Carriage bolt   Machine bolt

G L O S S A R Y

A

Abrasive Paper. Sandpaper.

Adjustable Try Square. See *Bevel Gauge.*

Adjustable Wrench. Tool designed to tighten or loosen nuts and bolts that relies upon a movable jaw to accommodate different-sized heads.

Allen Wrench. Hexagonal in section, tool used to tighten or loosen set screws. Also known as "allen key" and *Hex Wrench.*

Angle Bevel. See *Bevel Gauge.*

Anti-Kickback Fingers. Metal grippers found on many table saws that help prevent the workpiece from being propelled backwards and hitting the sawyer.

Auger. Drill bit for use in a *brace.*

Aviation Snips. See *Snips.*

Awl. A sharp, pointed tool used for marking or for making starter holes for nails or screws. Also known as a *Scribing Awl* or *Scribe.*

B

Backsaw. A flat-bladed handsaw with a reinforced spine that insures the blade remains rigid when sawing.

Ball Peen Hammer. Metalworking hammer with a head that has a hemispherical peen on the end opposite the face. Also called an *Engineer's Hammer.*

Basin Wrench. Purpose-made plumbing tool used to connect or disconnect the nuts that fasten the faucet or other fittings that provide water to a sink.

Beetle. Two-handed mallet used in timber framing.

Bevel. An angled edge of more or less than ninety degrees.

Bevel Gauge. An adjustable tool consisting of a handle and blade used for transferring and marking angles. Also known as a *Sliding Bevel, Angle Bevel, Bevel Square, Sliding T-Bevel,* and *Adjustable Try Square.*

Bevel Square. See *Bevel Gauge.*

Bird's-Mouth. The angled cut made in a rafter where the lumber intersects the wall.

Bit. The replaceable cutting tool used in a drill that performs the actual cutting.

Bitstock. See *Brace.*

Blind-Nailing. Nailing technique in which nails are driven at about a forty-five-degree angle into the tongue of the board; the groove of the next piece is slid over the tongue, obscuring the nail.

Blister Brush. Felt brush used by plasterers to apply water to a drying surface in order to extend the plaster's working time.

Block Plane. One-handed *plane* used for trimming end stock and in finish carpentry.

Board. Standard milled wood stock three-quarters of an inch thick. See also *Lumber* and *Timber.*

Board Foot. The unit of measure for wood equivalent to the cubic content of a piece of wood twelve inches by twelve inches square and one inch thick.

Boat Level. See *Torpedo Level.*

Bolster. See *Brick Chisel.*

Bolt Cutters. Heavy-duty cutting device with compound-action jaw used to cut metal stock, including bolts, nails, rods, and chains.

Bow Saw. A small frame saw, typically one with a blade tightened through the use of a toggle stick. See also *Frame Saw.*

Brace. A hand-powered crank device used with specialized blades called bits to drill holes. Various designs include joist braces and corner braces. Also called a *Bitstock.* See also *Bit* and *Drill.*

Breast Drill. Large hand-powered drill with a breastplate that is used to apply added pressure while drilling.

Brick Chisel. Chisel designed for use in cutting bricks. Also known as a *Bolster* and *Brick Set.*

Brick Set. See *Brick Chisel.*

Broad Knife. Taping knife with a blade in the four-to six-inch range.

Building Paper. The material, often asphalt-impregnated "tarpaper," applied to the sheathing prior to the application of the finished siding or roof material; also called "felt."

Burr. A small area of roughness produced in a smoothing or sawing operation.

Butt Chisel. Short, all-purpose wood chisel.

C

Cabinet Scraper. See *Hand Scraper.*

Cable Ripper. Cutting tool used to slice outer insulation from electrical cable.

Carbide. A hardening mixture of metals, especially tungsten carbide, used to strengthen cutting edges and teeth.

Carpenter's Level. A level, typically two or four feet in length, usually made of wood.

Carpenter's Pencil. A specially made pencil, rectangular in section.

Carpenter's Pincers. See *Nail-Puller.*

Carpenter's Square. L-shaped tool, usually sixteen by twenty-four inches, used for laying out and squaring workpieces. Also known as a *Framing Square.*

Carriage. See *Stringer.*

Cat's-Paw. A small-scale wrecking bar.

Caulk. Sealant used to close joints between two materials to make them watertight.

Caulk Gun. Hand-powered tool used to apply tube caulk, adhesive, or other materials.

Chalk Box. Tool consisting of a string with a hook on one end that is retractable into a case that contains chalk. When extended and held taut to a surface to be marked, the chalk-covered string is snapped to produce a line of chalk where it contacts the surface.

Chamfer. A beveled edge.

Checking. Fissures in wood that appear with age and weathering which at first are only superficial but eventually may penetrate deeply through the finish.

Chisel. A cutting tool with a sharpened end that is used to shape, dress, or work solid materials. See *Brick Chisel, Butt Chisel, Cold Chisel, Firmer Chisel, Mortising Chisel,* and *Paring Chisel.*

Chop Box. Common nickname for the power miter saw.

Chuck. The set of jaws on a drill or brace that grips the bit which does the actual cutting.

Circular Saw. A power saw utilizing a disk-shaped blade with its cutting edge along its circumference. See also *Reciprocating Saw.*

Clamps. Family of tools of various design used to apply pressure, especially during gluing, to hold workpieces firmly together. Varieties include pipe, bar, hand-screw, spring, belt, and C-clamps.

Claw Hammer. Hammer design that features a claw-shaped nail-pulling device on the end of the head opposite the face.

Clinch Nailing. Nailing technique in which a nail is driven through the pieces being joined, and the protruding tip is bent and nailed flush for extra holding power.

Club Hammer. A small, sledgehammer-like tool with a symmetrical head. Also known as a *Hand-Drilling Hammer.*

Cold Chisel. A metal-cutting tool.

Combination Saw. Multipurpose saw with teeth filed and sharpened in order to cut efficiently both across and with the wood grain. See also *Ripsaw* and *Crosscut Saw.*

Combination Square. An adjustable hand square, consisting of a steel rule with a headpiece that slides along its length.

Compass. A marking instrument with two legs joined at the top that is used to draw circles or arcs. See also *Dividers.*

Compass Saw. A narrow-bladed handsaw used to cut arcs or openings in boards or panels. The compass saw was once distinguished from the *keyhole saw* by having a broader blade, but today the names are used interchangeably. See also *Wallboard Saw.*

Coping Saw. A lightweight handsaw consisting of a U-shaped frame, thin blade, and handle, which is used to make tightly curved and angled cuts. See also *Fretsaw.*

Cornice. The decorative horizontal finish that projects at the crown of an exterior or interior wall.

Crosscut Saw. Saw with teeth filed and sharpened in order to cut most efficiently across wood grain. See also *Ripsaw* and *Combination Saw.*

Cutoff Work. The act of sawing wood or metal workpieces to length.

Cut Nail. Nails made predominantly in the nineteenth century with rectangular shafts, cut from sheet stock. See also *Wire Nail.*

D

Deadblow Hammer. A malletlike tool with a soft face and ballast within its head; the design minimizes rebound.

Dividers. An instrument closely resembling a compass that is used for marking off distances, dividing lengths into equal units, and other measuring and marking tasks.

Dovetail Nailing. Nailing technique in which pairs or sets of nails are driven at alternate angles.

Dovetail Saw. A small backsaw used for precise work like cutting dovetails. See also *Backsaw, Tenon Saw,* and *Gentleman's Saw.*

Dozuki. The Japanese equivalent of the dovetail or tenon saw. It cuts on the pull stroke and has diamond-shaped teeth.

Drain Auger. A plumbing tool consisting of a steel spring coil with a twisted wire hook and auger at one end, used to open clogged drains. Also known as a "snake."

Drawknife. Two-handed shaping tool used to chamfer or shape wood workpieces.

Drill. Any of the several types of tools used to drill holes; or the sharpened tools *(bits)* rotated within them, including twist drills, spade bits, brad point drills, countersink drills, Forstner bits, or masonry bits.

Droplight. Portable electric light with self-contained cord, socket, and protective housing.

Drywall. Finish material for walls or ceilings that consists of a layer of gypsum sandwiched between two layers of paper; called drywall because it is applied dry (unlike plaster, whose finish it resembles).

Drywall Screwdriver. A tool resembling an electric drill designed to drive drywall screws. See also *Power Driver.*

Duckbill Snips. See *Snips.*

E

End Grain. The cross grain at the end of a workpiece.

Engineer's Hammer. See *Ball Peen Hammer.*

Engineer's Pliers. Linesman's pliers without insulated handles.

Essex Board Measure. A table that gives board measure in feet.

F

Face-Nailing. Nailing technique in which the nail is driven straight into the face of the workpiece.

Featherboard. An adjustable arm fixed to the top of a table saw to brace the workpiece against the fence, holding the work in line while the saw is cutting.

Fence. A fixed or adjustable accessory to a saw that acts as a guide, positioning the workpiece with respect to the blade. See also *Rip Fence.*

Ferrule. A metal cap or ring fitted around the end of a shaft or handle to strengthen it.

Filling Knife. A wider-bladed version of the *putty knife.*

Finishing Knife. Taping knife with a blade eight to fourteen inches wide.

Firmer Chisel. All-purpose wood chisel used to form and shape wood elements.

Fixed Wrenches. Family of tools designed to tighten or loosen nuts and bolts, including box-end and open-end wrenches. See also *Adjustable Wrench.*

Flashing. Sheet metal (most often copper or aluminum) or other material used in roof and wall construction to protect the joints in a building from being penetrated by water.

Flat Bar. Steel tool with hook and claw at one end and sometimes a claw at the other that is used for removing nails or other demolition tasks. Also known as a *Pry Bar* and *Wonder Bar.*

Flats. The sides of a nut or bolt head.

Flexible Rule. See *Push-Pull Tape.*

Folding Rule. A jointed rule that folds up, usually made of wood or fiberglass. Also known as a *Zigzag Rule.*

Frame Saw. A broad category of saws including handsaws in which a narrow metal blade is drawn taut within a wooden or metal frame. See also *Bow Saw.*

Framing Square. See *Carpenter's Square.*

Fretsaw. A handsaw that resembles the *coping saw* in design but with a deeper throat. Also known as a *Scroll Saw.*

G

Gable. The end wall of a building formed by the eave-line of a double-sloped roof.

Gentleman's Saw. A small backsaw used for precise work. See also *Backsaw, Tenon Saw,* and *Dovetail Saw.*

Gimlet. A small tool with a screw point used for boring holes.

Glue Gun. Hand-held glue applicator that uses an electrically powered heating element to melt glue as it is applied to workpieces.

Grit. The abrasive particles on sandpaper; the size of the grit determines the abrasive value assigned to each grade of paper.

Grout. A thin, coarse mortar used to seal between tile joints.

Grout Float. Rubber-faced, trowel-like tool used to spread grout.

Grout Saw. Specialty saw used to remove old grout below the level of the tile.

Guard. Fixed or movable safety devices that prevent injury, especially in limiting exposure of sawblades. See also *Anti-Kickback Fingers* and *Splitter.*

Gullet. The trough between the teeth in a circular saw.

Gusset. A wood or metal reinforcement at a structural joint for added strength or rigidity.

Gypsum Board. See *Drywall.*

H

Hacksaw. A bow-shaped saw with steel blade and pistol-grip handle used to cut metal.

Hand-Drilling Hammer. See *Club Hammer.*

Handsaw. A hand-held saw powered by the muscle of the user. More specifically, the term *handsaw* is used to describe the traditional carpenter's saw. See also *Power Saw.*

Hand Scraper. A flat piece of sheet metal used to smooth wood, in particular, hardwood surfaces. Also known as a *Cabinet Scraper.*

Hawk. Plasterer's carrying device used to hold extra plaster in one hand while troweling with the other.

Hex Wrench. See *Allen Wrench.*

Hole Saw. A hollow, cylindrical drill bit with teeth on one end.

Hook Scraper. A scraping tool with a sharp metal blade fixed perpendicular to the long handle.

I

Impact Wrench. A purpose-made drill used for tightening or loosening bolts.

In-Line Driver. Hand-held cordless electric tool used for driving screws.

J

Jamb. The side or head lining of a door, window, or other opening.

Jigsaw. See *Saber Saw.*

Joint Compound. The premixed, plasterlike substance applied with a putty knife to cover nail holes and joints between sheets in gypsum board construction; also known as "spackle."

Joist. One of a series of parallel beams used to support a floor or ceiling.

K

Kerf. The cut made by a saw in a piece of wood; or the width of that cut.

Keyhole Saw. Narrow-bladed handsaw used to cut fine openings like keyholes. See also *Compass Saw.*

L

Lath. In wet-wall construction (i.e. when the plaster is applied wet rather than in dry gypsum boards), the lath is the wood, metal, or other material that is attached to the frame of the building prior to plastering to act as a base for the plaster.

Level. True horizontal, as determined by a level; or one of a variety of devices used to determine true vertical or horizontal. See also *Plumb, Level Vial, Line Level, Spirit Level, Transit Level* and *Water Level.*

Level Vial. A curved tube containing alcohol or other fluid. An air bubble within the vial aligns between two parallel lines at its center when the level in which the vial is mounted is positioned at true vertical or horizontal.

Line Level. A level vial suspended from a line, used to indicate true horizontal.

Line Tester. Pencil-sized electrical tester consisting of an indicator light and two leads, used to determine whether current is present.

Lumber. Milled wood stock thicker than one, but also thinner than six inches.

M

Machine Rule. A metal ruler, typically six inches long, most often used for reading drawings.

Magic Square. See *Speed Square.*

Mallet. Often made of wood, mallets are hammerlike tools used to drive other tools, like chisels, or wooden elements like dowels or pins.

Mandrel. A cylindrical shaft or axle on which a tool or blade is mounted.

Miter. An oblique surface shaped on a piece of wood or other material so as to butt against an oblique surface on another piece to be joined with it; a matching angle cut.

Miter Box. A frame or boxlike device that functions as a saw guide to enable its user to make accurate miter cuts.

Miter Gauge. An adjustable table saw accessory that enables workpieces to be presented to the blade at a variety of angles. Also known as a "miter fence."

Miter Saw. A power saw consisting of a circular saw mounted on a frame, designed to make accurate angle cuts. Sometimes referred to as a *chop box.*

Monkey Wrench. Common nickname for a pipe wrench.

Mortising Chisel. A wood chisel used for shaping openings called mortises in wooden workpieces.

N

Nailing Surface. A wood member fastened to an interior surface to provide an attachment point for another surface or element. Also called a "nailer."

Nail-Puller. Pliers-like tool with flat jaws that is used to remove nails. Also known as *Carpenter's Pincers.*

Nail Set. A flat-pointed punch used to countersink nails beneath the surface of a wooden workpiece.

Nippers. Pliers-like device used to trim off small shards from a piece of tile.

P

Paint Scraper. A flat-bladed tool with a plastic, metal, or wood handle that is used to scrape away paint, wallpaper, or other materials.

Paring Chisel. Fine chisel used for trimming or paring work. See also *Firmer Chisel.*

Peen. The end of the hammerhead opposite the face. The peen may be hemispherical, wedge-shaped, or of another form.

Pier. A masonry column used to support the structure.

Pinch Bar. See *Wrecking Bar.*

Plane. Carpenter's smoothing tool, usually consisting of a metal blade (*plane iron*) mounted in a hand-held frame. Many configurations for different purposes are (or have been) made, including the *block plane* as well as bench, bullnose, compass, jack, jointer, and rabbet planes.

Plane Iron. Flat blade that does the smoothing in a *plane.*

Plasterboard. See *Drywall.*

Plastic Pipe. A type of plumbing pipe, most often used for drainage, made of one of several compounds, among them polyvinyl chloride or PVC; acrylonitrile-butadiene styrene or ABS; and chlorinated polyvinyl chloride or CPVC.

Pliers. Family of hand-held, pincerlike tools used to grip, position, tighten, loosen, and cut metal elements. Varieties include *engineer's pliers,* as well as slip-joint, water-pump, linesman's, locking, and needle-nose pliers.

Plumb. True vertical, as determined by a plumb bob. See also *Level.*

Plumb Bob. A device used to determine true vertical, consisting of a weight suspended from a length of string or cord.

Plumb Cut. The vertical cut at the top of a rafter where it butts the ridgepole.

Plumb Square. Device used to determine true level or horizontal using a plumb bob hung on a string from a wooden frame.

Plumber's Tape. A sandpaperlike material also called "emery cloth," plumber's tape is used to polish copper pipe prior to sweating a fitting.

Plunge Cut. A cut made with a saber saw in which a hole is started in the interior of a board or panel by tilting the saber saw forward on its base, then tipping the blade back down into the workpiece.

Plunger. Plumbing tool consisting of a molded rubber cup mounted on the end of a wooden handle, used to unclog drains.

Pocket Cut. A saw cut made in the interior of a board or panel.

Pocketknife. A knife with one or more blades that fold into its handle, which fits into a pocket.

Pointing. The filling of open mortar joints between masonry units (brick, stone, block); when over time the mortar has deteriorated and has to be replaced, the process is termed *repointing.*

Power Driver. Tool resembling an electric drill designed to drive screws. Varieties include *Drywall Screwdriver* and *In-Line Driver.*

Power Saw. Any of several varieties of saws that are powered by electric motors. See also *Handsaw.*

Pricker. See *Awl.*

Propane Torch. Heating device powered by propane fuel used in sweating plumbing fittings, stripping paint, and other tasks.

Protractor Square. See *Speed Square.*

Pry Bar. See *Flat Bar.*

Pumps. Nickname for water-pump pliers.

Punches. Pencil-shaped metal tools with varying points that are used to puncture or indent metal, wood, or other materials when driven by a hammer or mallet. See also *Nail Set.*

Push-Pull Tape. A retractable, spring-loaded tape measure. Also known as a *Flexible Rule.*

Push Stick. A stick used to propel a workpiece through a tablesaw blade, enabling the sawyer to keep his or her fingers a greater distance from the saw. Also known as a "pusher."

Putty Knife. A scraperlike tool used to apply pastelike materials such as glazing compound and wood filler. A wider-bladed version is generally referred to as a *filling knife.*

R

Rabbet. A deep lip or channel cut from the edge of a workpiece, especially one intended for jointing to another piece.

Rafter Tables. The numerical chart found stamped on the *carpenter's square* that is used to calculate rafter dimensions.

Razor-Blade Scraper. Handled device designed to hold a single-edge razor-blade for cleaning and scraping smooth, hard surfaces like glass and tile.

Reciprocating Saw. A saw that cuts in an alternating, back-and-forth motion (see also *Circular Saw*). Also, a heavy-duty hand-held saw sometimes referred to by its proprietary name Sawsall. See also *Saber Saw.*

Resawing. Table-saw technique in which the two edges of a board are ripped in order to obtain a thinner workpiece.

Reversibility. An attribute of drills and drivers that allows the direction in which the motor turns to be reversed for withdrawing as well as driving.

Rip Fence. An adjustable guide on a table saw that is positioned to regulate the width of a workpiece being ripped.

Ripsaw. Saw with teeth filed and sharpened in order to saw most efficiently *with* the grain of the wood. See also *Crosscut Saw* and *Combination Saw.*

Rise and Run. The terms used to indicate the degree of incline (the rise is the vertical measure, the run the horizontal) in laying out rafters, stair carriages, or other construction elements.

Riser. The vertical board that closes the space between each tread of a stairway. See also *Tread* and *Stringer.*

Rotary Hammer. A specially designed drill that delivers its power in a hammering, as well as turning, motion for drilling holes.

Ryoba. A Japanese combination saw with rip and crosscut teeth on opposite sides of its blade.

S

Saber Saw. A small, hand-held reciprocating power saw used to cut curves and openings in boards or panels. Also known as a "power scroll saw "or "power jigsaw."

Sander. Power tool that uses sandpaper to smooth surfaces. A variety of power sanders are sold, including palm-grip, belt, disk, orbital, and other configurations.

Sanding Block. A block-shaped tool around which sandpaper is wrapped for sanding wood surfaces.

Sawhorse. A free-standing work surface used for supporting workpieces, usually made of wood and consisting of four legs and a flat, horizontal top.

Sawteeth. The sharp metal cutting points that line the edge of a saw.

Scraper. One of a family of tools with flat, sometimes flexible blades that are used to smooth or to scrape paint or other materials from a work surface. See also *Hand Scraper, Hook Scraper, Paint Scraper, Putty Knife, Razor-Blade Scraper,* and *Shave Hook.*

Screwdriver. One of a family of fastening tools used for turning screws.

Scribe. A tool used to mark lines or points on wooden workpieces. See also *Awl.*

Scribing Awl. See *Awl.*

Scroll Saw. See *Fretsaw* and *Saber Saw.*

Serrated. Marked with toothlike notches (serrations) at the edge.

Set. The bend given to sawteeth beyond the plane of the blade itself in order to prevent binding by insuring that the *kerf* cut will be slightly wider than the blade.

Sharpening Stone. Natural or artificial stone used to hone the cutting edge of a *chisel, plane iron,* or other cutting tool.

Shave Hook. A scraper with a sharp, profiled blade, metal shaft, and wooden handle, commonly used to remove paint or to smooth moldings or other curved surfaces.

Shears. Heavy-duty scissors.

Sheathing. The layer of boards or plywood that encloses the supporting structure of the house but lies beneath the final siding or roofing material.

Sheetrock. Proprietary name for *drywall.*

Shingle Remover. Thin-bladed demolition tool used for removing shingles, as well as for prying off boards and other elements. Also known as a *Slater's Ripper.*

Shop Knife. See *Utility Knife.*

Skew. The slight sway or dip in the back of a handsaw.

Slater's Ripper. See *Shingle Remover.*

Sledgehammer. A heavy two-handed hammer with a symmetrical head.

Slick. Oversized timber framer's chisel.

Sliding Bevel. See *Bevel Gauge.*

Sliding T-Bevel. See *Bevel Gauge.*

Snips. Scissors-like tool used to cut sheet metal. Varieties include *duckbill snips,* used for cutting screening or light-duty sheet metal, and *aviation* (or compound-leverage) snips.

Sockets. Cylindrical receptacles, generally sold in sets, that are mounted on ratchets to remove nuts or bolts.

Soffit. The underside of an overhanging cornice.

Soil Pipe. Pipe carrying waste from plumbing fixtures to septic system.

Speed Square. A triangular *try square.* Also known as a *Protractor Square*

and *Magic Square.*

Spirit Level. An instrument consisting of a level vial mounted in one or another of various sized bodies, which is used to identify true vertical or horizontal. Also known as a "bubble level." See also *Level Vial.*

Splitter. A fin-shaped piece of steel beyond the blade on a table saw, which separates the stock being ripped to prevent it from binding on the blade.

Square. Term applied to an assembly or workpiece with corners that are perfect right angles. Also, any of the several tools used to determine square.

Stair Carriage. See *Stringer.*

Staple Gun. Electric- or spring-powered devices used to propel staple fasteners.

Steel Wool. Loosely woven pad of steel thread used for smoothing.

Stillson Wrench. A pipe wrench.

Stringer. The side of the staircase onto which the risers and treads are affixed; also called *Stair Carriage.* See also *Riser* and *Tread.*

Story Pole. A purpose-made straightedge with markings for specific elements, like the tops and bottoms of openings and the courses of siding or masonry.

Subfloor. The plywood or boards laid over the floor joists on which the finished floor is applied.

Surfoam. A smoothing tool with a planelike body and filelike blade used on drywall and wood.

Sweat Fitting. A copper piping connection joined by solder.

T

Table Saw. A power saw in which a circular blade protrudes from a horizontal working surface. The height and tilt of the blade can be adjusted, as can the angle at which the wood is presented to the blade.

Tail Cut. The cut made at the lower end of a rafter.

Tang. A projecting shank or tongue from a file, chisel, or other metal blade that is fitted into a wood or plastic handle.

Taping Knives. Scraperlike tools of various widths used to apply joint compound in finishing drywall. See also *Broad Knife* and *Finishing Knife.*

Teflon Tape. Thin nonadhesive material applied over pipe threads to seal fittings.

Tenon Saw. A medium-sized backsaw used for such precise work as cutting tenons, usually with rip teeth. See also *Backsaw, Dovetail Saw,* and *Gentleman's Saw.*

Timber. Milled wood stock of a thickness greater than five inches.

Toe-Nailing. Nailing technique in which a pair of nails are driven at opposing forty-five-degree angles.

Torpedo Level. A nine-inch-long level tapered at the ends. Also known as a *Boat Level.*

Transit Level. A surveyor's instrument incorporating a telescope and spirit level, mounted on a stand, used to identify the relative positions of points and lines on a horizontal plane.

Trap. A **U**-shaped piece of pipe found beneath all plumbing fixtures; gravity holds a small amount of water at its base which prevents sewer gases from entering the home.

Traveler. Antique measuring device consisting of a simple wheel with a handle attached by a rivet to its center, which was rolled along the surface to be measured.

Tread. A horizontal board on a staircase; colloquially, the step. See also *Riser* and *Stringer.*

Tree Calipers. Oversized calipers used to measure the diameter of a tree and to calculate the amount of timber to be sawn from it.

Trimming Knife. See *Utility Knife.*

Trowel. Family of hand tools used to apply, spread, shape, or smooth mortar, plaster, adhesive, or other plastic substances.

True. Level, square, or concentric; precisely shaped, positioned, formed, or adjusted.

Try Square. An **L**-shaped tool used for checking or laying out right angles.

Tubing Cutter. Cutting tool used by plumbers and electricians to cut copper, plastic, or aluminum tubing.

Turnscrew. Outdated term for a *screwdriver.*

U

Utility Knife. A knife that uses replaceable, single-edged razor-blades that retract into the handle of the tool. Also known as a *Shop Knife* or *Trimming Knife.*

V

Variable Speed. An attribute of some drills, saws, drivers, and other power tools that allows the user to increase or decrease the speed of the tool by gradually depressing or releasing the trigger control.

W

Wallboard Saw. A narrow-bladed handsaw used to cut openings in wallboard.

Warrington Hammer. Cabinet maker's hammer with a cross peen opposite the face.

Waste. Excess portion of the raw material that will not be a part of the finished product.

Water Level. A device consisting of two plastic or glass cylinders connected by a flexible tube that contains water. The position of the water with respect to calibrations on the cylinders indicates whether the cylinders are level with one another.

Weather Stripping. Sections of metal, plastic, felt, or other material that is used to line the sides, top, or foot of doors or windows to prevent infiltration of air and moisture.

Wire Nail. Machine-made nail of the types generally available today. See also *Cut Nail.*

Wire Nut. A plastic cap containing a conical metal spring into which the twisted wires are tightened, both to fasten them together and to insulate them.

Wire Stripper. Purpose-made tool for removing insulation from wires.

Wonder Bar. See *Flat Bar.*

Wrecking Bar. Steel tool, usually octagonal in section, with a hook and claw at one end, used for removing nails or other demolition work. Also known as a *Pinch Bar* and, erroneously, as a "crowbar."

Wrenches. Family of tools used to tighten or loosen nuts and bolts. Varieties include *Adjustable, Allen, Fixed* (box-end and open-end), and pipe wrenches.

Worm-Drive. A screw-and-wheel drive mechanism used in certain heavy-duty hand-held circular saws.

Z

Zigzag Rule. See *Folding Rule.*

TOOL INDEX